Novelists and Their World
General Editor: Graham Hough
Professor of English at the University of Cambridge

Elizabeth Gaskell

The Novel of Social Crisis

Coral Lansbury

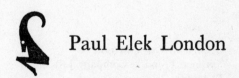

Paul Elek London

First published in Great Britain 1975 by
Elek Books Limited
54–58 Caledonian Road
London N1 9RN

ISBN 0 236 31147 6

For Caroline Robbins

Printed in Great Britain by
Latimer Trend & Company Ltd
Plymouth

Contents

Preface

Fame can distort a writer's achievements more radically than neglect. If *Cranford* had never been published, Elizabeth Gaskell's reputation would be as secure today as that of Thackeray or George Eliot, and she would be ranked without question amongst the major novelists of the Victorian period. Critics have been at some pains to explain the popularity of *Cranford* in literary terms, but the fundamental reasons for its success are the psychological consolations it offers for the fears of old age, particularly in women. *Cranford* obscured Elizabeth Gaskell's novels of social and psychological realism and her studies of social change. The clumsy narrative methods she employed in that work were regarded as typical, and critics persisted in reading the novels through the vagaries of *Cranford*. In a literary sense it is a splendid example of the city being evaluated in terms of the village, a practice not unknown to many sociologists. Nevertheless, *Cranford* remains the cracked touchstone that is used to define the subtle and various narrative strategies of the novels and short stories.

Long before it became the popular avocation of social historians, Elizabeth Gaskell was writing histories of the 'common people', describing how it felt to be poor, what it meant to be denied work and opportunity in an affluent society, and the means whereby the workers would eventually forge the trades-union into a hammer to smash the interlocking ranks of class and privilege. She also stated that the trades-union could become as oppressive and inherently conservative as the society that had forced it into being. As she remarked of the Camorra in 'An Italian Institution', movements that arise in violent opposition to a society all too often become mirror images of that society.

Friedrich Engels described Manchester, often inaccurately, in the language and theory of German social idealism. Elizabeth Gaskell's knowledge of the city and its people was derived from long experience and acquaintance—and Mancunians do not make friends easily. She knew the local dialect, impenetrable to strangers, and her friends extended from the wealthy Unitarian manufacturers to the inmates of workhouse and prison. No writer of the period could move so easily between all ranks of society, and be accepted by so many. Like her friend Florence Nightingale, she had the common touch that enabled her to converse as easily with a soldier of the line as with a duchess. And she could describe the domestic problems of the Countess of Cumnor in *Wives and Daughters* with the same sympathetic detachment that gave life to Alice Wilson, the washerwoman in *Mary Barton*.

Concerned with the needs of society, Elizabeth Gaskell never forgot that every human being was unique, a combination of male and female characteristics and often the better for it. Tennyson maintained that a good poet was part-woman. Elizabeth Gaskell believed that a captain of industry like John Thornton in *North and South* could arrive at self-understanding by appreciating female qualities in others as well as in himself. And no woman could be the worse for displaying strength, intelligence and independence. Elizabeth Gaskell never saw sex as being defined simply by gender.

It was in her delineation of the family that Elizabeth Gaskell is the least Victorian of novelists. Far from seeing the family as a heaven-ordained haven of bliss, she regarded it as a stifling and often blighting influence on children's lives. Men were encouraged to be despots and women were denied their natural intellectual instincts because of the demands of domesticity. Women's lives were stunted and children were forced to live with uncongenial siblings, like the unfortunate daughter in 'The Moorland Cottage' and the niece in 'The Crooked Branch'. Thus the happy families in the novels and stories have little in common with usual familial patterns. The family that Ruth finds refuge with in the novel of that name has no father, and Libbie Marsh lives in contentment with an elderly woman and her son in 'Libbie Marsh's Three Eras'. The most extreme example occurs in 'The Grey Woman', which depicts two women living lovingly together as 'father' and mother to a baby.

As a Unitarian Elizabeth Gaskell was unshaken by the

crises of doubt and faith that troubled so many Victorians. Her lack of concern with the after-life and the nature of sin deprived her work of the metaphysical and mystical qualities common to many writers of the period. When she wrote a ghost story, the ghost was always a manifestation of someone's troubled mind. Madness was a recurring theme in her work, but Elizabeth Gaskell argued that if people believed strongly enough in the irrational then the irrational would assuredly become a reality to them—and perhaps to others as well. Madness was not seen by her as divine punishment or a freakish anomaly of nature, but as a sickness of the mind often related to physical disease. She was not sentimental about the insane in the Wordsworthian manner, and she was aware that an idiot child could destroy a home more effectively than a vicious intruder. It is questionable whether Susan Dixon's life in 'Half a Lifetime Ago' was ennobled by her pledge to care for her mentally disturbed brother, or whether this sacrifice improved her erstwhile suitor's character. It was her lack of sentimentality in the study of human relationships that set Elizabeth Gaskell apart from so many of her contemporaries.

Perhaps Elizabeth Gaskell's most remarkable achievement as a novelist was to invent a narrative voice that reflected little of her own taste and feeling, but did correspond with her vision of the average middle-class reader of the day. Her opinion of this reader can be assessed from *Mary Barton*. Certainly, she was technically a subtle and inventive writer too often thwarted by the pressures of serial publication and the editorial demands of Charles Dickens. Nothing could be more unwise than to regard the authorial 'I' of the novels as the voice of Elizabeth Gaskell, particularly in the Manchester novels. There the narrator has a tendency to engage in false pleading and specious argument, while the workers demonstrate honesty and commonsense.

There have been many attempts to confirm Elizabeth Gaskell's place as a minor novelist and to account for her apparent artistic deficiencies. This work is a tribute to her success, and perhaps may offer some reasons why so many of her critics have been led astray down the winding road to Cranford. She is a master of psychological realism, comparable with Balzac, a writer who is concerned less with external realities than with the realities of feeling and mood. She does not describe physical appearance with originality or at length, but she does delineate with exquisite accuracy the convoluted patterns of emotion and thought. And she has accomplished this in works set in periods other than her own. As an historian of society she wrote with considerable perception of the changes and variations in the way people perceived reality at different periods of time. Elizabeth Gaskell was less concerned with describing events than with intimating the way in which people regarded those events and themselves. Rather than engage in the current fashion for depreciation of her talents, I would argue that it is high time that Elizabeth Gaskell was accorded her place in the company of Thackeray and Dickens, George Eliot and Jane Austen.

I
The woman, the writer and the Unitarian

To be born a woman in the Victorian era was to enter a world of social and cultural deprivation unknown to a man. But to be born a woman and Unitarian was to be released from much of the prejudice and oppression enjoined upon other women. Elizabeth Cleghorn Gaskell was born on September 29, 1810, at Cheyne Walk in Chelsea into a double tradition of Unitarianism. Her father, William Stevenson, had been a Unitarian minister for a time, but forsook the pulpit when he could not reconcile his faith with the acceptance of fees for preaching. A man of diverse talents, he worked as a farmer and as editor of *The Scots Magazine*; he also wrote a number of historical articles for *The Edinburgh Review* and *The Monthly Repository*, the main Unitarian journal of the day. Never poor but always pressed for money, Stevenson gratefully accepted the post of Keeper of the Records to the Treasury and held that position with distinction until his death in 1829. William Stevenson married a woman from a family with even longer Unitarian traditions. The Hollands had been active in political and religious reform since the eighteenth century, and Elizabeth Holland came from the Cheshire branch, from a family that was related in turn to the Darwins, the Wedgwoods, the Turners and Dr Peter Gaskell, the medical and social reformer.

Unitarians married more to find partners of like mind than for reasons of property or political advantage. They were a singular and distinct community in Victorian society, unaffected by the crises of faith that shook so many Christians and produced among them a profound and lasting pessimism. Claud Welch correctly describes the Victorian mind as being 'characterised by uncertainty and doubt',[1] but this is not the mood of Unitarianism. Their theology was an optimistic affirmation of man as a rational being who could ultimately attain a perfect state in this world without recourse to marvels and miracles. To the nineteenth century they brought a doctrine of rationalism that spoke in terms of the enlightenment of the preceding century. Further, they were untouched by the struggle between science and Christian doctrine. Indeed, in the contest between the apes and the angels, they gladly espoused the cause of the apes as further proof of man's capacity to evolve by reason and by will. For many Christians the Unitarian was the arch apostle of heresy, the one member of the Christian community who was beyond redemption. One of the most popular Methodist hymns was an appeal to the 'Triune God', imploring him to expel the Unitarian fiend and 'chase his doctrines back to Hell'.[2] If Elizabeth Gaskell was born to a heritage of political and social reform, and a passion for individual liberty and justice, she also knew that she belonged to 'a sect everywhere spoken against'.[3] Joseph Priestley regarded this as a statement of fact; he also saw it as a challenge.

The Unitarian rejected the divinity of Christ and with it belief in the Trinity. For men like Priestley and Theophilus Lindsey the Trinitarian formula was an impossible one, and in consequence, the doctrine derived from it was equally invalid. Christ was a man, albeit the best of men, and could not be worshipped. Socinus had rejected the doctrines of original sin, eternal punishment and the atonement, but he saw Christ as quasi-divine and thought it was permissible for him to be made the object of prayer. The Unitarians of the nineteenth century rejected even this limited form of worship as blasphemous and continually emphasised the simple humanity of Christ, his witness to the truth, and his death because of that witness. If many Christians regarded the Unitarians as heretics, more thought of them as less a religious sect than a political group, radical in temperament, reformers by design. It was difficult for a practising Unitarian to dissociate himself from social and political life. He was committed to social involvement as the visible expression of his faith. The Duke of Wellington despised Unitarians as atheists, and Lord Ashley saw them as lost souls, but despite persecution and derision they contrived to become leaders of reform, scientists, manufacturers, merchants and politicians.

Education was the right of every human being, male and female. When James Anthony Froude was appointed as tutor to the children of Samuel Darbishire, the wealthy Unitarian solicitor of Manchester, he was told that there was to be no distinction between the education of his sons and daughters. Unitarian schools flourished and their teaching methods of making learning a pleasure by means of games and dramatised scenes in the classroom were the most advanced of the century. The ideal was not the moulding of Christian gentlemen but the creation of individuals who would each in his and her own way find fulfilment as an active member of society. There is no record of Elizabeth Gaskell having been beaten as a child or at school. Reason and the birch could not exist together in the schoolroom according to Unitarian practice. If an adult was a rational being, then a child was only slightly less so, and no one had ever beaten understanding into a human being. Naturally, with these views, the Unitarians were to be leaders in the movement for women's rights. Eliza Fox, Barbara Bodichon, Harriet Martineau, Emily Shaen and Florence Nightingale were all Unitarians of varying degrees of faith. Of course, those degrees were never categorised since that would have necessitated an abridgement of individual liberty. Essentially, Unitarianism was a paradox, a collectivist movement in praise of the individual.

It was the incorrigible optimism of the Unitarian that most offended his fellow Christian. In the face of slums and poverty, crime and prostitution, the Unitarian maintained his faith in progress and perfectibility, in the power of reason to effect change. Naturally inclined towards Utilitarianism, a number of Unitarians became fervent statisticians, veritable Gradgrinds of religion in their insistence upon facts. William Gaskell was one of the founders of the Manchester Statistical Society and Florence Nightingale's genius for accountancy made her a revolutionary force in the Army Medical Service. Sustaining their life and work was a belief in the natural goodness of man. Theophilus Lindsey did not deny the existence of sin but declared emphatically that God 'never ordains or permits evil but with a view to the production of a greater good, which could not have existed without it'.[4] King David committed murder and sinned greatly when he took Bathsheba as his wife, but the fruit of that union was

Solomon. Unitarians were always careful to distinguish between the evil engendered by society and the suffering that men saw as evil but which was, in effect, part of God's plan for a greater goodness.

The only safe path to follow in life was one of absolute truth. For a man to lie was to obscure God's design for a world of virtue and knowledge. Truth to a Unitarian was the torch that would eventually illuminate the whole of mankind. Much of the abrasiveness people felt in the company of Unitarians was a result of their custom of speaking honestly. Because they could still believe, despite the problems of a new industrial society and the challenge of science, they were both the envy and the outrage of their day. It was not difficult for a Unitarian scientist like Charles Lyell or an industrialist like John Fielden to find a harmony between their work and their religion. Yet the fact that they remained so composed when the citadel of faith was crumbling around them seemed contrary to all sense of propriety. Froude found them infuriating. It was unsettling for the author of *The Nemesis of Faith* to find himself surrounded in Manchester with unfailing kindness and a certain indifference to his religious conflicts. Carlyle was converting many to religious despair, but Unitarians were not numbered among his disciples. Almost in hysteria, Froude wrote: 'We hate Manchester—Manchester in any form—Unitarian Manchester most of all. Vulgar and insolent: as they practise little virtue among themselves, so they pretend to even less than they possess, by the gracelessness of their manner; and when we leave the place, which we shall do in the summer, we shall leave it without breaking any ties except such as one might form with a prison cell.'[5] Froude and his wife had been frequent visitors to the Gaskell home, but Elizabeth Gaskell found it easier to maintain a friendship with Charlotte Froude, Kingsley's sister, than with her husband.

The insistence upon action, the refusal to take refuge in metaphysics or doctrine, was as trying for most Christians as it was for Froude. In 1801 the Unitarian John Cartwright met William Wilberforce, the Evangelical, in Westminster, and the exchange between them summarised the fundamental difference in religion between the two men. Cartwright recalled: 'Among other friendly expressions, he [Wilberforce] said he hoped we should meet in a better world: I answered that *I hoped we should first mend the world we were in.*'[6] Elizabeth Gaskell never doubted that she was born with the right and the ability to change society. Her novels and her life as a woman and social reformer were expressions of this theology of optimism. She was a religious writer, but her religion was at variance with most contemporary attitudes. Religious doubt is generally taken as an indication of some complexity of thought, while faith is regarded as the attribute of an unthinking mind. But the Unitarians confound this easy generalisation. Elizabeth Gaskell's religion was as closely reasoned as the denial of faith by Froude and Ruskin, but it was they who spoke to their age and found a sympathetic response. Elizabeth Gaskell has been consistently misunderstood because insufficient attention has been paid to her religion, and what it meant to be a Unitarian, isolated and privileged, dedicated to the principle of individual independence and yet determined to ameliorate society.

Elizabeth Gaskell was only thirteen months old when her mother died, and she was taken to live with her aunt at Knutsford. Mrs Hannah Lumb had been forced to have her husband committed to an asylum for the insane, and subsequently lived with her crippled daughter, Marianne, in a comfortable house on the outskirts of the village. William Stevenson remarried four years later but Elizabeth remained with her aunt, visiting her mother's relations at Holland Park and later spending five happy years at a remarkably fine school at Avonbank in Stratford-upon-Avon, run by Maria Byerley and her sisters. Nothing could have been more dissimilar from this school than the Lowood of Charlotte Brontë. At Avonbank, Elizabeth Stevenson was encouraged to write, and education was regarded as a woman's vocation not an adornment.

With no particular regard for her stepmother, Elizabeth chose to remain with her Aunt Lumb, her 'more than mother', until she was called to help with the nursing of her father in 1827. It was a period of great distress for the young woman, for her brother, John Stevenson, mysteriously vanished at sea on a voyage to India in 1828. Unlike Miss Matty's brother, Peter, nothing more was ever heard of him. After her father's death in 1829 she stayed for a time with her uncle Swinton Holland at Park Lane. No affection for her stepmother had developed, and the tie that remained was one of duty.

Throughout her life, Elizabeth Gaskell was to maintain that maternal love is not the natural attribute of every mother, that a woman may give birth to a child that she detests, and that it is possible for the love of parent and child to be established between strangers or distant relations. Aunt Lumb had become her mother and Elizabeth always thought of herself as her daughter. It was love that defined the relationship between mother and child, not an act of birth. That Elizabeth Gaskell grew to maturity in the security of love was a tribute to her aunt and her relations at Holland Park. She had been raised as an only child and she tried in later life to make her four daughters know the kinship of family without losing any sense of individuality. Elizabeth Gaskell sent her daughters to different schools because she regarded each child as unique, and believed that no spirit of competition or imitation should be permitted among them.

From London, Elizabeth went to stay with her cousin Anne Turner at Newcastle. The two travelled to Edinburgh to avoid an outbreak of cholera in Newcastle. It was in Edinburgh that Elizabeth's beauty was recorded in the miniature by Joseph Thompson and a sculptured bust by D. Dunbar. Anne Turner's sister had married John Robberds, senior minister to the famous Cross Street Unitarian Chapel in Manchester, and an invitation was soon forthcoming for the two young women to visit the Robberds in Manchester. Robberds's assistant minister was William Gaskell. The son of a manufacturer of sail canvas, William Gaskell had been educated at Glasgow University and the Unitarian Manchester College in York. From 1828 until his death in 1884 he was to preach from Cross Street. It is unlikely that the meeting between the two young people was wholly fortuitous. If marriages were not arranged, meetings were, and

John Robberds could have wished for nothing more than his friend's marriage to the daughter of a man who had once been a noted Unitarian minister. They were a remarkably handsome young couple. As their friends anticipated, the two fell deeply in love and their marriage was consecrated in Knutsford Parish Church on August 30, 1832.

It was an unusual marriage in which each was able to lead an individual life despite all the Victorian calls to wifely obedience and domesticity. Aina Rubenius, in *The Woman Question in Mrs Gaskell's Life and Works*,[7] devotes considerable attention to the part religion played in the subjection of Victorian women, but she does not differentiate sufficiently between Unitarianism and other forms of belief. Unlikely parallels are drawn between characters from the novels and William Gaskell to demonstrate an abiding resentment felt by Elizabeth Gaskell towards her husband.[8] And she finds confirmation of this in the occasional grumbling letter that was sent to her friends and relations. It would seem more likely to assume that a woman who feels she has the freedom to complain about her marriage, when so inclined, is one who has a reasonably stable relationship with her husband. Elizabeth Gaskell never idealised marriage, and never saw it as more than a working partnership between individuals with different tastes and inclinations. It is Charlotte Brontë's passionate effusions on her husband's virtues that should arouse a reader's suspicions, as they did Elizabeth Gaskell's. Her husband, like her children, was a person who often annoyed her but whom she loved very deeply. Certainly it was her husband's recognition of her creative genius that led Elizabeth Gaskell to become a professional writer. William Gaskell corrected her proofs and those of her friends (occasionally rendering a phrase grammatical), helped her collect material for her *Life of Charlotte Brontë* and never questioned her right to express views and opinions that were at variance with his own. William Gaskell epitomised Unitarian society when he preached to his congregation knowing that two prominent members had just burned his wife's novel *Ruth* as unfit for family reading. They were at liberty to burn the book but none there denied her the right to publish and write as she saw fit, and no one held William Gaskell responsible for his wife's opinions. It is to William Gaskell's honour that he resolutely refused to play the role of the typical Victorian husband.

Elizabeth Gaskell had always written, and her brother had once commended her for keeping, a diary.[9] The diary gives evidence of a characteristic that she once condemned to a young mother who wrote to her for advice: 'When I had *little* children I do not think I could have written stories, because I should have become too much absorbed in my *fictitious* people to attend to my *real* ones' (G.L. 515).[10] Her tendency to see her children as fictional characters in potential situations was evident throughout her life but was far stronger when she was a young mother who had already given birth to one stillborn child in 1833 and seen her little son die of scarlet fever in 1845. It was at this period that Elizabeth Gaskell wrote to her sister-in-law, Anne Robson, when she was 'sitting all alone, and not feeling over & above well', wondering if Marianne, her little daughter, had 'any *latent* disease in her' and continuing, 'Wm, I daresay kindly, won't allow me ever to talk to him about anxieties, while it would be *such a relief* often' (G.L. 16). Then, by the end of the letter, she had written herself out of the doldrums and was cheerfully relating a few items of local gossip and how she had recently taken up chess with William. For William Gaskell there was a clear distinction between reality and fiction, and he did not care to have the latter presented in the form of domestic anxieties. He was always prepared to discuss facts about the children, noting Marianne's tendency to dream and supervising Meta in her Latin, but he would not indulge in fancies about them. After the death of their son he urged his wife to sublimate her grief by writing a novel. Sorrow turned inwards, as he so often preached, was a dull and numbing emotion, but directed towards social grief, it could not only heal, but be healed in the process. In his sermons Gaskell spoke of the part of the individual in society, and in her novels Elizabeth Gaskell defined it as a fictional theme.

After moving from Dover Street to Plymouth Grove in 1849 Elizabeth Gaskell was in charge of her own money and frequently disagreed with her husband over the wisdom of certain contracts. He was convinced, for example, that she should have asked for royalties for the *Life of Charlotte Brontë*, but upon her insistence George Smith paid for it in a lump sum. Nevertheless she could inform Charles Dickens as editor that he would find nothing to correct or change in her manuscript since her husband had already checked it himself. Even more revealing of the relationship between the two than the correspondence over business, or the occasional complaint about her husband's solitary habits, is the hurried scrawl to Marianne from London: 'Has Papa got a library table for his study? because if not, I have found a very handsome, oblong, second-hand one at the Baker-Street Bazaar' (G.L. 234a). In Hyde Park, while being treated as one of the most engaging literary lions, Elizabeth Gaskell still had thoughts of her husband in Manchester. Neither saw marriage as a sacrament in which two souls mysteriously became one, preferably with the wife's being subsumed by the husband. Elizabeth Gaskell was never so happy as when surrounded by friends, and few people had a greater gift for friendship, but William Gaskell preferred the peace of contemplative rambles. It is surely revealing that she spent far more time away from home than her husband, travelling to France and Italy, Belgium and Germany, always with friends, often with one or more of her daughters. Occasionally she regretted that William chose to take his holidays alone, adding that a husband was such a convenience with the luggage when travelling. Her last business transaction in the year of her death, 1865, was to buy a country house where she could retire with her husband and family. It was clearly not the ideal Victorian marriage, but it endured with affection and respect to the end. May every marriage last so well.

It is difficult to find a harsh comment about Elizabeth Gaskell. Typically, Jane Welsh Carlyle attacked her for her lack of moral fervour and employed that old term of abuse, Socinian. To her own husband, Jane Carlyle wrote: 'She is a very kind cheery woman in her own house; but there is an atmosphere of moral dulness about her, as about all Socinian women.'[11] Tolerance was the measure of Unitarian life but to many it seemed like moral laxity. The evangelical call to righteousness was met on quite different terms by the Unitarian. Elizabeth Gaskell danced and played cards, she drank wine and enjoyed the theatre, but she was also a prison visitor, she conducted a ragged school in her home and she visited factories and mills. No writer of her day had travelled so far through all the ranks of society and been accepted in all of them. She was intimately acquainted with poverty and crime and she tended to see one as being the natural consequence of the other. Her letters provide an incisive commentary upon social work and education; certainly few writers showed more compassion for the outcasts of their society, the insane, the criminal and the prostitute.

Unlike George Eliot, who looked back to St Theresa as the glory of womankind, Elizabeth Gaskell revered Florence Nightingale. Before she had become the saint of the Crimea, she was accorded that title by Elizabeth Gaskell for her work among the prostitutes at Middlesex Hospital during the cholera epidemic. When one of the women prayed that Miss Nightingale would never know her despair, she replied: 'Oh, my girl, are you not now more merciful than the God you think you are going to?' (G.L. 217). It was the response of a Unitarian who sincerely doubted whether the God of inflexible morality revered by her fellow Christians was quite the same as the God of creation. Elizabeth Gaskell recorded the passage with fervent devotion to her friend Emily Shaen. Florence Nightingale, washing and dressing the sores of her cholera patients, embodied the Unitarian ideal of an individual serving the needs of society. It was not unreasoned praise that she accorded Miss Nightingale. In the midst of her eulogy she could pause and, with sympathetic detachment, commiserate with Mrs Nightingale who once said tearfully that she felt like a duck that had given birth to a wild swan.

Throughout her life Elizabeth Gaskell studied society, not as theorist, but as one actually involved in its crises. Most writers of the day dreaded the mob, but Elizabeth Gaskell laughingly recorded the fear of many Mancunians when troops were withdrawn from the city during the Crimean War. She did not see the workers as Carlyle's 'great dumb toiling class',[12] but as individuals who could often create a richer cultural life for themselves than the manufacturers. And for Manchester she shared all the ambivalent attitudes felt by any inhabitant of a great city. She detested the dirt and smoke, but she never failed to share her husband's pride in its people. When the opportunity came for him to be transferred to London, they both refused to move. He lectured on the Lancashire dialect and collected the songs and the poetry of the workers, while she recorded the drama of their lives.

Benjamin Disraeli's aphorism, 'what Art was to the ancient world, Science is to the modern', aptly described a city that numbered ten major scientific societies among its cultural institutions.[13] Art and science were combined in the Literary and Philosophical Society of which William Gaskell was a director and where he frequently spoke. And these societies, founded in the main by Unitarians, were not meeting places for a cultural elite. Their lectures were open to the public and the well-informed, astute Mancunian was quick to grasp the educational opportunities around him. Job Legh with his interest in etymology, Nicholas Higgins spending his earnings on books were workers in a unique industrial city. If the rich chose to live apart from the poor, and some Unitarians were as conservative as High Church bishops, it was still possible for them to share the same culture at public lectures and at Charles Hallé's concerts. Natural science was to be the aesthetic of Manchester as art had been of ancient Athens and Renaissance Florence. As a writer, Elizabeth Gaskell's preoccupation was with the behaviour of people in society, the problems of environment and the definition of social class. She was not simply the recorder of her times, but the defining voice of a city that would eventually alter the structure of English society.

2
Mary Barton: the condition of the working class in Manchester

From its publication in the revolutionary year of 1848, there was controversy and confusion of interpretation over *Mary Barton*, a confusion that has not been resolved today. Elizabeth Gaskell was never happy with Edward Chapman as either publisher or correspondent. Most writers found that his acknowledged personal charm did not extend to his business arrangements. He was dilatory both in his correspondence and his payments. With Elizabeth Gaskell, the relationship was uncomfortable from the beginning. She had been irritated when Chapman suggested a preface to the novel, relating its events to the revolutions in Europe. She had lived in Manchester since 1832, through its worst years of hunger, disease and industrial strife. To be told that she had written a 'relevant' book seemed absurd: 'I hardly know what you mean by an "explanatory" preface. The only thing I should like to make clear is that it is no catch-penny run up since the events on the Continent have directed public attention to the consideration of the state of affairs between the Employers, & their work-people' (G.L. 27). The novel was, she thought, self-explanatory. To her it was amazing that thinking people could have ignored for so long the new and troubled society in the industrial cities of England. Certainly, the problems of Manchester were not those of Paris or Berlin, and to conflate them would involve a distortion of fact. It would also encourage the reader to look abroad for the instigators of riot and strike in Manchester. This was not her intention.

The original title of the novel was *A Manchester Love Story*, but at Chapman's suggestion this became *Mary Barton*, subtitled *A Tale of Manchester Life*. Critics have indulged themselves at the expense of the novel because of a statement Elizabeth Gaskell later made that her initial idea had been to compose a tragic poem about a working man, John Barton. It was to the wife of William Rathbone Greg, the Unitarian industrialist, that she recalled having first decided to write a work around 'an ignorant man full of rude, illogical thought' (G.L. 42). The letter refers not so much to the novel as it later became, but to the antagonistic review Greg had written about her delineation of industrial life in Manchester.[1] Elizabeth Gaskell wanted to placate Greg who was, after all, one of the more enlightened cotton manufacturers. It was always her hope that more manufacturers would see that it was in their own interest to make concessions to their workers, to understand that the sharing of labour in a mutual enterprise was essentially a co-operative undertaking. Nevertheless, in her letter to Mrs Greg she would not abandon her belief in the moral justification of her theme. Manchester may have been the marvel of the manufacturing world, but its wealth was spun from the lives of men, women and children, as well as from cotton. John Barton is not a rude or illogical man in the novel, and his tragedy is that not even courage, intelligence and great determination can withstand a famine of the body and the spirit imposed by a capitalist society.

As was customary in all Elizabeth Gaskell's major works, although its original conception may have been the story of a man—just as 'Mr Harrison's Confessions' (1851) is a tentative prelude to *Wives and Daughters* (1864)—it became, in the course of development, the story of a young woman. Mary the child becomes Mary Barton the woman, who acquires an understanding of herself and society from misfortune and death. It is Mary who redeems both Jem and her father, by saving one from the gallows and the other from committing a double crime, of murder and allowing an innocent man to hang. This redemptive power is not the passive grace exerted by the angel in the house, not the mellifluous goodness of Agnes Wickfield who taught David Copperfield the meaning of domestic love. Instead, Mary confronts society at every turn and eventually overcomes it. Whether she is running in delight to the local shop as a child, proud in her possession of the money to buy the tea for her parents and the Wilsons, or racing against time and tide to bring Will Wilson back to Liverpool assizes to give evidence on Jem's behalf, she is the active force in the novel. It is her actions for good or ill that provide the catalyst for events. Her flirtation with Harry Carson causes Jem to be suspected of his murder, but it is her flight to Liverpool that leads to his rescue.

The emphasis upon Mary Barton does not eclipse the significance of her father. An able, quick-witted and conscientious working man, Barton is driven to opium addiction and murder by the oppression of a social system that denies him work and eventually life itself. As Adam Smith cogently remarked, slaves were better treated than workers because replacing a slave meant an expenditure of capital whereas workers, in time of depression, could be hired or dismissed at the owner's pleasure. They were not even dignified by a title of status, lowly as that of slave might be. Instead they were 'hands', truncated objects of labour to be retained or discarded at the whim of the employer. John Barton is not an object; he thinks and feels, and when deprived of all hope, he will kill for bread and justice. It is a novel of two narrative themes. Love and courage do eventually surmount disease and death, but the victory is won at the price of a certain loss. Jem and Mary emigrate to the simpler world of Canada. In one sense they have triumphed, but in a deeper sense it is Manchester that has defeated them by destroying John Barton, and by driving the two lovers out of its darkness into the serene light of a Canadian forest. The myth of Eden is reversed. Manchester will not tolerate those who have transgressed its iron laws. The punishment it metes out is death or exile. Like the workmen marked down at every mill because they are trades-unionists, Jem is driven out because he has broken the law of the city and survived.

Elizabeth Gaskell had already written about Manchester before she began *Mary Barton*. With her husband she had composed *Sketches among the Poor* (1837), which she stated to be in the style of Crabbe, but with a 'more seeing-beauty spirit'. The qualification is important. Crabbe's poetry, as Raymond Williams observes,[2] was blunted by the ambiguities of his moral and social position, domestic chaplain to the Duke of Rutland and priest to a congregation that included the destitute farm labourer as well as the landowner. But no matter how deeply Crabbe felt for the poor he could not forget his stipend was paid by the Duke of Rutland and that fact alone placed bounds upon his sympathies. Elizabeth Gaskell was never troubled by these restrictions. Her problem was one of eliciting her readers' sympathies for the poor without alienating them with her belief that poverty was not a natural condition but a state engendered by a capitalist society. Her solution was a narrative strategy of considerable subtlety. The poor are never objectified in her work, either by pity or the declamatory reforming zeal of the writer— they speak for themselves, and often at variance with the narrative commentary. Elizabeth Gaskell herself assumes the narrative stance of what may be described as a concerned middle-class reader. In effect she assumes the role of the reader, so that the characters may reveal themselves. Their individuality is preserved because the narrative voice so often contradicts the characters' thoughts and actions. The result is what Elizabeth Gaskell desired: her own voice becomes fiction, while the fictional characters assume reality. The tension is deliberately induced and becomes her most typical narrative technique.

The novel begins in the traditional mood of arcadian retrospect made fashionable by Carlyle and Disraeli. 'There are some fields near Manchester, well known to the inhabitants as "Green Heys Fields", through which runs a public footpath to a little village about two miles distant' (Ch. 1). It is the landscape of a lost world that can be visited only on holidays and in the dreams of nostalgia. Elizabeth Gaskell appreciated that an industrial society walked forward while looking back to an imaginary golden age of rural simplicities. The romantic poets had endowed nature with a visionary quality that illuminated the prophecies of Carlyle and Disraeli. Both saw the ideal age as a restoration of a 'merrie England', a medieval, feudal Eden where stalwart yeomen stood in pride on their ancestral acres and charitable squires looked to the needs of their tenants. Having spent her childhood in the country and being well acquainted with village life, Elizabeth Gaskell did not follow the contemporary vogue for judging the present by appeals to an imperfectly recollected past. Memory, as she shows with Alice

Wilson, can be a web of illusions, particularly when those memories are derived from childhood experience. Certainly she could not accept the myth of a happy peasantry. The peasantry she remembered had more in common with Crabbe's than Kenelm Digby's rustic yokels in *The Broadstone of Honour*. Disraeli, who knew less of country life than most writers, never failed to recall the days when 'the people were better clothed, better lodged, and better fed just before the war of the roses . . .' (*Sybil, or the Two Nations*, Bk 3, Ch. 5). In *Coningsby* the problems of an industrial society are apparently resolved by a marriage between the aristocratic hero and the daughter of Millbank, the manufacturer. Unfortunately it is always memory, deceptive or actual, that helps to shape man's vision of the real world. Elizabeth Gaskell had no need to recall the Lake Poets or novelists like Digby and Disraeli when she wrote of the town and the country. Both were part of her own experience.

For the workers, the quality of their daily life in the factory or the mill would always be measured against the country that now existed for them as a place of holidays and infrequent leisure. In Green Heys Fields, the town is only half-a-mile away, but workers can walk and play there, and 'Here in their seasons may be seen the country business of hay-making, ploughing, etc., which are such pleasant mysteries for townspeople to watch' (Ch. 1). There is a note of irony punctuating the noncommital prose. It always is pleasant to watch other people working, particularly when the work seems quaint, jovial and linked with the traditions of one's own past. Country labour now seemed part of the whole holiday atmosphere for the city worker, much as tourists find peon labour in South America a picturesque subject for photographs. Popular fiction still extolled rural virtues and deplored the vices of the city. The country as a place of work had passed beyond the experiential understanding of most readers. The rural landscape portrayed in the early novels of Dickens, or by Disraeli, lacks the visionary quality of a Renaissance pastoral but shares its basic unreality. Elizabeth Gaskell never used the country in this way. It is never a stick to belabour the city. She is always aware of the beauty of trees and flowers, the changing of the seasons, but she also knew that Caliban toiled on an island that seemed a paradise to strangers.

Critics of the city and its problems were caught in the dilemma of wondering what standard of values could be applied. Frequently there are contradictions in their own writings that point more directly to an appeal to fiction than to demonstrable facts. Peter Gaskell wrote of the stability of country life, of generations living in the same village, frequently as 'one great family',[3] of children growing up under the watchful care of parents engaged in domestic manufacture, and stressing the essential unity of the family as the priceless jewel of the golden age. It was, like most discussions of family structure, a fiction bearing less relation to life than most. In his evocation of rural life he was troubled by death rates that were often higher than those of the city, but offset them against the city worker's life that was, in his opinion, one long disease. He admitted the sexual licence of many rural areas but declared that premarital intercourse was always sanctioned by a later marriage. In the city among industrial workers he could discern only the grossest immorality and sexual promiscuity resulting from the dissolution of family life. Peter Gaskell was an honest and reliable witness to events. As a doctor he had practical experience of city life in poor areas, but his attempt to draw statistical evidence from the past was based more on wishful thinking than historical evidence. On the size of families, Adam Smith was closer to the truth when he wrote that in the Highlands of Scotland it was not uncommon for a woman to bear twenty children and see only two live to be adults.[4] Elizabeth Gaskell makes plain in *Mary Barton* that although death could strike the city in holocausts of famine and disease, life could still, given steady employment, be infinitely richer than the existence of the country labourer.

It was, however, Peter Gaskell's vision of country life that prevailed, given added force by Friedrich Engels's *The Condition of the Working Class in England*, written in Germany in 1844 after twenty months spent in Manchester. Engels was inspired by Peter Gaskell and Carlyle, both social catastrophists, both predicting the imminent collapse of industrial society in revolution. The full impact of Engels's work did not reach the United States and England until 1887 and 1892 when translations first appeared in those countries. By that time Peter Gaskell's works and Kay and Ridgeway's studies of industrial Manchester were all out of print, and Elizabeth Gaskell had become the Mrs Gaskell of *Cranford*. Peter Gaskell was absorbed by Engels's work, but the links between the two are obvious. Engels borrowed from the former his view of rural society living at peace under the 'free, the balmy, and the uncontaminated breath of heaven', a way of life producing 'a sluggish mind in an active body'[5] and proceeded to summarise it in the line: 'They vegetated happily and but for the Industrial Revolution would never have left this way of life, which was indeed idyllic.'[6] Making good use of Peter Gaskell's denunciation of sexual promiscuity, Engels described the libidinous city workers taking refuge from their toil in drink and sex. It would seem from Engels that a virtuous woman in the cotton mills was as rare as a flower in a furnace, an attitude determined, perhaps, by the fact that Engels's mistress at this time was a millworker.

Elizabeth Gaskell accepted neither her kinsman's nostalgia for the past nor his belief in a catastrophic end to industrial society. And she rejected his denunciations of indiscriminate working-class immorality. What led strangers to draw false conclusions, she implies, was the free and open manner of the women workers. Against the background of an arcadian past in the first chapter of *Mary Barton* the millworkers laugh and play on a holiday that may have been granted by the employers, but may equally well have been taken by them as 'a right of nature and her beautiful spring time'. These are not mindless drudges despite the arduous work and long hours. The women reflect the independence that comes from being wage-earners in their own right: 'Groups of merry and somewhat loud-talking girls, whose ages might range from twelve to twenty, came by with a buoyant step. . . . Their faces were not remarkable for beauty; indeed, they were below the average, with one or two exceptions: they had dark hair, neatly and classically arranged, dark eyes, but sallow complexions and irregular features. The only thing to strike a passer-by was an acuteness and intelligence of countenance, which has often been noticed in a manufacturing population' (Ch. 1). And when Jem steals a kiss from Mary Barton he receives a resounding slap, a blow she regards as the correct response to impertinence, and no cause for repentance, as Eleanor Bold regretted slapping Mr Slope's face in Trollope's *Barchester Towers*. Unlike Eleanor, Mary's natural instincts had never been blunted by the need to behave like a lady. In John Barton's view, ladies were a plague to themselves and everyone else, and the desire to become one the reason why Mary's aunt had run away from home. When he recalls how Esther had promised to make Mary a lady one day, his anger is voiced in a biblical cadence: ' "I'd rather see her earning her bread by the sweat of her brow, as the Bible tells her she should do, ay, though she never got butter to bread, than be like a do-nothing lady, worrying shopmen all morning, and screeching at her pianny all afternoon, and going to bed without having done a good turn to any one of God's creatures but herself" ' (Ch. 1).

Mary has, however, never forgotten her aunt's promise and she knows instinctively how a good-looking shopgirl can become a lady. She must sell herself at the altar to a gentleman, and the transaction need not be as grim and heartless as Edith's marriage to Mr Dombey when the lover is young and handsome like Harry Carson. Her virginity has a price and it must not be sold for less than marriage. Nothing, as Mary knows, was more reckless than to live with a man in the hope that marriage would follow in due course. She is reason and commonsense, and tough shrewdness of Lancashire that prefers 'brass' to stardust and dreaming. Mary knows precisely what she wants from marriage with young Carson and love is a secondary consideration. She can even convince herself that she will be able to play Lady Bountiful to her friends and her family when she is Mrs Carson. As for Jem, her faithful lover, he too may share in her good fortune with something profitable in the business line being put in his way. Her dreams are of riding from the church in finery, to take up 'her astonished father, and drive away from the dim work-a-day court for ever, to live in a grand house, where her father should have newspapers, and pamphlets, and pipes, and meat dinners, every day . . .' (Ch. 7). It is not an idle dream, not a little milliner longing for a prince, but Mary

Barton, dressmaker's apprentice, who is fully aware that Harry Carson's parents worked in a mill like her father, and that, in effect, Mrs Carson's place in working-class society had been rather lower than her own. It is clear to her that her father will never be able to give up his radical pamphlets, his Chartist petitions, but she sees no reason why he should not combine them with a few luxuries provided by his daughter.

John Barton cannot break free from the prison of industrial society. It is only when he has tried every means possible that violence becomes his only recourse. For Mary, there is the escape possible for a woman, a marriage chosen for its material benefits. It was the escape planned by Esther, her aunt, who leaves Manchester with a young army officer, but instead of insisting upon marriage becomes his mistress and gives birth to a child. When her lover is posted to Ireland, Esther is left with the child and £50. Poverty forces her onto the streets and Esther becomes a prostitute and an alcoholic. There is no sense of a fall from virtue in Esther, she has simply tried to improve her position in society by the only method she knows, and she fails. Mary, on the other hand, is quite prepared to marry for money and a modicum of affection, but not when she finally knows that Jem is the man she loves. Harry Carson has no intention of marrying Mary, but is prepared to bargain, 'feeling that at any price he must have her, only that he would obtain her as cheaply as he could' (Ch. 11). The 'cash nexus' affected the relationship between employer and worker less intimately than it did young lovers from different social ranks. Sally Leadbitter, the self-appointed matchmaker, is delighted when Harry Carson is forced to propose and Mary refuses him. Sally takes great pleasure in reminding him what had led Mary to think that he was planning a proposal of marriage from the very beginning. Harry explains:

'My father would have forgiven any temporary connexion, far sooner than my marrying any one so far beneath me in rank.'
'I thought you said, sir, your mother was a factory girl,' reminded Sally, rather maliciously.
'Yes, yes!—but then my father was in much such a station; at any rate there was not the disparity there is between Mary and me' (Ch. 11).

And when Harry consoles himself with the notion that women always have second thoughts and that Mary will return to him, there is the final gratifying thought: ' "Mind! I don't say I shall offer her the same terms again." ' In a society of cash transactions, Mary's innate shrewdness tells her that there are some human relationships that are best not defined by money.

Elizabeth Gaskell, as a prison visitor and social worker, knew more about prostitution than most writers of the day. It was not innate virtue that saved a working girl from the streets but commonsense and intelligence. Esther, like Ruth Denbigh, is a simple soul whose yearnings do not extend beyond fine clothes and a release from factory work. She is seduced, not so much sexually as socially. It is for this reason that John Barton cannot forgive her. To try to become a lady is to desire all that he despises most in life. Bedraggled and forlorn, Esther is known to the local police as 'the Butterfly', being picked up regularly for disorderly vagrancy. But stupidity is not, in Elizabeth Gaskell's canon, a crime meriting punishment. So in her novels a young girl who is seduced does not meet the same fate and is not delineated in quite the same fashion as the 'fallen woman' of Victorian fiction.

Mary's most remarkable attribute as a woman in Victorian literature is her independence. From the night of her mother's death in childbirth she has been mistress of the house, and a breadwinner as well. Engels saw working women disrupting family life, an attitude he shared with Peter Gaskell, but Elizabeth Gaskell saw a woman deriving strength and dignity from the ability to earn her own living. This is not stated in the narrative commentary but through Mary herself, using her own money to run the home and buy food for her father, capable of making decisions without recourse to advice from others. Far from families being broken by city life they are fortified by the ability of all adult members to find work. Unlike Engels and Peter Gaskell she saw the fragmentation of family life brought about by rural conditions. In the country it had always been customary to place young children in service, or to send them out to earn their livings as soon as they reached adolescence. George Wilson and his sister Alice indicate this in the novel. Tom Wilson left the family farm first and found work in Manchester. Then, as Alice continues, he ' " . . . sent word what terrible lots of work was to be had, both for lads and lasses. So father sent George first . . . and then work was scarce out toward Burton, where we lived, and father said I maun try and get a place. And George wrote as how wages were far higher in Manchester than Milnthorpe or Lancaster . . ." ' (Ch. 4). The pattern of rural migration to the city was dictated not only by the impoverishment of farm life but by the attraction of high wages and the vitality of urban culture. The loneliness of the country labourer can be far more acute than that of the city worker. A man ploughing an empty field does not know the companionship of the factory, but often hungers for it. It is intellectualised romanticism to argue otherwise.

In the city, families lived in small units unless forced by extreme poverty to share dwelling-places. Alice Wilson lives alone until her brother dies; she then moves in with her sister-in-law, but even with young Jem Wilson, it is still only a family of three. Demographers would approve Elizabeth Gaskell's representation of family size. The comparison is drawn sharply between the workers' homes and families, and the household of Carson with four adult daughters, a son, and a flock of servants living under the same roof. It is emphasised that in Manchester the working-class population was effectively regulated by disease and death. But families among the workers were not confined to near relations; there was no sense of alienation, rather a feeling of mateship, which binds John Barton to George Wilson and sends them both to the bedside of Davenport, the Methodist millworker dying of typhus. 'The poor mun help the poor' is the creed of these men, and they can and do stand by each other. Elizabeth Gaskell understood the nature of working-class solidarity long before most socialist theorists. Families were united by mutual adversity and friends often became closer than family. When Sturgis, the old boatman, picks up the bemused Mary Barton from the dockside in Liverpool and takes her home to his wife, she immediately suspects that Mary may be a prostitute, but even this does not cast out compassion: ' "Well-a-well! It's the bad ones as have the broken hearts, sure enough; good folk never get utterly cast down, they've always getten hope in the Lord: it's the sinful as bear the bitter, bitter grief in their crushed hearts, poor souls; it's them we ought, most of all to pity and to help" ' (Ch. 31). The old couple take Mary in and treat her like a daughter. The virtues of friendship and sympathetic generosity were not attributes of country life denied the city dweller.

It is in Alice Wilson that Elizabeth Gaskell subtly reveals the relationship between town and country for the poor. Living in a cellar under No 14, Barber Street, a short distance from the Wilsons and the Bartons. Alice has devoted her life to the care of others and to the recall of her childhood. It is after Mary's probing questions that certain discrepancies are disclosed in her story. All her life in Manchester Alice has dreamed of the farm where she grew up, but there were always reasons why she could not go back, reasons that partially obscure the real one. When Mary touches upon this, Margaret, Job Legh's granddaughter, immediately intervenes. Alice speaks of the time when as a domestic servant she had to look for another place.

'Well, but,' interrupted Mary, 'I should have thought that was the best time to go home.'
'No, I thought not. You see it was a different thing going home for a week on a visit, may be with money in my pocket to give father a lift, to going home to be a burden to him. Besides, how could I hear o' a place there. Anyways I thought it best to stay, though perhaps it might have been better to ha' gone, for then I should ha' seen mother again;' and the poor old woman looked puzzled.
'I'm sure you did what you thought right,' said Margaret, gently (Ch. 4).

Alice was forced to leave home because the farm could not support three adults. Her father was pleased when George wrote from Manchester and Alice was 'all agog to go'. Only her mother silently grieved to see her leave home. But the reason was there in the idyllic countryside that Alice remembers every waking hour of her life. To the two girls she describes a scene that has become like a coloured etching in her mind.

> 'Well, and near our cottage were rocks. Eh, lasses! ye don't know what rocks are in Manchester! Gray pieces o' stone as large as a house, all covered over wi' moss of different colours, some yellow, some brown; and the ground between them knee-deep in purple heather, smelling sae sweet and fragrant, and the low music of the humming-bee for ever sounding among it. Mother used to send Sally and me out to gather ling and heather for besoms, and it was such pleasant work! And then mother would make us sit down under the old hawthorn tree (where we used to make our house among the great roots as stood above the ground), to pick and tie up the heather. It seems all like yesterday' (Ch. 4).

The landscape Alice describes so rapturously is a barren waste. The Wilson farm was on a shaded hillside, stone covered and eroded, where heather flourished but not crops or cattle. And two children spent their days making gorse brooms. It is a scene of bleak poverty, but in memory it can become a lost paradise. Wisely, Alice always found excuses for not returning to test the dream against reality. This is not made apparent through narrative commentary, but in dialogue. The voice of the narrator describes a romantic fiction, and Alice in her own words shows how memory can translate hardship and rejection into a treasured sanctuary of the mind. It can also, as Mary perceives, provide an effective barrier to action. She, all commonsense and reason, has her own dreams, but they are ones that seem well within her grasp. A proposal of marriage from the infatuated Harry Carson does not seem improbable. Alice Wilson is neither shrewd nor quick witted, and in a lifetime of domestic drudgery it is only the reverie of the Burton farm that has provided meaning to her life. But this deliberate retreat to the past, this cherished memory, has never permitted her to become an adult. She is still a child, and when she dies it is with appeals to her mother and babbled talk of a linnet's nest and a hawthorn tree. The narrator intrudes awkwardly, affirming Alice's deep faith in God and then provides the Nunc Dimittis for the old washerwoman. The profusion of

34

Christian sentiments point to the narrator's embarrassment that Alice should die without recourse to formal religious phrases. The apologetic tone of the narrative gives added point to the psychological and social implications of Alice Wilson. The best and most devoted people may well be seeking atonement for a passage in their lives that has passed beyond their rational comprehension. Alice Wilson's abiding grief was that she did not go back to see her mother before she died, that she did not even attend her funeral, and again, the reasons she gives are confused and inconsistent. But as she dies, she does not call upon God to forgive her, but her mother. This is what Mary understood when Alice explained why she could not go home, and what Margaret would not let her make known.

The narrative commentary has two functions in *Mary Barton*; it is descriptive and analytic, or homiletic. The latter occurs when an event has to be extenuated or excused —the Nunc Dimittis for Alice Wilson, for example—and the former when a social condition is examined or a character's emotions are observed. The homiletic voice uses religious references to pacify and appease; the analytical voice frequently reveals religion as a radical and revolutionary force in people's lives. Religious conformity could call upon a congregation to pray that all men should be kept in their proper stations, but the voice of radical dissent could seek to know whether those stations should be determined by God or man. In Manchester, Engels failed to observe that while Methodism could well comfort the millowner in the acquisition of wealth and authority, it could also inspire the millworker to rebellion. The links between religion and trades-unionism are forged from the experience of the past in England. The Levellers and Diggers who sought a new society in the days of the Commonwealth were succeeded by the Methodist preachers in the Kentish Weald who served as agents for the labourers in the Captain Swing risings.[7] John Barton's religious faith is grounded in certain texts that castigate the rich and condone his determination to change the condition of the poor. It is in Green Heys Fields that the pattern of social action is established, and it is expressed in biblical terms. As Wilson says, John Barton never 'could abide the gentlefolk'. They had never been benign or paternalistic to him. In consequence Barton feels that the owners have denied the workers the basic right to live, common to all humanity.

'Don't think to come over me with the old tale, that the rich know nothing of the trials of the poor. I say, if they don't know, they ought to know. We are their slaves as long as we can work; we pile up their fortunes with the sweat of our brows; and yet we are to live as separate as if we were in two worlds; ay, as separate as Dives and Lazarus, with a great gulf betwixt us; but I know who was best off then,' and he wound up his speech with a low chuckle that had no mirth in it (Ch. 1).

It is not John Barton's intention to wait for the next world to rectify this situation. His passionate resolve to demand change has grown from a lifetime of frustration and death. He knew he was a man when, as a child, he had enough strength to conceal his own hunger so that his younger brothers and sisters might eat. For John Barton the religion of the rich is a pious humbug, but his faith is a confirmation of social change. His words echo Rainborough's in the debate at Putney: ' "I would fain know what the soldier hath fought for all this while? He hath fought to enslave himself, to give power to men of riches, men of estates, to make him a perpetual slave." '[8] Slavery is the condition of life that John Barton will not accept. And like John Middleton in 'The Heart of John Middleton', he can justify his rebellion from the Bible. But a pacifying narrative voice intervenes to assure the reader that Barton's rage was not aroused by society but by the death of his wife. It is this voice that speaks for middle-class conservatism and is self-condemnatory. Too many voices have been heard, too much evidence has been given to the contrary to make it seem credible. The dimensions of reality and fiction are sharply defined as between the characters and the narrator, whose veracity has been weighed and found wanting. Yet it is this voice that expresses contemporary opinion and is, in a sense, like a mirror turned to reflect the reader.

It is over the deathbed of Ben Davenport, the Methodist

millworker, that John Barton most succinctly sets out the philosophy of labour. Carson's mill has burnt down, conveniently so, for it was a slack season, and his workers have been left idle. Among them is the devout Ben Davenport now dying of typhus in a cellar with a sick wife and starving children. His faith may have sustained him in life but now, in delirium, Davenport curses and swears until his frenzy passes into exhaustion. George Wilson goes to fetch an infirmary order for the dying man from Carson, who lives some distance from the town in a suburban villa. Carson signs the order readily enough and young Harry Carson, eager to be off and away in the chance of seeing Mary, even gives Wilson five shillings for Davenport and his family. It is precisely the amount that John Barton received from the pawnbroker when he put his coat and silk pocket handkerchief in pledge, using the money to buy food and medicine. The contrast is drawn as starkly as it appears to Barton.

The rural labourer seldom had the opportunity of evaluating his worldly goods by comparison with the landowner's. The country poor were not encouraged to visit the manor house. But John Barton is constantly made aware of his own poverty and the wealth of the owners. When his son was dying,

> He thought it would be no sin to steal and would have stolen; but he could not get the opportunity in the few days the child lingered. Hungry himself, almost to an animal pitch of ravenousness, but with the bodily pain swallowed up in anxiety for his little sinking lad, he stood at one of the shop windows where all edible luxuries are displayed; haunches of venison, Stilton cheeses, moulds of jelly—all appetising sights to the common passer by. And out of this shop came Mrs Hunter! She crossed to her carriage, followed by the shopman loaded with purchases for a party. The door was quickly slammed to, and she drove away; and Barton returned home with a bitter spirit of wrath in his heart, to see his only boy a corpse! (Ch. 3).

Hunter was Barton's employer who had closed his gates a few weeks earlier, giving notice of impending bankruptcy. Business failures, like fires, did not always operate to the detriment of the owner. Barton knew that what may appear as a temporary reverse to the employer could well lead to eventual profit, while for the worker it meant starvation.

From this continuing disparity of fortune, Barton derives the philosophy that makes him a trades-unionist and a militant Chartist. If he should falter he can always walk down those crowded streets where the rich go to shop and the poor to feed their eyes and imagination. Barton knows that he can never hope to achieve Carson's status as a millowner. Rags had a tendency to remain rags in the 1830s and 1840s. In the early years of the century it was common enough for the cotton men to begin modestly, buying a few mules, knocking down the inner walls of a cottage to make a factory, perhaps employing six or seven helpers. This was how Carson began, but now it required a minimum capital investment of £5,000 to establish the smallest mill. It is for this reason that Barton does not dream of becoming a capitalist. He knows that he must accept the wage system; he asks only that he be given the opportunity to work and a just wage. Wilson, amiable and good-natured, reminds his friend that God is their provider and the father of all men, to which Barton replies: ' "Don ye think he's th' masters' father, too? I'd be loath to have 'em for brothers" ' (Ch. 6). Unlike the 'rude, illogical man' that may have been Elizabeth Gaskell's first conception, Barton can reason with all the logic of a confirmed Socialist:

> 'You'll say (at least many a one does), they'n gotten capital an' we'n gotten none. I say, our labour's our capital and we ought to draw interest on that. They get interest on their capital somehow a' this time, while ourn is lying idle, else how could they all live as they do? Besides, there's many on 'em as had nought to begin wi'; there's Carsons, and Duncombes, and Mengies, and many another, as comed into Manchester with clothes to their back, and that were all, and now they're worth their tens of thousands, a' getten out of our labour; why the very land as fetched but sixty pound twenty year agone is now worth six hundred, and that, too, is owing to our labour: but look at yo', and see me, and poor Davenport yonder; whatten better are we? They'n screwed us down to the lowest peg, in order to make their great big fortunes, and build their great big houses, and we, why we're just clemming, many and many of us. Can you say there's nought wrong in this?' (Ch. 6).

And Wilson can only equivocate.

Elizabeth Gaskell presents a spectrum of working-class life in *Mary Barton* that is as varied as it is clamorous in its demands. Men and women speak for themselves, frequently in argument over what is required to ameliorate their condition, but it is their hunger and their want that makes a union not only necessary but inevitable. It was easy in the 1830s and 1840s to translate a religious assembly into union organisation. At the early Owenite union meetings chapters were read from the Bible vindicating the rights of the poor and praising the strength of union. Oaths were taken and socialism was preached with all the confidence of a new faith.[9] John Barton becomes a follower of Feargus O'Connor and his paper, *The Northern Star*, the most radical journal of the Chartist press. But he is not a dupe of conniving political agents. He always assesses what he reads and hears against his own experience. Thus, he approves an article in *The Northern Star* calling for shorter hours by his recollection of an episode at the infirmary where he had been given the task of sorting the surgeon's papers. Examining the admission sheets he soon realised that the greatest number of factory accidents occurred in the last two hours of work (Ch. 8).

Mary Barton is an unwilling witness to meetings of union delegates who come to the house planning the presentation of the Charter in London. John Barton now believes that since all appeals to the owners have failed, they must march to Westminster and demand justice from the queen and parliament. Because of his union activities he has been refused work at the few mills remaining open and he is being supported by Mary's meagre earnings. Slowly starving, he begins to chew opium to still the pangs of hunger and once in despairing rage he beats Mary and throws her out of the house. Every incident, every action indicates a man being driven to violent crime. Murder was not uncommon in Manchester, and Elizabeth Gaskell knew the story of young Ashton, the son of one of the principal cotton manufacturers, who had been shot during the strike of 1831–32. Peter Gaskell left a record of it[10] and Elizabeth Gaskell used the incident and the circumstances in the death of Harry Carson. But whereas Peter Gaskell regarded the crime as brute assassination, she saw it as the anguished consequence of misery. All hope rested with a petition to parliament. And in the year 1839 John Barton is chosen as one of the delegates to present the case for the poor of Manchester to the legislators. Every man and woman has a particular wish to be fulfilled, a need to be answered. One wants machines done away with, another wants a short hours' Bill, and Mrs Davenport wants the restrictions against child labour repealed so that her thirteen-year-old son can get work in the factory instead of roaming the streets. Peter Gaskell and Engels both predicted that children would be the major working-force in the factories, but Elizabeth Gaskell had seen the inspectors regulating child labour and knew how effective they were. She also knew how bitterly many parents resented this restriction of their authority over their own children. The advice to Barton runs from the ludicrous to the sage, but everyone holds firm to the conviction that, as Barton says, ' "yo see now, if better times don't come after parliament knows all" ' (Ch. 8).

John Barton returns to Manchester from London to learn that his old friend George Wilson is dead and there is no hope of redress from parliament. The poor will remain poor and those who are starving will die. London has been a grotesque nightmare for Barton in which the postilions seemed like gentlemen wearing parsons' wigs and the horses were sleeker than the delegates from the manufacturing towns. When Barton tried to cross Oxford Street he was knocked back by the police who accused him of frightening the horses. In despair, he says to his daughter: ' "Mary, we mun speak to our God to hear us, for man will not hearken; no, not now, when we weep tears o' blood" ' (Ch. 9). Having little acquaintance with a God of loving kindness, Barton calls upon the Lord of Hosts, and knows there is sufficient biblical writ to sanction violence. It is when parliament, the voice of the people, remains mute that the trades-union becomes a militant force in society.

Determined to break the union's resistance the owners advertise for labour, but at lower rates than had ever been previously offered. There is a demand, even for starvation wages, from the country labourers. 'Foot-sore, way-worn, half-starved looking men they were, as they tried to steal into town in the early dawn, before people were astir, or late in the dusk of evening' (Ch. 15). These are the knobsticks, strike-breaking weavers from the country areas; they are waylaid by the Manchester unionists and many of them beaten and burned with vitriol. Every means of intimidation is used to keep cheap labour out of the city and to hold out against the owners. It is John Barton who sees the futility of attacking men poorer than themselves when it is the masters who should be forced to yield. A meeting between the workers and the owners has led to an obdurate refusal on Carson's part to compromise. When some of the owners are prepared to conciliate, he insists that no member of a trades-union or affiliated society should be employed by any Manchester mill. And every delegate at the meeting is a unionist. Exacerbating them even further, Harry Carson sketches a cartoon of the workers that is passed around amongst the owners with amused approval. It is 'the jesting picture' that makes the young artist the chosen victim. The cartoon is torn up, one piece is marked, and each member of the union draws. It is John Barton who is elected the murderer.

The crime committed, John Barton flees from the city, while the police arrest Jem Wilson. The evidence points to him; it was his gun found near Carson's body, and a police spy disguised as a working-man has already ascertained this from Jem's mother. But Mary knows the identity of the murderer from the scrap of paper her aunt Esther found in the hedge near the spot where the gunman stood. She must save Jem, not only because he is her lover, but in order to spare her father from the guilt of having a second murder laid to his account. When she returns to Manchester, she finds her father sitting by the cold grate, a dying man. John Barton calls for Carson and confesses, but although the narrator stresses his repentance and grief, there are certain facts that Barton does not reveal. He makes no mention of the union or the oath taken by its members to commit murder, and he does not try to clear Jem Wilson until after the court has acquitted him. Not even Job Legh will enlighten Carson on the union's part in the murder. When Carson questions him after Barton's death, demanding to know if his son was murdered in consequence of the part he had played in the strike, Job answers slowly: ' "Well, sir . . . it's hard to say: John Barton was not a man to take counsel with people; nor did he make many words about his doings. So I can only judge from his way of thinking and talking in general, never having heard him breathe a syllable concerning this matter in particular" ' (Ch. 37). Repentance did not extend to the implication of fellow workers in a crime, nor could Barton confess without involving the union. So his silence was unbroken, even though it meant sacrificing the life of a man he had come to regard as a son. Elizabeth Gaskell knew how strong the sense of loyalty could be within a union, but she reveals it by implication, not statement.

It is Jem Wilson who can shoulder his way through the new society much as John Carson did at an earlier time. The cotton magnates were being challenged as leaders of industry by the engineers in the 1830s. Textiles were yielding to the revolution in transport with railroads making the demand for iron seem insatiable. And the increasing complexity of machinery required trained workmen who were often inventors in their own right. Jem Wilson as overseer of the open hearth at Duncombe's has patented a new crankshaft for which he received a handsome royalty. When his father is thrown out of work Jem's earnings keep the family, but he cannot return to his old job with the suspicion of a murder trial still lingering about him. Duncombe suggests that he take a post in Canada, and Jem's only fear is that Mary may still want to remain in Manchester, 'the old smokejack'.

In 'Libbie Marsh's Three Eras', written in 1847, a year before *Mary Barton*, the workers on holiday in Dunham Park had looked back towards Manchester:

> Far, far away in the distance, on that flat plain, you might see the motionless cloud of smoke hanging over a great town, and that was Manchester—ugly, smoky Manchester; dear, busy, earnest, noble-working Manchester; where their children had been born, and where, perhaps, some lay buried; where their homes were, and where God had cast their lives, and told them to work out their destiny (Era 2).

That the destiny of the city worker need not have been one

of unrelieved misery was apparent to all those who enjoy
the high wages that were paid in the mills when trade w
prosperous. Power-loom weavers were the highest-paid indu
trial workers of the day. Archibald Alison and James Kay
were both agreed that it was not enclosures that were driving
people from the country, but the attraction of good wages
in the city. Industry brought with it a revolution of rising
expectations, a cornucopia of manufactured household goods
and the railroads to provide cheap transport across England.
Jem and Mary can both recall the days when the Barton
home was brightly furnished and a tea of eggs and Cumber-
land ham was served in front of a red-hot coal fire (Ch. 2).
In 'Libbie Marsh's Three Eras', Mrs Dixon thought nothing
of adding eggs to thicken the cream and rum to warm the
tea (Era 1). In good times the millworkers enjoyed a luxury
of material things that was unknown in a country village.
Jem knows that he could make a reasonable living in Manchester, but emigration is forced upon him after his acquittal.
There was only one man more despised in a workshop than
a knobstick and that was a convict. It is enough for Jem's
mates to know that he has stood in the shadow of the gallows
to shun his company. It was a situation that Elizabeth Gaskell
knew from the experience of her friend Thomas Wright, the
prison reformer and foreman of an iron foundry. When an
ex-convict was discovered in the workshop the men demanded
his dismissal, and Wright only secured his employment by
depositing £20 with the owners as security for the man's
good behaviour. For Jem, there was no Thomas Wright, and
emigration or ostracism are his only alternatives. The choice
is not an easy one and the young lovers do not leave Manchester without regret.

Death walks more closely with life in *Mary Barton* than in
most novels of the period. As a social realist, Elizabeth
Gaskell knew that death took the children first, but seemed
indiscriminate in its choice of grown men and women.
George Wilson dies suddenly in the street but his wife,
crippled by a factory accident in her youth, lives on to
accompany Jem and Mary to Canada. It is the wanton
destruction of life that records most faithfully actual conditions in Manchester. Typhus and cholera were regular

visitors to the slums of Ancoats and Ardwick, while the Medlock often seemed like the Styx oozing between charnel houses. It is made quite clear in the novel why Carson chooses to live two miles from his factory and the tenements of his workers. Manchester was already becoming the home of those not rich enough to live beyond its confines. Children were always the first to die in epidemics, and it is children, lost and injured, who punctuate the narrative of *Mary Barton*. They are the small accusing consciences of society: the Italian boy starving near Mary's home, the lost child that John Barton guides on his way, and the little girl who unconsciously echoes Christ's message from the cross to Carson.

All too often death does not accompany childbirth, age or chronic disease; it is not an act of God, but the sentence of a morally irresponsible society upon the weak and defenceless. Death was the not unnatural consequence of starvation in houses that were like foetid caves in a morass of ordure and stinking garbage. When Elizabeth Gaskell describes the Davenports' cellar she is engaging in her customary pictorial restraint. The reports of the sanitation commissions were less reticent and more detailed. As Asa Briggs has noted, 'Literature is much more revealing than economic data for the understanding of the attitudes of contemporaries to the social gulfs of the 1840s.'[11] Undoubtedly Elizabeth Gaskell was as much concerned with the subjective representation of events as she was with social attitudes. Peter Gaskell and Kay, commissions of enquiry and medical reports could all provide statistics for typhus and housing standards; Elizabeth Gaskell wanted to express the feeling of poverty, the hopeless anger at being out of work and unable to feed a family. The definition of external reality, the analysis of the form and movement of society is given deeper significance by her exploration of the psychological motivation of social and individual behaviour.

The workers of *Mary Barton* are not cartoon figures in varying attitudes of defiance and despair, and they have little in common with the Carlylean mob. They do not, like Stephen Blackpool in *Hard Times*, feel that society is ' "aw a muddle! Fro' first to last, a muddle!" ' Elizabeth Gaskell's workers think and reason, and above all, they respond passionately to social injustice. Within the context of an industrial society demanding conformity, they retain their individuality and their personal tastes range widely from Job Legh's etymological research to John Barton and George Wilson's contests at the shooting gallery. It is the complexity of human response that Elizabeth Gaskell reveals in the constant recall of the past, as the mind is drawn back in time even as the clock of conscious time moves forward. It is seen in John Barton after his wife's death, listening to a neighbour blundering about for soap and water as she lays out his wife's body upstairs; then there is a rush of memory that makes all physical action on his part impossible (Ch. 3). Or Mrs Wilson's reaction when Mary assures her that some means will be found to prove Jem's innocence, that the law will never hang him. ' "But I tell thee they will," interrupted Mrs Wilson, half-irritated at the light way, as she considered it, in which Mary spoke; and a little displeased that another could hope when she had almost brought herself to find pleasure in despair' (Ch. 22). It is these ambivalences of thought and feeling that give reality to the characters and make the narrative voice seem so inconsequential.

Honesty was Elizabeth Gaskell's touchstone for literature as it was for Matthew Arnold. And this honesty required a certain creative humility, particularly when Arnold insisted that the main function of the critic and writer was 'to see the object as in itself it really is'. For Arnold, to see was also to experience, to know the sense of being as well as to appreciate the actuality of vision. For the middle-class writer composing a novel of the working class, the desire for truth generally resulted in a tone of sympathetic patronage, the note that constantly jars a working-class reader in Charles Kingsley and Disraeli. Elizabeth Gaskell had lived amongst the poor of Manchester, she had seen her son die, but not of hunger, and while she had observed, she had certainly not experienced the famine years of the hungry Forties in Manchester. What she desired most was that, in her novel, the Mancunian workers would be able to speak for themselves; she wanted people to hear the resonant cadence of their speech and to give some impression of men and women who could sing as well as curse. The poor in *Mary Barton* are never poor in spirit. They can laugh at Job Legh's indignation as Will Wilson spins out his seafaring yarns of mermaids and other wonders, and they can listen rapt as Margaret sings the traditional laments of the city. They are shown to have a culture and a capacity for pleasure that is more refined than the Carson girls yawning over their piano. Who would not prefer to spend an evening with Job Legh and his friends rather than with the Carsons?

Only once does the restrained persona of caution break, and Elizabeth Gaskell speaks in a voice that is a call to action, a clear statement of the difference between acts of God and social crimes:

> Of all trite, worn-out, hollow mockeries of comfort that were ever uttered by people who will not take the trouble of sympathising with others, the one I dislike the most is the exhortation not to grieve over an event, 'for it cannot be helped'. Do you think if I could help it, I would sit still with folded hands, content to mourn? Do you not believe that as long as hope remained I would be up and doing? (Ch. 22).

Elizabeth Gaskell had buried her son but not her grief. The suffering she saw around her could be alleviated; there was no need for children to die of hunger when the city shops displayed every variety of food. If her own child could not be saved then it was possible for others to grow up in health and comfort. *Mary Barton* is not an elegy to the dead but an accusation of guilt.

It is not weakness but the deliberate evasion of the truth that reduces Mary to nervous hysteria after Jem has been acquitted. She knows she has certain proof that her father murdered Harry Carson and, by saving Jem from the gallows, she may lead to her father's conviction. So her illness is a refuge from a reality that has become unendurable. In Manchester, despite all her repugnance for her father, she chooses to send Jem away and nurse him in his last days, protecting him from arrest. It is, as Elizabeth Gaskell first stated, a love story in which a girl grows into a woman who can save in turn her lover and her father. Mary Barton's silence, her rejection of friends and betrothed, permit John Barton to die in his own home and not in prison. Barton's death is melodramatic, a tableau of industrial reconciliation, but Mary Barton's character and behaviour at this time are not. And Mrs Wilson's reaction is typically one of pettish annoyance that Jem could not have paid more attention at the death bed:

'Jem!' she was saying, 'thou might'st just as well never be at a death-bed again, if thou cannot bring off more news about it; here have I been by mysel' all day (except when oud Job came in), but thinks I, when Jem comes he'll be sure to be good company, seeing he was in the house at the very time of the death; and here thou art, without a word to throw at a dog, much less thy mother: it's no use thy going to a death-bed if thou cannot carry away any of the sayings!' (Ch. 36).

The sentimentality dissolves when characters complain like this with the grit of Lancashire in every syllable.

Elizabeth Gaskell was concerned with more than reproducing a dialect in *Mary Barton*; she wanted to give the richness of Lancashire speech and justify the pride Mancunians felt in their own tongue. *Mary Barton* shows Manchester looking at London, and finding it, as Mr Openshaw did in 'The Manchester Marriage', a city of fine, lazy people keeping late hours and ruining good English. Just as it is Manchester and not London that has the quality of historical place in the novel, the language of its people is more vibrant and resonant than the commonplace English of the narrative. John Barton was laughed at in London for his accent because dialect always had a comic or rustic connotation. Lancelot's reaction to the speech of the local farmers in Kingsley's *Yeast* was the customary one:

To his astonishment he hardly understood a word of it. It was half articulate, nasal, guttural, made up almost entirely of vowels, like the speech of savages. He had never before been struck with the significant contrast between the sharp, clearly defined articulation, the vivid and varied tones of the gentleman, or even of the London street-boy when compared with the coarse, half-formed growls, as of a company of seals, which he heard round him (Ch. 13).

It is, of course, typical of Kingsley that he does not record the reaction of those farmers to Lancelot's own impeccably modulated vowels. Elizabeth Gaskell not only gives the quality of Mancunian speech, but her husband carefully footnoted regional words and phrases, tracing them to sources in Chaucer and Skelton. The conclusion is obvious. As Mr Openshaw knew, Manchester spoke good Saxon, London a bastard Norman, and if London did not care for the comparison then it could lump it.

The contemporary criticism of *Mary Barton* was that Elizabeth Gaskell had been partial, and indeed prejudiced, in favour of the working classes in her novel. Lady Kay-Shuttleworth had written to her, gently deploring the absence of any socially responsible millowners in the novel and complaining that there was a complete absence of middle-class concern for the condition of the poor. Elizabeth Gaskell replied with some asperity:

> In the first place whatever power there was in Mary Barton was caused by my feeling strongly on the side which I took; now as I don't feel as strongly (and as it is impossible I ever should,) on the other side, the forced effort of writing on that side would end in a weak failure. I know, and have always owned, that I have represented *but one* side of the question, and no one would welcome more than I should, a true and earnest representation of the other side. I believe what I have said in Mary Barton to be perfectly true, but by no means the whole truth; and I have always felt deeply annoyed at anyone, or any set of people who chose to consider that I had manifested the whole truth; I do not think it is possible to do this in any *one* work of fiction (G.L. 72).

If the novel was fiction then Elizabeth Gaskell meant it to have more serious intent than was commonly accorded the term. John Barton was not a creation of her imagination, as she assured her dear friend Eliza Fox, but an actual person whose character and speech she had attempted to reproduce (G.L. 48). Like the historian seeking a veridical imitation of reality by continual reference to known characters and events, Elizabeth Gaskell was determined to achieve the same measure of reality by means of a combination of representational and fictional types that embodied the quintessence of an historical period. She was writing a history of the common people, before it became a popular subject with historians.

There were failures of technique in *Mary Barton* which arose from her insistence on recording feeling and thought in a literary form that was increasingly dominated by the spectacular visual tableaux of Thackeray and Dickens. There are dissonances between the sequential movement of thought in her work and the logical order of event. Elizabeth Gaskell always saw character inwardly and in *Mary Barton* her plight was one of attempting to express this externally. The visual aspects of her characters, like their names, tend to waver. They are known to the reader not by appearance, but by idiosyncracies of mind and speech. It is difficult to recall what John Barton looked like, but one knows exactly how he thought and felt.

The conclusions to be drawn from the novel were disturbing for most readers. Carson's reformation was hardly credible and certainly inconsistent with the man who had embarked on a struggle with the workers as though preparing for a battle with the enemy. There was an alternative society, and Carson saw Barton as its representative: ' "You mean he was an Owenite; all for equality, and community of goods, and that kind of absurdity" ' (Ch. 37). Robert Owen's Grand Consolidated Trades Union had collapsed in 1832, but Owen's social philosophy endured to mould the whole labour movement in England. Socialism—and the term was probably first used in Owen's *Cooperative Magazine* in 1827 —was to become an active force in English life. The creation of a welfare state was eventually accomplished not only by militant trades-unionists, but by the group that Elizabeth Gaskell had ignored in *Mary Barton*—middle-class reformers and capitalists shrewd enough to know that compromise is more profitable than revolution. George Watson quotes William Cunningham, later Archdeacon of Ely and professor of economic history, writing in 1879 that it is 'not as remedy for the miseries of the poor, but rather as an alleviation of the cares of the rich, that socialism is coming upon us'.[12] Thornton of *North and South* was the new man of business just as Carson represented the methods of an earlier time.

And in *North and South* Elizabeth Gaskell completed the examination of industrial society that she began in *Mary Barton*. It is a study of social compromises, of middle-class people becoming aware, for reasons both altruistic and self-interested, that if capitalism were to survive, it had to be civilised. Peter Gaskell, Engels and Carlyle had all predicted imminent revolution, but Prince Kropotkin saw the nature of English socialism being qualified by 'the considerable number of middle-class people who gave it their support, in different ways, some of them frankly joining it while others helped from outside'.[13] It was never difficult for the English to find a middle road between Christianity and Socialism.[14] As Elizabeth Gaskell herself said, one part of her was a true Christian, 'only people call her socialist and communist' (G.L. 69). The solution was not a restoration of past values that Carlyle and Disraeli discussed with varying degrees of fervour, but a new relationship between conflicting groups in contemporary society and the awareness that profits won at the cost of social justice will always be a dangerous short-term investment.

3
Ruth: moral depravity and capital gain

Prostitution was one of the most lucrative trades in Victorian England, as George Bernard Shaw observed in *Mrs Warren's Profession*. It flourished, despite vociferous condemnation, and was even condoned for a time by government ordinance under the Contagious Diseases Act of 1864. Elizabeth Gaskell, like Florence Nightingale, did not regard it as a symptom of moral depravity but as the glaring example of society's reluctance to provide women with employment at a living wage. Better organised than many areas of industry, prostitution ranged from the palatial brothels of the West End to stews by the docks, from the kept mistresses looking forward to pensions when their services were no longer required to the women who walked the pavements either from desperation or with a cool resolve to make sufficient capital to set themselves up in a business of their own. It was the only trade in which a woman could acquire capital quickly. In domestic service a woman could drudge for a lifetime and end, like Sally in *Ruth*, with £40 to her name.

Arthur Munby, the poet and member of the Ecclesiastical Commission, records an instance of a servant girl, Sarah Tanner, who was a maid-of-all-work to a tradesman in 1854. A year later he met her in the Strand gorgeously dressed and she told Munby that 'she had got tired of service, wanted to see life and be independent; and so she became a prostitute, of her own accord and without being seduced. She saw no harm in it: enjoyed it very much, thought it might raise her and perhaps be profitable.'[1] Later Munby met her again, but this time she was dressed respectably, like an upper servant:

'How is this?' said I again. 'Well, I've left the streets and settled down,' she said quietly. 'Married?' I asked. 'Oh no! But I'd been on the streets three years, and saved up—I told you I should get on, you know—and so I thought I'd leave, and I've taken a coffeehouse with my earnings—the Hampshire Coffeehouse over Waterloo Bridge.' I laughed, incredulous. 'Quite true,' said she simply. 'I manage it all myself, and I can give you chops and tea—and anything you like: you must come and see me.' 'That I will,' said I; for her manner was so open and businesslike that I saw it was true: and with a friendly goodbye we parted.

Sarah Tanner would have been regarded as a 'hardened' prostitute while she was on the streets, but in her own opinion and Munby's she was selling the only thing of value she possessed in a discriminative capitalist society. When Annie Besant was taxed with the fact that many of the match-girls became prostitutes, she replied that there seemed little difference to her between slaving for four shillings a week and dying of phosphorous poisoning, or taking to the streets and succumbing to syphilis.

Elizabeth Gaskell believed that most women became prostitutes because they were unable to find a decent well-paid job in England. Like Dickens, she helped prostitutes to emigrate, and one girl, Pasley, the model for Ruth Denbigh, was recommended to the care of Caroline Chisholm and went to Australia. England had become a predatory sexual society in which women were disadvantaged by their numbers. Census figures from 1801 to 1841 showed a steady surplus of between 500,000 and 600,000 adult women over men in England and Wales, and this period included years of depression and unemployment. There seemed little point in preaching reformation to a prostitute, or reproaching her with the error of her ways, unless she could be given a job. A man, with the aid of his union, could fight his way in industry to a reasonable wage. But it was always apparent to Elizabeth Gaskell that women provided the most dangerous threat to organised male labour. In *Blackwood's Magazine*, Charles Mackay noted that the 'despotic unions' were refusing to permit women to be employed 'and how, in consequence, they make themselves the instruments of driving the superabundant female population, unable to find either husbands or work, into the ranks of that awful prostitution which is the great scandal of our age'.[2] William Fox had written in 1832 that woman 'is vested with the entire power of the State, or not entrusted with its meanest function. She is a divinity or a slave.'[3] Slaves were sexually promiscuous and worked, divinities were chaste and idle. The function of a lady in Victorian society was increasingly being defined in passive terms. Ladies did not work and earn money. If a woman desired to improve her position in society then she had to marry a gentleman and immediately his rank would be conferred upon her. This had been Esther's hope in *Mary Barton*, but because she had relinquished her virginity without receiving a marriage certificate in return, she had become not a lady but a 'fallen woman'.

Parents with a surplus of marriageable daughters were the most stringent critics of 'fallen women'. There was always the chance that sexual compliance by a rival woman could lead to marriage with a prospective suitor, as Henry James observed in *The Spoils of Poynton*. Marriage for a Victorian girl was a sexual stock-market in which selling at what seemed the right moment could achieve a proposal or, alternatively, ruin, while a refusal to take advantage of a market offer might raise the value of the stock to the desired price or result in a refusal to bid. Mary Barton's persistent reluctance to be seduced has the effect of wringing a proposal of marriage from Harry Carson, but Esther is abandoned with £50 by her lover when she is pregnant. Nevertheless, if women were sexually exploited, it was not easy for young men, who could not think of marriage until they had earned or inherited enough to support a wife. The marriage age was always lower in areas where a high percentage of women worked. Men married women for their money as often as women aspired to be the wives of rich husbands. Respectable families kept their daughters well guarded, and so it is not surprising that parents were prepared to accept their sons' seductions of pretty milkmaids or mill-girls, but were constantly alert to the danger of these affairs being sanctified by marriage. Harry Carson knew that his father would tactfully have ignored an affair with Mary Barton, but he would have incurred parental wrath had he married her. To marry profitably was as much a man's concern as it was a woman's, and the occasional sexual use of working girls was regarded as fair sport and a young man's privilege. It was this state

53

of affairs that aroused Elizabeth Gaskell to fury and occa-
sioned the writing of *Ruth*.

Elizabeth Gaskell and Charlotte Brontë had become close
friends by 1853 when *Ruth* was published in three parts by
Edward Chapman. Charlotte Brontë deliberately held back
publication of *Villette* at Elizabeth Gaskell's request so that
Ruth would not have an immediate competitor. It was an
arrangement that suited both writers. Charlotte Brontë
warmly approved the subject and its treatment in *Ruth*,
finding it a most salutary and moral work. But *Ruth* became
Elizabeth Gaskell's most controversial novel and, as she told
Elizabeth Fox, with some irony: 'I think I must be an
improper woman without knowing it, I do so manage to
shock people. Now *should* you have burnt the 1st vol. of
Ruth as so *very* bad? even if you had been a very anxious
father of a family? Yet *two* men have; and a third has for-
bidden his wife to read it; they sit next to us in Chapel and
you can't think how "improper" I feel under their eyes'
(G.L. 150). Ruth Denbigh was a 'fallen woman' who had
perpetuated and confirmed her shame by producing a
bastard, but in Elizabeth Gaskell's novel, the shame is not
Ruth's, but society's. Dickens hedged when he dealt with this
subject, and at the same time as Elizabeth Gaskell was using
the words 'bastard' and 'illegitimate' with considerable freedom in *Ruth*, he was expunging the word 'prostitute' from
the preface of *Oliver Twist*. Essentially, *Ruth* is a study of
the martyrdom a woman had to endure before she could
make society accept her illegitimate child. Oliver's mother
expiated her guilt by dying at his birth.

It is not sexual passion or a 'depraved appetite' that makes
an unmarried mother out of Ruth Hilton, but ignorance
and poverty. More knowing young women would have made
use of the 'working girl's friend', the crochet needle, or paid
a few shillings down a back alley to be aborted. It was a
commonplace for women to present themselves at charity
hospitals with a showing of blood and then be curetted, the
familiar ICM (incomplete miscarriage) of more recent times
was then termed a voluntary abortion. Methods of abortion,
like means of birth control, were handed down in many
families like recipes for good marmalade. The important

social issue was that an affair could be concealed but a child was a noisy testament to its mother's behaviour. Miss Benson, who is quite prepared to pity Ruth with all her heart, is seriously concerned for the girl's character and common-sense when she announces her intention of having and keeping her baby. When Lizzie Leigh gives birth to a child in the story of that name, she puts the baby into the arms of a kindly young woman at night, returning secretly to put a few shillings on the doorstep for it. A baby was a considerable inconvenience for a street-walker, and Lizzie knew there was no alternative for her other than prostitution. Miss Benson was ready to sympathise with Ruth when she was not revealing any visible sign of her affair with Bellingham, but her reaction upon hearing that Ruth is pregnant is predictable:

'Oh, I was just beginning to have a good opinion of her, but I'm afraid she is very depraved. After the doctor was gone, she pulled the bed-curtain aside, and looked as if she wanted to speak to me. (I can't think how she heard, for we were close to the window, and spoke very low.) Well, I went to her, though I really had taken quite a turn against her. And she whispered, quite eagerly, "Did he say I should have a baby?" Of course I could not keep it from her; but I thought it my duty to look as cold and severe as I could. She did not seem to understand how it ought to be viewed, but took it just as if she had a right to have a baby. She said, "Oh, my God, I thank thee! Oh, I will be so good." I had no patience with her then, so I left the room' (Ch. 11).

It is incomprehensible to Miss Benson that any young woman in Ruth's plight would not be praying for kindly death to intervene and save her child from a life of shame, or at least be quietly planning for its disposition on the parish.

Ruth's family and background are given with considerable detail just as her age is emphasised—she is fifteen when Bellingham seduces her. The daughter of a farmer, and an unsuccessful one at that, Ruth is an only child who has never been to school and always lived with people much older than herself. Simple, uneducated, she is the prototype of the country girl who comes to the city to find work and finds herself pregnant before the year is out. Her mother had died when she was twelve, and her father three years later. Typically, her mother was a faint and fragile woman who had married beneath her, but being the orphan of an impoverished Norfolk curate, marriage with a farmer many years older than herself at least offered her the security of a home. When Ruth was born, Mrs Hilton had taken to her bed, never to leave it again until she was carried to her grave. This type of invalidism is examined by Elizabeth Gaskell with some care in her novels and stories. Frequently the victim died, like Mrs Hamley in *Wives and Daughters* or Mrs Buxton in 'The Moorland Cottage', but invariably the husbands of these women were similar. Bluff, hearty, domineering men from whom their wives took refuge in chronic illness. It was a form of flight that was socially condoned and widely practised, and not by married women alone. Harriet Martineau took to her bed until family affairs were settled to her approval, and Florence Nightingale escaped her domestic obligations by the same means. She could write reports for the India Office on a pillow, but she was not well enough to arrange flowers or pay calls. Ruth's only memory of her mother was that of a sweet and pretty woman gradually relinquishing her grasp upon life. Her father became deranged after he had buried his wife and, upon his death, Ruth found that her future had been entrusted to a casual acquaintance of his, who was considerably embarrassed to find himself burdened with a ward. However, he did his best and paid the little money Hilton had left to Mrs Mason, the local dressmaker in Fordham. Ruth was to serve a five-year apprenticeship in her workroom.

Factory girls had their hours regulated by government ordinance, and the larger the factory, the more likely that hours and conditions were under the supervision of inspectors. But the millinery and dressmaking industry still abided by older standards; the girls worked until the orders were completed, and then they rested without pay. Some concern for religious proprieties gave them Sunday free, but on this day no provision was made for their food. It was a situation common to all small shops and workrooms employing women. Mary Barton's hours were no different from Ruth's, and had not improved when George Gissing wrote about Monica's service as a shop assistant in *The Odd Women*. At the height of the ball season Ruth finds herself working an eighteen-hour day in a badly lit room, too tired to eat, too exhausted to undress when she finally collapses on her bed. And Mrs Mason's establishment was the best in Fordham; there were others less congenial. In every large town there were sweatshops and hovels where outworkers stitched disease and death into their work, like the typhus coat that came from Jacob's Island and killed its tailor and the shop-man who sold it, the valet who brushed it and its owner, Alton Locke's cousin, in Kingsley's novel. By contrast with Jacob's Island, Mrs Mason's establishment was a model of cleanliness and agreeable conditions. Dressmaking, if not the occupation of a lady, was a refined trade in popular opinion, and since refinement, like virtue, was its own reward, it remained one of the poorest paid and most exploited. Ruth's guardian was quite satisfied that he had done the very best for a girl in her situation. If Ruth had been endowed with native wit, or had been as mature as Mary Barton was at twelve, it is likely that she would have been able to resist some of the miseries imposed upon her, but Ruth was inexperienced and docile. Her artlessness was as much the result of stupidity as it was of her lack of education.

Ruth is not a young woman of resolution and determination. Nothing could be further from the character of Margaret Hale, planning and advising, than Ruth taking refuge in dreams and refusing to look beyond the present moment. In Mrs Mason's workroom, the old drawing-room of a decayed mansion, Ruth chooses to sit in the darkest corner because there she can dimly see the gilt panels on the opposite wall, and the painted garlands remind her of the flowers around her old home. Lonely and afraid, all she knows with any certainty about herself is that she is very pretty, but it is not a fact that has any meaning for her beyond expressing the opinion of others: ' "Did you hear Ruth Hilton say she knew she was pretty?" whispered one girl to another, so loudly that Ruth caught the words. "I could not help knowing," answered she, simply, "for many people have told me so" ' (Ch. 2). In the jungle of Victorian sexual life, Ruth is a predetermined victim made all the more vulnerable by her beauty and inexperience. She is tractable because she has so little will of her own, her opinions are those she derives from others, her morality that which is imposed upon her by circumstance and training. When her son is a grown lad, Mr Farquhar offers to send him to school, but Ruth temporises. Farquhar asks Benson, ' "What does she look forward to making him into, finally?" ', and Benson replies: ' "I don't know. The wonder comes into my mind sometimes but never into hers, I think. It is part of her character—part perhaps of that which made her what she was—that she never looks forward, and seldom back. The present is enough for her" ' (Ch. 32). Ruth's only desire is to please and be loved. Argument and discussion frighten her and when Mr Benson has explained why she should accept Mr Bradshaw's gift of white muslin for her baby she agrees without further consideration, ' "I will do what you wish me", she said, after a little pause of thoughtfulness. "May we talk of something else?" ' (Ch. 15).

If they were shrewd and insensitive, the Sarah Tanners did remarkably well for themselves as prostitutes. Elizabeth Gaskell knew that there was no hope of redeeming women like this with prayer. They were interested in making sufficient money to be economically independent. Money carried a certain distinction even in the most fastidious areas of society. But for every Sarah Tanner, there were hundreds of Ruth Hiltons, women who were made social outcasts because they had conceived a child out of wedlock. It was not uncharacteristic that Bradshaw should regard Ruth as a whore when he discovers her past, or that Mrs Pearson thought it unlikely that the Ruth Hilton she had met in her sister-in-law's workroom at Fordham could be the Ruth Denbigh of Eccleston. After all, as Mrs Pearson confides to Jemima, there was only one occupation open for a girl like Ruth Hilton, and that would hardly permit her to be nursery governess in the Bradshaw home. However, Elizabeth Gaskell was committed to the belief that it was not natural depravity that made women promiscuous, but the whole environment of society. In the care of the Bensons, Ruth becomes an assured young woman who is given sufficient courage by her training to refuse Bellingham's last desperate proposal of marriage.

Bellingham's seduction of Ruth is not related at great length in the novel. For him it is merely the acquisitive desire to possess a remarkably pretty young girl who offers none of the prospective dangers and expenses of a prostitute. Ruth is deeply grateful for his companionship on one of those lonely Sundays when Mrs Mason abandoned her apprentices to God and their hunger. Ruth is oblivious to Bellingham's intentions when he takes her back to see her old home, and what is immediately obvious to Thomas, her father's old servant, is not apparent to her. What follows is less a passionate wooing than an episode of trifling coincidences that baffle Ruth. She is observed with Bellingham by Mrs Mason on her way back from the farm, and since Mrs Mason is in a considerable rage from the misbehaviour of her eldest son, she is delighted to be able to expend her feelings upon Ruth. Without being given any opportunity to explain, Ruth finds herself dismissed on the spot. And as she weeps hysterically, Bellingham sees the opportunity he has long awaited. He offers to take her to London with him. When he goes off to fetch a carriage, Ruth waits at the inn drinking a cup of tea that the maid has ordered for her and trying to decide what she should do. Knowing that she could return to the farm and seek shelter with Thomas and his wife, she determines to leave:

She put on her bonnet, and opened the parlour-door; but then she saw the square figure of the landlord standing at the open house-door, smoking his evening pipe, and looming large and distinct against the dark air and landscape beyond. Ruth remembered the cup of tea that she had drunk; it must be paid for, and she had no money with her. She feared that he would not let her quit the house without paying. She thought that she would leave a note for Mr. Bellingham, saying where she was gone; and how she had left the house in debt, for (like a child) all dilemmas appeared of equal magnitude to her; and the difficulty of passing the landlord while he stood there, and of giving him any explanation of the circumstances (as far as such explanation was due to him), appeared insuperable, and as awkward and fraught with inconveniences as far more serious situations. She kept peeping out of her room, after she had written her little pencil-note, to see if the outer door was still obstructed. There he stood, motionless, enjoying his pipe, and looking out into the darkness which gathered thick with the coming night. The fumes of the tobacco were carried by the air into the house, and brought back Ruth's sick headache. Her energy left her; she became stupid and languid, and incapable of spirited exertion; she modified her plan of action, to the determination of asking Mr. Bellingham to take her to Milham Grange, to the care of her humble friends, instead of to London. And she thought, in her simplicity, that he would instantly consent when he had heard her reasons (Ch. 14).

The passage carries Elizabeth Gaskell's conviction that society, which should protect the simple of heart and mind, is the first to oppress them. Ruth lacks every quality that would enable her to defend herself. Her finest qualities, her gentleness and kindness, make her more vulnerable than if she had been selfish and callous.

There is no account given of their brief sojourn in London, or the loss of Ruth's virginity, because these are irrelevant to the nature of Bellingham's relationship with her. In the little village in North Wales where they have taken rooms at the inn, Ruth has become a toy that is beginning to bore Bellingham, while her only regret is that she lacks 'the gift of being amusing; it must be dull for a man accustomed to all kinds of active employments to be shut up in the house. She was recalled from her absolute self-forgetfulness. What could she say to interest Mr. Bellingham?' (Ch. 5). Ruth regards herself as being as great a source of tedium as a wet day, and her lover does nothing to disillusion her of this fancy. Ruth has no sense of herself, she is a mirror reflecting other people's moods, seldom her own. She is distraught when Bellingham becomes ill with a fever and his mother, arriving in state to nurse him, forbids Ruth to see him. It is not when she is desired sexually that Ruth becomes most passionate but when she can assume a maternal role with Bellingham. She does not yearn to be his lover, but his nurse. And Elizabeth Gaskell is at pains not to conceal this aspect of Ruth's personality.

When she is deserted and left with the customary £50 to console her for any suffering she may have endured, Ruth is befriended by a crippled dissenting minister, Thurston Benson. The relationship between Thurston and his sister is one in which she has taken the male role and he the female. There is never the slightest indication that Benson has fallen in love with Ruth, or that his feelings are more than those of guardian and friend. Indeed, it is Faith Benson who displays all the customary masculine characteristics. It is she who '. . . had the power, which some people have, of carrying her wishes through to their fulfilment; her will was strong, her sense was excellent, and people yielded to her' (Ch. 11). It could be a description of a perfect Victorian gentleman. She is devoid of maternal instincts and the thought of a crying baby in the house appals her. Her feelings are expressed less delicately by Sally, their old servant, who cries out in horror at the first mention of the child: ' "Lord bless us and save us!—a baby in the house! Nay, then my time's come, and I'll pack up and begone. I never could abide them things. I'd sooner have rats in the house" ' (Ch. 13). Miss Benson and Sally have both accepted single life with a great deal of satisfaction, sustained in one case by a sense of duty (Miss Benson had rejected a suitor to care for her brother), and Sally in the knowledge that she had received and refused two proposals of marriage in her life, admittedly one from a lunatic who had the disconcerting habit of crawling around the floor on all fours. Having socially acceptable reasons for leading celibate lives, each is contented with her lot.

The feminine characteristics of Mr Hale, the erstwhile minister in *North and South*, serve to accentuate his inability to confront life and its problems, but Thurston Benson's womanly nature gives him the strength and sensitivity to act with judgment and compassion. Carefully avoiding a utilitarian interpretation of the situation, Benson argues that in Ruth's case her sin is quite distinct from its consequences, that there can be no guilt attached to any child. It was a favourite and reiterated saying of Mary Mohl's that she wished everyone was a bastard, and William Fox argued that every child born should be regarded as legitimate but it was not the way of the world to accept such a generous morality. Thurston Benson's words are mere sophistry to his sister, and in the course of their discussion, it is she who speaks with authority for accepted moral standards. When Benson becomes quite excited as he considers the social implications of his thoughts, his sister interrupts: ' "These are quite new ideas to me," said Miss Benson, coldly. "I think you, Thurston, are the first person I ever heard rejoicing over the birth of an illegitimate child. It appears to me, I must own, rather questionable morality" ' (Ch. 11).

The morality is a vexed one for Benson because there seems no possible way in which Ruth can be protected without taking refuge in falsehood. Having appealed without success to Mrs Bellingham—her reply to Benson is to remind him of the £50 she left for Ruth and a note that would procure her admission to the Fordham Penitentiary—Benson is at a loss to know how to provide for the girl and her unborn child. It is his sister who suggests that they pass her off as a young widow, a relation of theirs who has been left to their charge. Telling a lie is disturbing to Benson. His religion is essentially a profession of the truth, and to present Ruth in Eccleston as a widow and his own relation is to commit a grievous sin, but he is equally determined that the child shall not endure social obloquy. When Miss Benson complains that Ruth has not shown any gratitude for being offered a home, her brother replies in accord with the necessarian doctrine of Joseph Priestley:

'It is better not to expect or calculate consequences. The longer I live, the more fully I see that. Let us try simply to do right actions, without thinking of the feelings they are to call out in others. We know that no holy or self-denying effort can fall to the ground vain and useless; but the sweep of eternity is large, and God alone knows when the effect is to be produced. We are trying to do right now, and to feel right; don't let us perplex ourselves with endeavouring to map out how she should feel, or how she should show her feelings' (Ch. 12).

Benson never ceases to be troubled by the lie he has told, but he is content to let divine providence determine its consequences.

Sally, the servant in the Benson household, is a magnificent creation in the long tradition of comic domestics. She is next-of-kin to Juliet's Nurse and has a nodding acquaintance with Fielding's Mrs Deborah Wilkins, who had similar views on strumpets and their offspring. Sally's misgivings about Ruth are for the reputation of Mr Benson and his sister, both of whom she regards as unworldly in the extreme. Miss Benson provides Ruth with her grandmother's ring to wear when she hears Sally's muttered complaints, but this is not enough to calm the rising storm of Sally's indignation. At first it is only 'The low mutterings of the thunder in the distance, in the shape of Sally's soliloquies, which, like the asides at a theatre, were intended to be heard' (Ch. 13). Then Sally confronts Ruth with a pair of scissors and informs her that if she is to be passed off as a widow, she must look like one, and that means cutting her hair and wearing a widow's cap. It is a 'fancied necessity' on Sally's part, but Ruth submits to the loss of her hair without complaint, and immediately Sally is repentant. She has humiliated Ruth, and has demanded a sacrifice in atonement for her sexual behaviour, and when Ruth is so submissive Sally is confused and a little ashamed of herself. It is a subtly drawn scene of considerable psychological perception, concluding with Sally's decision to keep Ruth's hair. 'Sally had carried away the beautiful curls, and she could not find it in her heart to throw such lovely chestnut tresses away, so she folded them up carefully in paper, and placed them in a safe corner of her drawer' (Ch. 13). Few writers have been able to grasp the ambiguities of sexual response so incisively in such a brief compass.

Sally not only comforts herself with having refused two proposals of marriage but with her status in religious life, which she regards as being considerably higher than that of the Bensons. She was the daughter of the parish clerk and is a member of the Established Church while the Bensons are Dissenters. De Tocqueville once remarked of the English that they were never happy unless they had inferiors while the French resented superiors. Sally knows with all the certainty of conviction that she enjoys a state of grace that is more pleasing to God than the faith of her employers, and she takes pains to remind them of this on occasion. When

63

Miss Benson convinces her brother that Ruth's young son should be whipped for telling stories, it is Sally who intervenes like an avenging angel quoting scripture. Even Ruth has agreed that Leonard should be punished, but Sally carries the day when Mr Benson takes shelter behind the text that 'He that spareth the rod, spoileth the child'. In a tirade embellished with biblical reference Sally retorts:

'Ay, I remember; and I remember a bit more than you want me to remember, I reckon. It were King Solomon as spoke them words, and it were King Solomon's son that were King Rehoboam, and no great shakes either. I can remember what is said on him, II. Chronicles, xii. chapter, 14th v.: "And he," that's King Rehoboam, the lad that tasted the rod, "did evil, because he prepared not his heart to seek the Lord." I've not been reading my chapters every night for fifty year to be caught napping by a Dissenter, neither!' said she triumphantly. 'Come along, Leonard' (Ch. 19).

The Bensons and Sally are responsible for educating Ruth. It is Mr Benson who teaches her so that she may in turn give her young son the rudiments of learning; Miss Benson acquaints her with household management, but it is Sally who gives Ruth a sense of personal identity. After the birth of her baby, Ruth undertakes many of the household tasks to relieve Miss Benson, but she goes about them, as Sally says, ' "a-sighing and a-moaning in a way that I can't stand or thole" ' (Ch. 16). For Sally it is not enough to drift through life, complaining of one's fate and taking flight from reality in daydreams and a regretted past. Life requires gumption, and this is what she teaches Ruth. Always tractable, Ruth listens patiently to Sally and the result is that 'henceforward Ruth nursed her boy with a vigour and cheerfulness that were reflected back from him; and the household work was no longer performed with a languid indifference, as if life and duty were distasteful' (Ch. 16). As a Unitarian, Elizabeth Gaskell firmly believed that every human being could be developed by education to the full capacity of his intelligence. Some people were born less intelligent than others, but even they could be made valuable members of society. Thus Ruth, vapid, on the verge of illiteracy, deprived

of the sense of family and friendship in her life, is transformed into a capable and courageous young woman. These
qualities were not innate; they are the result of her life with
the Bensons, a family that is contrasted at every point with
Mr Bradshaw's moral tyranny.

A family, as Elizabeth Gaskell never ceased to insist, need
not be the accustomed group of two parents and their children. It could be like the Bensons, brother and sister, a servant
who is part of the family and a young woman and her child.
In the Benson household there is love, and a warmth of
companionship in which Sally shares every detail of her
employers' lives, and a child that has, in effect, not two
parents, but four. Leonard, despite the shattering knowledge
that he is illegitimate, a fact concealed in his early years,
grows up to be an accomplished and intelligent lad who is
apprenticed to the leading surgeon of Eccleston. The Brad-
shaws, on the other hand, represent the conventional family
of father and mother, a son (who becomes a forger) and three
daughters. It is a mockery of familial love, a model for
hypocrisy, neurosis and crime. Outwardly Mr Bradshaw is
a pattern of rectitude, a man who takes daily comfort in the
contemplation of his own virtues. Like Jane Eyre's bleak
inquisitor, Mr Brocklehurst, he is continually alert to the
failings of others and prompt to caution them. Ruth Hilton,
known in Eccleston as Ruth Denbigh, makes the most
favourable impression upon him by her silence and the
poverty of her dress. She has used the clothing Bellingham
bought her to make garments for her baby, and bought the
cheapest cloth in the market to make dresses for herself.
Nothing delights Bradshaw more than the poor making a
public demonstration of their acceptance of poverty in this
way. It is not long before he plans to appoint Ruth as nursery
governess to his two young daughters, Mary and Elizabeth.

Ruth's background has been accounted for by Miss Benson, who quietly tells Mrs Bradshaw that Ruth is the widow
of a young surgeon. When her brother cautions her against
lying in this fashion, Faith replies spontaneously: ' "I do
think I've a talent for fiction, it is so pleasant to invent, and
make the incidents dovetail together; and after all, if we are
to tell a lie, we may as well do it thoroughly, or else it's no

use. A bungling lie would be worse than useless. And, Thurston—it may be very wrong—but I believe—I am afraid I enjoy not being fettered by truth!"' (Ch. 14). Benson is concerned, and makes his sister promise that she will not add one additional word to the account that is not strictly true, but Faith Benson consoles herself with the thought that Mrs Bradshaw will speedily embroider Ruth's story to the satisfaction of the town. Mrs Bradshaw escapes from life in sentimental romances, and whenever possible, she makes her life conform to the latest lachrymose novel.

The outstanding characteristic of the Bensons is the freedom with which they can voice their thoughts to each other, a freedom that extends to Sally and later to Ruth and her son. There are dark moments in their past, but these are not permitted to cloud the present. Sally's devotion to Thurston Benson is not simply one of affection but derives from the day when she dropped him as a young child, crippling him for life. Unlike most households where she would have been instantly dismissed or given in charge, Sally is kept on by the Bensons' parents. Similarly, Ruth is not encouraged to look back in the guise of repenting of her alliance with Bellingham, but inspired to look towards her own future and that of her son.

As was customary in most Dissenting chapels, it was the richest member of the congregation who paid the most pew rent. A fifth of Mr Benson's annual income of £100 is provided by Mr Bradshaw. The system of seat rents, which deterred many of the working class from attending Methodist chapels,[4] was the exception and not the rule in Benson's church.

The congregation consisted of here and there a farmer with his labourers, who came down from the uplands beyond the town to worship where their fathers worshipped, and who loved the place because they knew how much those fathers had suffered for it, although they never troubled themselves with the reason why they left the parish church; and of a few shopkeepers, far more thoughtful and reasoning, who were Dissenters from conviction, unmixed with old ancestral association; and of one or two families of still higher worldly station. With many poor, who were drawn there by love for

Mr. Benson's character, and by a feeling that the faith which made him what he was could not be far wrong, for the base of the pyramid, and with Mr. Bradshaw for its apex, the congregation stood complete (Ch. 14).

In the minds of rich and poor alike there is no doubt that Bradshaw is a leader in the community as he is master in his own home.

His wife, 'thoroughly broken into submission', lives in constant dread of offending her husband. The household revolves around subterfuges and schemes whereby he may not be roused to anger. Unlike the Benson home where freedom of speech is indulged in by everyone, and by no one more freely than Sally, the Bradshaw household is a place of furtive whispers and unspoken thoughts. Mrs Bradshaw devours gossip and trivialities but in her husband's presence,

A sort of constant terror of displeasing him made her voice sharp and nervous; the children knew that many a thing passed over by their mother when their father was away, was sure to be noticed by her when he was present; and noticed, too, in a cross and querulous manner, for she was so much afraid of the blame which on any occasion of their misbehaviour fell upon her. And yet she looked up to her husband with a reverence, and regard, and a faithfulness of love, which his decision of character was likely to produce on a weak and anxious mind. He was a rest and a support to her, on whom she cast all her responsibilities; she was an obedient, unremonstrating wife to him; no stronger affection had ever brought her duty to him into conflict with any desire of her heart (Ch. 20).

Implicit in such a passage is the statement that a domineering bully is created as much by the weakness of others as he is by his own temperament. Richard, his son, is a pious, mealy-mouthed prig in his father's presence and a spendthrift lout in his absence. Richard later justifies his father's faith in him by forging a number of share certificates, including a number belonging to Mr Benson. Elizabeth and Mary are two quiet, and not very bright, little girls who cling to Ruth as a most welcome substitute for their mother. They are what George Eliot was quite incapable of creating, perfectly natural children who are rendered as neither grotesque nor sentimental little beings. It is Jemima, the eldest daughter, who openly rebels against her father and, in so doing, establishes her right to be treated as an individual and not as an extension of her father's will and desires. It was a relationship that inspired Dickens in his delineation of Gradgrind and Louisa.

From the first, Jemima is drawn to Ruth who seems the embodiment of all that is beautiful and romantically tragic. With a sharp ear and a shrewd intelligence, Jemima is at first a little puzzled when Mr Benson beseeches the world to show pity on Ruth's child at the christening. But her suspicions are soon lulled as she develops a 'crush' on the young woman little older than herself. Ruth is appointed as a nursery governess to take care of Mary and Elizabeth, and Jemima spends as much time as possible with her new friend. Mr Bradshaw wholeheartedly approves. There is nothing more gratifying to him than to have the object of his charity under his approving gaze and that of his associates. Never loquacious and incapable of argument, Ruth is the model of what a young woman should be, a pattern for Jemima and her disconcertingly rebellious spirit. It is Jemima who has won the reluctant admiration of Mr Farquhar, Bradshaw's partner. He is at a loss to know why he should be so attracted to a young woman who seems the antithesis of everything he has decided his wife should be. When Farquhar occasionally reproves Jemima, she blazes out in anger, to the chagrin of her father who has long dreamed of consolidating the family business by marrying Jemima to his partner. So Bradshaw seeks to enlist Ruth's aid by asking her to remonstrate with Jemima and draw her attention to all Farquhar's admirable characteristics. At first incapable of understanding quite what Mr Bradshaw wants, Ruth is about to refuse, but he takes her inarticulate response for agreement and bows her from the room.

Jemima becomes a rebel when she learns from her mother that Ruth has agreed to beguile her into a more amiable relationship with Mr Farquhar. The account Mrs Bradshaw gives is garbled and confused, but the effect upon Jemima is immediate. Her love for Ruth becomes a passionate loath-

68

ing, and every act of kindness on Ruth's part becomes a treacherous attack upon her freedom. Jemima enjoys little enough liberty in her father's house, but she is determined to maintain one privilege, and that is her right to refuse the suitor chosen for her by her father. Her feelings are complicated because she does love Farquhar and when he begins to consider Ruth as a prospective wife, Jemima's anguish becomes unbearable.

> She would so fain have let herself love Mr. Farquhar; but this constant manoeuvring, in which she did not feel clear that he did not take a passive part, made her sick at heart. She even wished that they might not go through the form of pretending to try to gain her consent to the marriage, if it involved all this premeditated action and speech-making—such moving about of every one into their right places, like pieces at chess. She felt as if she would rather be bought openly, like an Oriental daughter, where no one is degraded in their own eyes by being parties to such a contract (Ch. 21).

Ruth, troubled by Jemima's coldness, is quite unaware that Farquhar has deliberately transferred his affections to her. It has not been easy for him, but he convinces himself that Ruth's 'shy reserve, and her quiet daily walk within the lines of duty' are what he has always desired most in a wife. Not unnaturally, he commences his courtship by winning her son, and Ruth takes this as simple tribute to Leonard's undoubted charm and intelligence. Even Mary and Elizabeth are aware of the charade that is taking place before them, but Ruth remains unconscious that she has been singled out for the honour of becoming Mrs Farquhar. Elizabeth Gaskell never fails to make apparent that the simple charm which men find so attractive in Ruth is derived from her lack of intelligence, not her personality.

Bradshaw's rectitude is compromised when he seeks to extend his influence beyond his home and his church to engage in politics. As the foremost merchant and manufacturer of the town he resents the influence of the Cranworth family, which has consistently ignored 'the growing power of the manufacturers, more especially as the principal person engaged in the trade was a Dissenter' (Ch. 21). So he decides to buy himself a Liberal candidate and defeat the Tory Cranworths at their own game. In London, Bradshaw finds a parliamentary agent, 'a man whose only principle was to do wrong on the Liberal side; he would not act, right or wrong, for a Tory, but for a Whig the latitude of his conscience had never yet been discovered' (Ch. 21). It is disturbing for Bradshaw when he discovers that every election involves bribery, but he is equally determined to succeed. Success can always outweigh conscience in Bradshaw's scale of values, and he gladly accepts the agent's suggestion of a wealthy young candidate who is looking for a parliamentary seat.

'A Liberal?' said Mr. Bradshaw.
'Decidedly. Belongs to a family who were in the Long Parliament in their day.'
Mr. Bradshaw rubbed his hands.
'Dissenter?' asked he.
'No, no! Not so far as that. But very lax Church' (Ch. 21).

And Bradshaw does not bother to enquire whether this laxity extends to matters other than his religious interests. He is jubilant with the acquisition of Mr Donne, who is none other than Bellingham. Bellingham has changed his name to acquire some property, just as Florence Nightingale's father had once been a Shore. Upon acquaintance, Bradshaw is a trifle nettled by Bellingham's obvious assumption of rank, and decides to take him down to the seacoast house that he is planning to buy. The house costs £14,000, a price that Bradshaw mentions on every possible occasion. If he cannot display his breeding, he is determined to make a show of his money. Besides, Mr Benson has announced that he will preach on the Christian view of political duties, and Bradshaw considers that a short Sunday visit to the coast will save his candidate's ears and his own from exposure to any vexing scruples.

Ruth is placidly preparing for Bradshaw's descent upon the house with Donne and Hickson, the parliamentary agent. Untroubled by any need except to keep the children quiet and 'out of the way', she is suddenly thrown back into the past when Donne speaks to her on the sands at dusk. She recognises his voice immediately, but he is unaware to whom he has spoken. It is from this moment that Ruth's ordeal of temptation begins. Her first thought is to plead with him for some explanation of his desertion. He is still her 'darling love', made dearer to her as Leonard's father, and if he left her it must have been because she had angered him, or his mother had forced him to leave her behind in that Welsh village. It is the Ruth of Mrs Mason's dressmaking establishment who first pleads with her present self, but slowly, and in anguish, all that she has learned from the Bensons, and the courage she has acquired from her religious faith overcome the longing to see her lover again. She recognises that 'Leonard's father is a bad man' (Ch. 23) and that she would degrade herself and her child by seeking him out. So she determines, that if circumstances bring about their meeting, she will neither question him nor reveal any curiosity about the past. She sits behind the tea-urn at breakfast, 'the very model of a governess who knew her place', and is able to observe the Bellingham who has become Donne and acquired more than wealth in the process. He, in turn, is at a loss to recall Ruth in the woman at the end of the table. She has seen a restless and dissatisfied man, but he admires a woman of singular grace and dignity. Something in her face causes him to remember Ruth, and as each watches the other they judge by reference to the past. For Donne it is a puzzling enigma, because he knows with certainty what must have happened to Ruth.

> Poor Ruth! and, for the first time for several years, he wondered what had become of her; though, of course, there was but one thing that could have happened, and perhaps it was as well he did not know her end, for most likely it would have made him very uncomfortable. He leant back in his chair, and, unobservedly (for he would not have thought it gentlemanly to look so fixedly at her, if she or any one noticed him), he put up his glass again (Ch. 23).

And the glass is not an affectation but a necessity; Bellingham has become very short-sighted.

Recognition follows, but Ruth still refuses to speak to him. In church she gazes fixedly at a carved stone face, a gargoyle, in which the agony depicted was proof that 'Circumstance had conquered; and there was no hope from mortal endeavour, or help from any mortal creature, to be had. But the eyes looked onward and upward to the "Hills from whence cometh our help" '. Outside the church Bellingham whispers to her, pleading to be given the opportunity to explain, and Ruth is tempted again: 'She earnestly desired to know why and how he had left her. It appeared to her, as if that knowledge could alone give her a relief from the restless wondering that distracted her mind, and that one explanation could do no harm.' But Ruth has not prayed for strength without avail, and her resolution comes in part from the consolation she has received in church, but more from the conscious awareness that she herself has changed. She knows that

> . . . during the time of her residence in the Benson family, her feeling of what people ought to be had been unconsciously raised and refined; and Mr. Donne, even while she had to struggle against the force of past recollections, repelled her so much by what he was at present, that every speech of his, every minute they were together, served to make her path more and more easy to follow (Ch. 23).

Elizabeth Gaskell had no faith in miraculous conversions and instantaneous changes of heart, but she was convinced that religious training, and an education in love and self-respect over a long period, could radically change the personality. It is not the lesson read in the church that helps Ruth, so much as the sermon serving to recall the Benson household and the person she had become there. Her refusal to reply serves to rebuff Bellingham most effectively until he learns that Ruth has a child, and then he knows that he has the means to make her listen.

A Molly Gibson was not beyond threatening blackmail when confronted with a similar man to Bellingham, but it does not occur to Ruth that Leonard represents as great a threat to his father's reputation as he does to her own. A political candidate supported by the Eccleston Dissenters would have been painfully embarrassed to be known as the father of a bastard son. But Ruth is neither shrewd nor worldly, and all she knows is that a father had every claim to a child, whether legitimate or not. It was one of the legal scandals of the age that exploded when George Norton demanded not only his children but his estranged wife's earnings. Elizabeth Gaskell was a friend of Caroline Norton, and she felt acutely for the woman who had not only lost custody of her children to a husband whose sanity was, at the best of times, a matter of public contention, but who had been sued in court by him for the money she earned as a writer. Ruth's fears were not without foundation.

On the sands, Ruth waits for Bellingham, unable to refuse to see him now that he has learned they have a child. At first speaking of their past love, he soon becomes aware that Ruth's only vulnerable point is Leonard. What he hoped would be a passionate declaration of feeling becomes a matter of sordid bargaining over the boy. ' "What have you to say about him?" asked she, coldly. "Much!" exclaimed he— "much that may affect his whole life. But it all depends upon whether you will hear me or not" ' (Ch. 24). What follows is largely incomprehensible to Bellingham, for she does not express any anger or resentment for his desertion of her, and when she speaks of being penitent he can only conclude that she is referring to the loss of her virginity. But Ruth's sense of shame is that she could once have loved a man who is despicable, and it is this truth that Bellingham finds intolerable. He is driven to the last resource of pleading with her to marry him, promising to legitimise the child and provide him with every material advantage. To try and buy her with promises of a golden future for her son are more than she can endure:

'If there was one thing needed to confirm me, you have named it. You shall have nothing to do with my boy, by my consent, much less by my agency. I would rather see him working on the roadside than leading such a life—being such a one as you are. You have heard my mind now, Mr. Bellingham. You have humbled me—you have baited me; and if at last I have spoken out too harshly too much in a spirit of judgment, the fault is yours. If there were no other reason to prevent our marriage but the one fact that it would bring Leonard into contact with you, that would be enough' (Ch. 24).

Ruth's answer is sufficient to quench any passion Bellingham feels for her, and all he can do is assure her that he will never trouble her or the boy again.

The truth about Ruth and her son is not revealed by Bellingham, but as a result of Jemima's gossip with the new Eccleston dressmaker, Mrs Pearson, a relation by marriage to Mrs Mason. It is a time of considerable disquiet for everyone. Ruth has been made aware of Farquhar's feelings for her, and does her best to avoid him when he calls with gifts for Leonard. She resents every effort to manipulate her feelings by bribing her son. And Bradshaw feels tainted by the success of his election campaign. He has helped to present the triumphant Liberal candidate to parliament, he has defeated the Cranworths, and he lives in constant fear of an 'indictment for bribery, and of being compelled to appear before a Committee to swear to his own share in the business' (Ch. 25). Consequently he feels impelled to adopt a more rigorous profession of public and private morality than before. Jemima has guessed Ruth's identity, but she remains silent even though her jealousy of Ruth has become a sort of madness, a 'sullen passion which seethed below the stagnant surface of her life' (Ch. 26). When Bradshaw hears the local rumours about Ruth's past, she provides a convenient means whereby he can expiate his sense of guilt over the election. And because of Ruth, Jemima at last finds sufficient cause to defy her father. It is a scene in which Bradshaw can exercise his favourite passion, righteous indignation, concluding with the pious hope that his children have not been contaminated by their association with Ruth's bastard. Ruth is almost mute, she makes a faint effort to defend her child, but she realises that Bradshaw has spoken the truth. She will be made to suffer for her past but her son will be made to endure far more from society. Though Ruth chooses to tell Leonard the truth herself, she makes no reference to his father, nor does she inform Bradshaw or the Bensons that the Liberal candidate of Eccleston has very close ties indeed to his electorate.

When Bradshaw confronts Benson with Ruth's 'profligacy' Benson makes no attempt to defend his deception. But he does demand that society must change: ' "What have the world's ways ended in? Can we be much worse than we are?"' (Ch. 27). There is no casuistry, and no cautionary note is allowed to intrude into the dialogue or the narrative commentary. It is morally wrong that a child should be stigmatised because his parents disregarded a social and religious convention. And from this point, the emphasis of the novel rests not upon Ruth, but on Leonard. Ruth's first thought is to run away, to go to Helmsby where she vaguely remembers her mother was born. Elizabeth Gaskell knew that the first retreat is always to the past, and Ruth is now beyond reason and understanding. Even Benson is broken emotionally after he has persuaded Ruth that she must stay with them and care for her son. When his sister returns he can only pour out the story disjointedly, punctuating his account of Bradshaw's indignation with the words, '"I did so want you, Faith!"'. Leonard is afraid now to go outside, and when he does, he returns angry and silent from the jeers of other children and the patronising stares of their parents.

Only Mr Farquhar can take some comfort in the situation, being quite convinced that no one was aware of the affection he had once felt for Ruth. He is an amiable and expedient man who is now 'most thankful, most self-gratulatory, that he had gone no further in his admiration of her' (Ch. 28). Nevertheless he is grateful that Jemima should defend Ruth since this makes it morally permissible for him to help the woman he had once planned to marry. The weak find their strength in others, and in Elizabeth Gaskell's novels it is generally women who provide the courage for men to do good. Farquhar persuades Leonard to come to his house every day to fetch *The Times* for Mr Benson, a short journey that forces the lad to risk the streets where he has become 'an object of remark' to everyone. It is this mutual concern for Leonard that reconciles Farquhar and Jemima, and the moment that Jemima promises to marry him, Farquhar immediately forgets that he had ever loved Ruth and chooses to regard himself as having been 'a model of constancy'. However Jemima knows that by marrying Farquhar she will surrender something very precious to her. The obvious reasons are clear enough, but there is a motive that she is unable to formulate in rational terms. Nonetheless, it is the major determinant of her action when Farquhar asks for permission to speak to her father:

No! for some reason or fancy which she could not define, and could not be persuaded out of, she wished to keep their mutual understanding a secret. She had a natural desire to avoid the congratulations she expected from her family. She dreaded her father's consideration of the whole affair as a satisfactory disposal of his daughter to a worthy man, who, being his partner, would not require any abstraction of capital from the concern; and Richard's more noisy delight at his sister's having 'hooked' so good a match. It was only her simple-hearted mother that she longed to tell. She knew that her mother's congratulations would not jar upon her, though they might not sound the full organ-peal of her love. But all that her mother knew passed onwards to her father; so for the present, at any rate, she determined to realise her secret position alone (Ch. 28).

Jemima feels that the first person she should tell is Ruth, just as Ruth 'yearned all the more in silence to see Jemima' (Ch. 29). It is clear that the raging jealousy which tormented Jemima for so long was not a simple antagonism towards a woman who had won the affection of a former lover, but a complexity of feeling for Ruth herself. Just as sexuality is not the natural and inevitable concomitant of gender, it is possible for a woman to love passionately either man or woman, but it is not within Jemima's experience to comprehend androgyny.

Two years later, Jemima comes to see Ruth on the eve of her wedding.

. . . in the gloom of the apartment she recognised Jemima. In an instant they were in each other's arms—a long, fast embrace.
'Can you forgive me?' whispered Jemima in Ruth's ear.
'Forgive you! What do you mean? What have I to forgive? The question is, can I ever thank you as I long to do, if I could find words?'
'Oh, Ruth, how I hated you once!'
'It was all the more noble in you to stand by me as you did.

You must have hated me when you knew how I was deceiving you all!'

'No, that was not it that made me hate you. It was before that. Oh, Ruth, I did hate you!'

They were silent for some time, still holding each other's hands (Ch. 29).

It is a love scene and one that carries more implied passion than Walter Farquhar's proposal to Jemima. The love between women was to become a dominant theme in Elizabeth Gaskell's work, being stated most explicitly in 'The Grey Woman'.

When Ruth is unable to find any work in Eccleston, Mr Wynne, the parish doctor, suggests that she should go out nursing. It is Jemima who is most distressed that this degrading occupation should be imposed upon Ruth. Jemima cannot bear to think that her adored Ruth should be compelled to work among the diseased and dying, but Ruth is resolute. It was, after all, the one occupation in which a flawed background was more an asset to a woman than a disadvantage. Florence Nightingale was to change the whole vocation of nursing for women, but in 1852, when Elizabeth Gaskell was writing *Ruth*, it was still Sairey Gamp who visited the sick and not the Lady with the Lamp.

Florence Nightingale was a scandal to her family and an embarrassment to her friends by insisting on studying nursing at Kaiserswerth in Germany and with the Sisters of Charity in Paris. As Florence Nightingale observed, the apparently insuperable barrier to her studying nursing was the notorious immorality of hospital nurses. Her decision was as outrageous as a young woman today deciding to study domestic economy in a brothel. ' "It was *preferred*," wrote Miss Nightingale, "that the nurses should be women who had lost their characters, i.e. should have had one child" '.[5] Florence Nightingale always preferred Bluebooks to fiction, but she made an exception for *Ruth*. Hilary Bonham Carter, Florence Nightingale's companion at the time, wrote to Elizabeth Gaskell in 1859: 'She said of your *Ruth* this morning, "It is a beautiful novel, and I think I like it better still than when I first read it six years ago." '[6] Nonetheless there were specific aspects of Ruth's career as a nurse that Florence

Nightingale had sought to change. There is no sense of profession in the work she undertakes, and no period of training is required. When Ruth mildly tells Jemima that her slight knowledge of Latin will at least enable her to read the prescriptions, Jemima reminds her that the last quality a doctor looked for in a nurse was educated initiative. Education, which Florence Nightingale regarded as the basic requirement in a nurse, would make Ruth quite unfit for the task of tending the sick, in Jemima's opinion. But Ruth perseveres and wins the respect of the poor of the town, just as Florence Nightingale's first and most devoted patients were the prostitutes suffering from cholera whom she nursed in the Middlesex Hospital in 1854.

When Bradshaw discovers that his son Richard has forged a number of share certificates belonging to Benson, his humiliation is deepened by the minister's refusal to prosecute. His only consolation, barely voiced, is that there must be some 'innate wickedness' in the boy derived, of course, from his mother. Once more the two argue on a point of social morality, with Bradshaw demanding that Benson take action to have Richard brought to justice. The minister refuses,

'I should think it right to prosecute, if I found out that this offence against me was only one of a series committed, with premeditation, against society. I should then feel, as a protector of others more helpless than myself——'
'It was your all,' said Mr. Bradshaw.
'It was all my money; it was not my all,' replied Mr. Benson (Ch. 30).

Kind people can be pitiless as Bradshaw finds to his grief. As everyone seeks to help him, his anguish becomes the greater. His family is in ruins around him and the only voice of reproach is his own. Richard is sent by Farquhar to a Glasgow office where he can be employed as a clerk and Mr Bradshaw returns, with some reluctance, to the chapel. It is now Farquhar who controls the business and makes decisions. Bradshaw must learn to forgive himself before he can forgive others.

It required the holocaust of the Crimea to make Florence

Nightingale's family accept her career as a nurse, and it needs an epidemic of typhus in Eccleston before Ruth is regarded as a decent woman. The typhus occurs first in the Irish lodging houses, in the poorest part of the town. The alarm is given by the priests, but it is then too late to stem the virulence of the infection. Ruth decides that she must nurse in the infirmary where the customary nurses have abandoned the patients and fled. Leonard, standing outside the hospital, hears his mother's name blessed by the crowd as a saint. There is a biting irony in the procession of visitors who come to the chapel-house when the fever has abated and Ruth has returned home. Mr Grey, the rector, arrives with a letter of commendation and thanks from the Board, and takes great care to address Ruth as Mrs Denbigh. And Mr Davis, the senior surgeon of Eccleston, comes with an offer to make Leonard his bound apprentice, so that in the course of time he will become a partner and eventually succeed him in the most lucrative medical practice in the town. Almost inadvertently, Mr Davis announces that he must leave them to attend Mr Donne who has succumbed to the fever at the Queen's Hotel. Ruth immediately says that she must go and nurse him.

It is a crucial moment that does not dissolve in sentimental rhapsodies of self-abnegation and mortification because Davis, acerbic and stringent, proceeds to question Ruth's motives. It is not love that takes her to Bellingham's side, but a sense of duty, the fulfilment of a task she once undertook but was unable to complete. When Davis tells her that he doubts if it is worth risking the health of a paid London nurse for Bellingham's life, Ruth replies: ' "We have no right to weigh human lives against each other" ' (Ch. 34). As Davis continues to argue, she is forced to confess Bellingham's relationship to her, answering with honesty that even if she no longer loves him she does feel the need to care for him. Drily, the doctor shares secret for secret with Ruth, telling her that he is himself illegitimate and for this reason he had always sympathised with Leonard.

Ruth dies as a result of nursing Bellingham, but there is no reconciliation over his sick-bed, no opportunity made for explanation or forgiveness. Instead the commentary upon the succeeding events is given to Davis, who devotes all his time and skill in the effort to save Ruth.

He called on the rival surgeon, to beg him to undertake the management of Mr. Donne's recovery, saying, with his usual self-mockery, 'I could not answer it to Mr. Cranworth if I had brought his opponent round, you know, when I had such a fine opportunity in my power. Now, with your patients, and general Radical interest, it will be rather a feather in your cap; for he may want a good deal of care yet, though he is getting on famously—so rapidly, in fact, that it's a strong temptation to me to throw him back—a relapse, you know' (Ch. 35).

Despite all Davis's care, Ruth dies in a gentle delirium, singing the tunes her mother had taught her as a child. 'She never looked at any one with the slightest glimpse of memory or intelligence in her face; no, not even at Leonard' (Ch. 35). As Leonard calls out for his mother, there is the unspoken thought that a child had once given birth to a child and now that mother was returning to the childhood she had lost. In death, Ruth is what she had always been, a faithful, obedient and loving child whom society had insisted on treating as an adult. She is not a tragic heroine capable of shaping events and making decisions for herself and others. Even when she goes to the Infirmary she says that it is because the Bensons have taught her to serve others, that the idea was not hers since she had seen how the minister had gone out and tended the sick.

Bellingham made her a toy, Bradshaw saw her as the visible object of his charity, but the curious family of the Bensons and Sally made her a heroine despite her lack of intelligence and commonsense. Some of Elizabeth Gaskell's friends were well advised to burn *Ruth*, but not necessarily on moral grounds. The real threat in the book lies in the clear statement that even the dull and underprivileged can be of greater value to society than the clever and the rich. And society, assuming a collective voice, will make that fact known to the dismay of those who claim authority by reason of wit and wealth.

4
Cranford: old age and Utopia

Cranford has always bedevilled Elizabeth Gaskell's reputation, providing an incongruous touchstone for the major works and fully justifying her subsequent status as a minor novelist. It is a slight piece, a series of vignettes written to please the current taste for semi-comic reminiscence, but prolonged and composed under the direction of Charles Dickens, that baleful influence on her creative method. On 13 December 1851 a short story entitled 'Our Society at Cranford' was published in *Household Words*. As Elizabeth Gaskell later wrote to John Ruskin, 'The beginning of "Cranford" was *one* paper in "Household Words"; and I never meant to write more, so killed Capt Brown very much against my will . . .' (G.L. 562). However, the readers were delighted and Dickens persuaded her to continue the story of the surviving characters. It is foolish at this point to speak of artistic integrity; Elizabeth Gaskell wrote for money and, like every Victorian novelist, she had to keep a watchful eye on the lending libraries, the demands of serial publication and fluctuations in popular taste. Many novels were improvised from week to week according to the sales of the magazine, and a work that failed to capture an audience was bundled to a quick conclusion as was *North and South*. (The writer of television serials is accustomed to precisely the same weekly testing of his material.) Frequently a Victorian novelist, while engaged in the comfortable and leisurely fashioning of his plot, found himself in the awkward position of a music-hall singer halfway through his song, suddenly hearing the orchestra playing the last chorus and finding the next performer waiting in the wings. Writing a novel in these circumstances became almost a co-operative enterprise between the author and his readers.

It is quite remarkable that Elizabeth Gaskell was able to resist so many of Dickens's editorial directions. Dickens's journals were like orchestras that he conducted according to

81

his own choice of mood and tempo. The music was supplied by others, but he controlled its presentation. Elizabeth Gaskell was remarkably resistant to his proffered comments. For example, in one of her best ghost stories, 'The Old Nurse's Story' (1852), an old woman, Miss Furnivall, is haunted by the cruel revenge she once exacted from her sister. Maude Furnivall and her child had been driven from the house by an enraged father and an implacable sister. A child who has come to stay in the house is the first to see the ghosts and then wakes the living dead. The climax is reached when the great door of the house is blown down in a winter gale, and the violent scene from the past is re-enacted before their eyes. Miss Furnivall sees herself, and falls dead before this image of 'relentless hate and triumphant scorn'. Brokenly, as she lies dying, she mutters over and over, ' "Alas! alas! what is done in youth can never be undone in age! What is done in youth can never be undone in age!" ' Dickens was delighted with the story but his suggestions for its conclusion were firmly rejected by Elizabeth Gaskell. She had written, he told her,

'A very fine ghost-story indeed. Nobly told, and wonderfully managed. But it strikes me (fresh from the reading) that it would be very new and very awful, if, when the narrator goes down into the parlour on that last occasion, she took up her sleeping charge in her arms, and carried it down—if the child awoke when the noises began—if they all heard the noises—but *only the child* saw the spectral figures, except that they all see the phantom child. I think the real child crying out what it is she sees, and describing the phantom child as shewing it all to her as it were, and Miss Furnivall then falling palsy-stricken, would be a very terrific end.'[1]

It would also have blurred the conclusion by destroying the spectral affirmation of Miss Furnivall's guilt. It is Miss Furnivall who is the source of the apparitions, the child is only the recipient, and at the old woman's death the hauntings cease.

Whenever Dickens could emphasise the role of a child in a story he did so, but Elizabeth Gaskell had a less sentimental regard for children. Those who cherished the most tender feelings for them were, in her opinion, those who had never had any, like Miss Matty dreaming of the little girl who never changes, never grows older or fails to love her. 'A terrific end' to 'The Old Nurse's Story' would have satisfied most readers, but it would have compromised Elizabeth Gaskell's sense of the inner logic of her plot, so she refused. *Cranford*, on the other hand, won Dickens's wholehearted approval, despite his shrewd and well-founded suspicion that she was dismissing his praise as 'soft sawder'.

The first part of *Cranford* contained all the ingredients Dickens regarded as necessary for the composition of the Christmas pudding novelette—a good measure of pathos in the form of Captain Brown and his family, a death scene, some robust humour in the shape of Miss Betsy Barker's cow clad in flannel drawers, and Elizabeth Gaskell's own original addition to the approved recipe. The ingredient that flavoured the whole commonplace mixture was solace for some of the deepest and most infrequently expressed human fears. It was never intended to be more than the usual Christmas piece expected of all popular novelists and written in a tradition that Anthony Trollope despised. He felt that the magazine treatment of Christmas was humbug,[2] something that Dickens had done more to inspire than dispel. But despite the trite formulation of plot and the lack or organic structure, *Cranford* was an astonishing success. It was read, and is still read, to the neglect unfortunately of Elizabeth Gaskell's major works. Not only was it reprinted more often than any of the other novels, but it became, in time, a popular stage play, a musical, a film and a television serial. There are reasons for popularity of this magnitude. Certainly, Elizabeth Gaskell assured Ruskin that it was her favourite work, the one that she could always read again with pleasure and most readers would be prepared to share her delight with its warm good humour. But on another occasion she reminded W. S. Williams that 'authors are so easily deceived about their own things!' (G.L. 499). It is not difficult for a writer to enjoy the praise of an audience given freely and without criticism.

Cranford, which all readers immediately associate with Knutsford, has less relationship with reality than had Monkshaven and Milton. As A. W. Ward observed, the book had many affinities with Crabbe's *Tales of the Hall*. Elizabeth Gaskell's first poems had been composed in the style of Crabbe. It was then her intention to write of working-class people in a way that revealed their inherent dignity, but in *Cranford* the working class is scarcely visible except as servants. What she does achieve is a transformation of the people who had been cast aside by the new industrial society, and in particular, those who had always been singled out as objects of derision. The women, and the few men of Cranford, with the exception of Dr Hoggins and transients like Signor Brunoni, are all old, or at least retired from life. Captain Brown makes it clear that he has chosen to live in Cranford because he cannot afford to do so anywhere else, and even the narrator of the story, barred by her youth from permanent residence in the village, vibrates back and forth from the city of Drumble. Age is neither disfiguring nor a time of loneliness and pain in Cranford. There is occasional bitterness and frequent acrimony, but the old live and play cards, give parties and pay calls, creating their own society in a place ignored by the city with its demands for change and progress. And this is the main reason for the work's enormous success. All of us fear death, and many fear old age even more, but Cranford reveals old people devising their own entertainments, contriving to enjoy themselves on reduced incomes and making 'elegant economy' a matter of pride.

Age has always held more terrors for women than for men, and for the single woman it still looms with bleak uncertainties and social isolation. Not in Cranford: there it is Miss Pole's daily prayer of thanks that she has never succumbed to matrimony, and Miss Deborah Jenkyns maintains her belief that woman is man's superior by a dogmatic manner and a jockey's cap worn at a masculine angle. The characters are neither sentimental nor idealised, but it is impossible to deny their satisfaction with themselves and Cranford. Undoubtedly it is the atmosphere that developers and investors hope to achieve in 'sun cities' and other havens for those who have 'retired' from what is described, with a mordant sense of humour, as 'life'. It should be possible now to ask why Cranford brims over with life and humour, while the sun cities of California and Florida creak with a grotesque vitality that is more terrifying than death.

Cranford is itself, not created by social workers or reformers to serve any particular function, or shield a group of old women from active society. It is sustained by its own patterns of behaviour, as hierarchical and as arbitrary as those of the court of Louis XIV. Yet it is a social structure that responds to the needs of those who live within it, and it is flexible enough to admit the occasional new member. When the narrator smiles at the foibles of Cranford, we can laugh with her, but pause to wonder where today it is possible to grow old without being made to feel like a social outcast. The macabre horror of a Florida retirement settlement lies in its determination to provide an imitation of youth, with old men wearing plaid trousers and old women concealing the scars of cosmetic surgery under pony tails and aviator sun glasses. But there is no emulation of youth in Cranford, and the women dress as they have always done, with only one concession to fashion—a new cap for great occasions.

> The expenditure on dress in Cranford was principally in that one article referred to. If the heads were buried in smart new caps, the ladies were like ostriches, and cared not what became of their bodies. Old gowns, white and venerable collars, any number of brooches, up and down and everywhere (some with dogs' eyes painted in them; some that were like small picture-frames with mausoleums and weeping-willows neatly executed in hair inside; some, again, with miniatures of ladies and gentlemen sweetly smiling out of a nest of stiff muslin), old brooches for a permanent ornament, and new caps to suit the fashion of the day (Ch. 8).

The ladies of Cranford have so ordered their society that a new dress, unless warranted by circumstances of immense social magnitude, would have appeared as vulgarly ostentatious as a tiara at tea-time in Belgravia. Their dress, like their behaviour, is an expression of their independence modified only slightly by regulated custom. '. . . as they observe, "What does it signify how we dress here at Cranford, where everybody knows us?" And if they go from home, their reason is equally cogent: "What does it signify how we dress here, where nobody knows us?" ' (Ch. 1). The ladies of Cranford are sustained not only by their own sense of self-sufficiency but by a society that condones 'individuality, not to say eccentricity, pretty strongly developed' (Ch. 1). It is essentially a society of their own creation, run by rules and proscriptions of their own choosing, which may appear petty and occasionally spiteful to the outsider. Nevertheless it functions, responding to emergencies that affect the community as a whole, or individual members. It is, quite remarkably, a society that fully expresses the temperament of those who have created it. Cranford is as much a Utopia as any devised by a social reformer. The point, so often disregarded by Utopian theorists from Plato onwards, is that no one society can ever accommodate the needs and desires of everyone. Somebody will always be dissatisfied. There can never be an earthly paradise in which some of its inhabitants do not feel alienated and oppressed. But Cranford is the joyful expression of the liberty of the few in the midst of general conformity. If called upon to define the work in terms of literary genre, it would be necessary to see *Cranford* as Utopian fiction.

The fear of age has no place in Cranford where everyone is old. Jane Austen's world was one of young people where the occasional old woman is a figure of fun, like Miss Bates in *Emma,* but in *Cranford* Miss Deborah Jenkyns is the arbiter of the social and intellectual life of the village. And her influence continues beyond her demise. One of the many inconsistencies of the work is provided by Miss Matty's death at the end of the second chapter (the conclusion of 'Our Society at Cranford') and her resurrection in the succeeding narrative. The authorial strategy here is so apparent as to embarrass the reader. There could be few complexities of plot with Deborah Jenkyns in control of Cranford, but to recall Miss Matty to life and dispose of Deborah provided a far more sympathetic and malleable heroine. Deborah remains a ghostly witness to events, the patron saint that must be appeased and appealed to in death as in life. But it is disconcerting when the writer is forced to reveal her intentions quite so openly.

Sexual love between the middle-aged and old has always

been regarded as disgusting or a source of broad comedy. The Victorians knew instinctively that an elderly woman was a figure of fun in her own right, but as a victim of passion she became ludicrous. Dickens provided a gallery of old maids and widows, each more ferociously bent on matrimony than the next, and each more hilarious in her determined charge to the altar. Elizabeth Gaskell, on the contrary, showed the middle-aged capable of deep and enduring love with Lady Glenmire marrying Mr Hoggins, the local doctor, and Miss Matty choosing to wear a widow's cap when Mr Holbrook, the love of her youth, has died. She also gives us women who have decided to lead single lives, and never ceased to rejoice in the decision. If there is comedy, it is not at the expense of the characters, but of the reader's prejudices. It is impossible to deny that Miss Jenkyns, Miss Barker and Miss Pole enjoy their lives to the full. It is not immaterial to the theme of *Cranford* that Mary Smith begins her narration as a young unmarried woman, but at its end she has grown old with the women she has chosen to make her friends. There is no hint of resignation when the narrator accepts the life of the characters she has described so lovingly. For a Mary Smith, who can shiver deliciously when it is rumoured that robbers have besieged the village and who collects pieces of string with assiduous care, Cranford is the perfect society. Through her narrator's admissions of preference, Elizabeth Gaskell makes it quite clear that her village is not for everyone.

Nowhere do the heroines collapse into matrimony with greater relief than in Charlotte Brontë's novels. Caroline Helstone's visit to the 'old maids' in *Shirley* is a study in frustration and despair, a confirmation of all her abiding dread of the spinster's lot. In the nineteenth century a single woman beyond the age of twenty-five was felt to be socially anomalous, a burden upon her family that could only be alleviated when she accepted the role of a superior servant in the household. But Elizabeth Gaskell was always convinced that single women could lead lives that were as satisfying as those of married women, with one stipulation—those lives had to be led apart from their families. Throughout her work she gives instances of women who choose to live together, creating 'families' of their own devising, like Libbie Marsh who leaves the Dixon family in order to be with the widowed Mrs Hall and her son, or Miss Matty who establishes herself with Martha Hearn and her husband, and presumably with her brother and the narrator, Mary Smith. Conversely, Elizabeth Gaskell portrays the traditional family as a source of frustration and oppression, like Lizzie Leigh's home or the Huntroyd family in 'The Crooked Branch'. (Yet nothing was held more sacred in Victorian life than the family, and a broken home was felt to be like a bottomless pit of misery and insecurity.) The existence of servants meant that it was quite possible for a single woman to maintain a household without living alone. It is typical of Elizabeth Gaskell's social irony that Miss Matty becomes in effect Martha's lodger, but the result is a family ranging from the old to Martha's baby, named after Miss Matty. It is also a family that cuts across class and social barriers to search out mutual affinities and common interests. These odd families that seem to provide so much comfort and security to those who find shelter in them have nothing in common with the household presided over by a patriarchal father delegating his authority from wife to children and servants. Mrs Jamieson attempts to recreate this pattern by permitting Mulliner, her butler, to tyrannise over her, but Mrs Jamieson's torpid stupidity is also one of the comic themes of the work. The real family life of Cranford is found at the parties and morning calls, when the old ladies trip from one house to the next as though entering different rooms of their own homes. No writer has ever placed a higher value upon friendship than Elizabeth Gaskell, and no one realised better that a good friend is worth a dozen indifferent relations. In the context of Victorian society it was a singular heresy to be endorsed quite so openly.

Cranford is, as the narrator states in the famous opening lines, a society of women: 'In the first place, Cranford is in possession of the Amazons; all the holders of houses above a certain rent are women' (Ch. 1). These women, proud of their idiosyncrasies, profess to despise men and only gradually agree to tolerate the company of Captain Brown. He proves to be a paragon of 'excellent masculine common sense', according to the narrator, and all save Miss Deborah are prepared to find no fault in him. But, of course, in Cranford it is women's commonsense which has a tendency to prevail. This is established in the first two chapters by a joke involving the narrator and Charles Dickens that is resolved at the expense of the unfortunate Captain Brown. Miss Deborah Jenkyns and the Captain have long disputed the respective merits of Boz and Dr Johnson. When the Captain insists on reading aloud from the latest number of *Pickwick Papers*, Miss Jenkyns responds with a chapter from *Rasselas*. Now Dickens suspected that Elizabeth Gaskell was pulling his leg and changed *Pickwick Papers* to the poems of Hood. Elizabeth Gaskell promptly restored her original reference when the novel was published in book form. Captain Brown is killed by an onrushing train while absorbed in reading the adventures of Mr Pickwick, and it is not only his commonsense that is called in question but the respective merits of the two works. No instance has ever been recorded in history or fiction of anyone being run down by a train while reading *Rasselas*. Perhaps, in the long run, Miss Deborah Jenkyns was right, but unquestionably for the wrong reasons, in true Cranfordian fashion.

The whole of Cranford society is thrown into a delightful panic by the rumour of thieves abroad, and Miss Pole becomes the chief authority on the outrages the ruffians have committed. When she hears that Mr Hoggins has been way-laid and robbed on his own threshold she submits to having a tooth pulled in his surgery so that she may hear the true story. But the facts according to the local doctor are not to Miss Pole's taste and she gives vent to her chagrin in a characteristic passage:

'Well, Miss Matty! men will be men. Every mother's son of them wishes to be considered Samson and Solomon rolled into one—too strong to be beaten or discomfited—too wise ever to be outwitted. If you will notice, they have always foreseen events, though they never tell one for one's warning before the events happen. My father was a man, and I know the sex pretty well' (Ch. 10).

Now, of course, the robbery at Hoggins's house was no more than the disappearance of a neck of mutton from a yard meat-safe, but Miss Pole's indignant outburst has a considerable degree of relevance to another situation. It was Miss Pole who had always cautioned Miss Deborah Jenkyns against investing her savings in the Town and Country Bank and when Miss Matty is ruined by the bank's failure, she gathers the women of Cranford together and arranges a fund to be paid to her out of their own slight resources. Miss Pole may have been wrong about the neck of mutton, but she was right in her apprehensions about the Town and Country Bank.

Mary Smith's father had also warned Miss Jenkyns about the bank and arrives to investigate Miss Matty's affairs with a fine sense of vindicated business acumen. But it is Miss Pole who has settled matters quietly with her friends, and Mary has devised the means whereby Miss Matty should set herself up as a purveyor of fine teas in the village. Nevertheless, despite everything having been arranged decorously and with a sensitive regard for Miss Matty's feelings, Mr Smith insists on displaying that 'excellent masculine common sense' which had cost Captain Brown his life. The narrator, like Miss Matty, is quite crushed by Mr Smith's professional manner:

I am not going to weary you with the details of all the business we went through; and one reason for not telling about them is, that I did not understand what we were doing at the time, and cannot recollect it now. Miss Matty and I sat assenting to accounts, and schemes, and reports, and documents, of which I do not believe we either of us understood a word; for my father was clear-headed and decisive, and a capital man of business, and if we made the slightest inquiry, or expressed the slightest want of comprehension, he had a sharp way of waying, 'Eh? eh? it's as clear as daylight. What's your objection?' And as we had not comprehended anything of what he had proposed, we found it rather difficult to shape our objections; in fact, we never were sure if we had any. So presently Miss Matty got into a nervously acquiescent state, and said, 'Yes', and 'Certainly', at every pause, whether required or not; but when I once joined in as chorus to a 'Decidedly', pronounced by Miss Matty in a tremblingly dubious tone, my father fired round at me and asked me, 'What there was to decide?' And I am sure to this day I have never known (Ch. 14).

There was considerably more clarity and a great deal more sympathy, when Miss Pole conducted the meeting that ensured Miss Matty's financial security. Miss Matty's tea business flourishes despite her moral reservations about green tea and its effect on the health, but as the narrator notes artlessly and almost in an aside: '. . . I fancy the world must be very bad, for with all my father's suspicion of every one with whom he has dealings, and in spite of all his many precautions, he lost upwards of a thousand pounds by roguery only last year' (Ch. 15). The ladies have a rare talent for being wrong about necks of mutton and similar trifles, but in the larger concerns of life they are invariably right. The logic is indeed Pickwickian, but it works.

A long-lost brother returning from distant climes was a cliché of fiction that was drawn from the experience of everyday life. Travel was uncertain, and the Book of Common Prayer beseeched God to protect those in danger at sea. It was a prayer that had a painful significance for many of the supplicants. The frequently disputed point in *Mansfield Park* concerning the moral implications of the play being rehearsed in Sir Thomas Bertram's absence in Antigua can be resolved quite simply. If Sir Thomas had been lost at sea or died in the Indies (no word had reached the family to the contrary), then it would have been harrowing for his children to discover later that a merry comedy had been played out when their father was dead. The point was not lost upon Sir Thomas when he returned home unexpectedly. Dickens's son Sydney was lost at sea in 1872 as Elizabeth Gaskell's own brother had vanished earlier in the century. The dangers of travel and the uncertainties of the mails made any voyage by sea a challenge to fate. Thus, the magnificent white shawl that Mrs Jenkyns had longed for when she was married is sent to her by her son Peter in time for her to be buried in it. However, the homecoming of Peter Jenkyns is arranged less by chance than as a result of the investigations of Mary Smith, aided by Mrs Brown.

Mrs Brown embodies the endurance and initiative of a working-class woman. As the wife of a sergeant in India, Mrs Brown has already lost six children in the intemperate climate and, determined to save her seventh baby, she sets off to Calcutta to buy a passage back to England, carrying with her a small picture of the Virgin and Child given to her by a Roman Catholic. After stopping to pray in a Hindu temple, Mrs Brown is sheltered by a certain Aga Jenkyns before taking ship for England. After long questioning, Mary discovers the address of the mysterious Englishman in India and writes to him. There is no answer, and Mary has almost forgotten her first hopes until a stranger arrives in Miss Matty's little shop—a white-haired, middle-aged man whom she can hardly recognise as the young brother who ran away from home so long ago. Now, if the incident is trite in the extreme, its implications within the context of the story are not. Peter does not arrive to save his sister from penury; her business is flourishing and she is managing to live within the bounds of that 'elegant economy' required of Cranford society. She does, upon his return, give up the shop, but only after it has been clearly established that Miss Matty can support herself with the aid of her friends.

Peter does not change Cranford, instead Cranford absorbs him into its society, making him a welcome guest at the parties and the endless round of calls. The main service he renders to the village is to heal the breach between Mrs Jamieson and her erstwhile sister-in-law, now Mrs Hoggins. As Mary notes with considerable approval: 'I don't believe Mr. Peter came home from India as rich as a nabob; he even considered himself poor, but neither he nor Miss Matty cared much about that. At any rate, he had enough to live upon "very genteelly" at Cranford; he and Miss Matty together' (Ch. 15). The stories Mr Peter tells of his travels in India are as exotic as those of Baron Munchhausen but they blend well with those of Miss Barker's cow in flannel drawers, and Mrs Forrester's cat which swallowed the lace. Time and place are deliberately vague in *Cranford* but it seems as though the little village is mysteriously drifting towards Cockayne and the vale of Avalon. It is the nature of Cranford to find it difficult to accept Mr Hoggins's creaking boots, but not the magic of Signor Brunoni or Mr Peter's shooting of a cherub in the Himalayas.

It is difficult to describe *Cranford* as a novel of country life, since there is so little that is uniquely rural about it.

Unlike *Sylvia's Lovers* and *Wives and Daughters*, there is no evocation of scenery to complement and modify the lives of the characters. Instead, *Cranford* is deliberately set in the context of fiction, and there is no reality beyond the card tables, the tea tray underneath the sofa and the pattens clattering from one house to another in rainy weather. When the world ventures to intrude in the form of a bank failure or a railway it is immediately translated by Cranford into terms acceptable to itself. Peter knows instinctively that his years in India have significance for this society, but only when they are adapted to conform with its own vision of distant lands. The gossip flows continually, traversing the past, recalling the dead and probing the future, but the atmosphere is always timeless and static. All that comes to Cranford is changed, but Cranford is changeless. This is the paradox of fairy tale and romance.

The writing is often clumsy in *Cranford*, with a repetitiveness that grates upon the reader. Miss Matty, Captain Brown and Mary's father all drum their fingers upon the table as though Elizabeth Gaskell were thinking of the next incident while the last was dragging itself out in verbal clichés. Nothing can alleviate the structural flaws in the work or the recourse to the tried and true techniques of the serial novelist —the long-lost brother, the bank failure, the railway accident, the death scene and comic lower-class courtship. Analysed as a series of incidents, the novel is embarrassingly banal and commonplace. Yet *Cranford* is still a pleasure to read and we are captivated by reasons that lie beyond the reach of critical cognition. (When Elizabeth Gaskell attempted a sequel entitled *The Cage at Cranford*, published in *All the Year Round* (November 1863) almost ten years after *Cranford* was completed as a novel, the episode was trite and unappealing. The magic of *Cranford* had vanished from the humorous little account of Miss Pole mistaking a French dress cage for a bird cage, and being set to rights by Peter and Mr Hoggins. It is quite clear that the whole world of *Cranford* has disappeared when Miss Pole needs to be advised and proven wrong by two men.) The delight of the novel is that a group of middle-aged and old women can order a society to their own pleasure. Men are accepted as unavoid-

able but hardly respected, eccentricity is indulged and condoned and every accepted social prejudice is turned on its
head. Old women can live joyfully without children or husbands, friends are a better source of security than families,
and old age need have no fear of loneliness. Nothing could
be further from the outlook of a novel like Muriel Spark's
Memento Mori, where age and decay, disease and death totter
to the grave.

It is not the old who are closest to death in *Cranford* but
the young, like Miss Brown, and the middle-aged, like her
father. Miss Matty is mysteriously resurrected and Miss
Deborah lives on as the Johnsonian guardian of Cranford
society. Stirring softly within us all there is the fear of age,
of being jostled aside while the young rush past to an uncertain future regardless of our needs and opinions. *Cranford*
alleviates that fear, and offers the hope that, somewhere, we
too may find a society which not only respects age but is
prepared to accommodate all our whims and predilections.
To see the old eagerly greeting every new experience is to
present age with a sympathy seldom found in literature. It is
exemplified not simply by Miss Matty buying a new gown
but by the exuberance of Thomas Holbrook suddenly
announcing that he is going to Paris: ' "To Paris!" we both
exclaimed. "Yes, madam! I've never been there, and always
had a wish to go; and I think, if I don't go soon, I mayn't go
at all; so as soon as the hay is got in I shall go, before harvest
time" ' (Ch. 14). Old bachelors, like old spinsters, do not find
a fountain of youth in Cranford—Miss Pole would laugh any
such nostrum to scorn—but they do come to a grateful understanding of age as the fulfilment of life and of the individual
personality. It is little wonder after all that Elizabeth Gaskell
told John Ruskin that *Cranford* was the one book she always
chose to read again when 'ailing or ill' (G.L. 562). It is the
most comforting book for those growing old—as we all of
us are.

5
North and South: civilising capitalism

North and South was Dickens's title for Elizabeth Gaskell's novel *Margaret*, which appeared in *Household Words* between September 1854 and January 1855. Elizabeth Gaskell was under the impression she was to be given twenty-two episodes but Dickens insisted on twenty. A compromise was effected with the twenty-second number being a breathless compression of plot and incident. It was a painful introduction for her to all the stringencies of weekly serial publication. She had already published *Cranford* and a number of short stories with Dickens when she agreed that he should have the story of Margaret Hale. Serial publication was inimical to every strength she possessed as a writer, requiring her to concentrate on dramatic episodes, theatrical vignettes of suspense and tension, when all her creative ability lay in the delineation of emotion and thought. Dickens's evocation of reality against a moral landscape of symbolic forms was apparent in *Hard Times,* the novel that preceded Elizabeth Gaskell's. Nothing could have been more alien to Elizabeth Gaskell's Milton-Northern than Dickens's Coketown, painted red and black like the face of a savage and twined with serpents of smoke. Her sense of reality was never translated into a realm of symbolic metaphor. Smoke remained smoke in Manchester, just as no Mancunian doorknob could ever have become a ghostly face on Christmas Eve, or New Year's Eve, for that matter. The two writers lived in different visionary worlds and Dickens's attempts to bring Elizabeth Gaskell's into conjunction with his own resulted in acrimonious argument between them. He shaped what he saw into figurative and symbolic allegories that had the power to change the world's image of itself. She transcribed reality into literal forms. Dickens was the alchemist of literature, Elizabeth Gaskell, the chemist, whose works always disclosed their original sources. When Dickens borrowed from Elizabeth Gaskell, as he did in *Hard Times*, reality was changed to

parable. The scene in *Ruth* where Bradshaw informs Jemima
of his plans for her future marriage to an elderly suitor
becomes the superlative theatre of Gradgrind informing
Louisa of Bounderby's proposal. But Dickens's influence
upon Elizabeth Gaskell produced only melodrama and
bathos. The ghost stories she wrote in imitation of Dickens
are among her worst, and the effort of straining after conscious visual effect resulted in constraint and artifice. She
had no inclination towards the theatre and made no attempt
to write a play, but Dickens's literary technique was essentially dramatic. She was soon aware of these differences and
argument became the keynote of their discussions. It was
typical of Dickens to amend the title of Elizabeth Gaskell's
short story from 'A Night's Work' to 'A Dark Night's Work',
and equally consistent with their relationship for her to
resent the change and to insist, without success, that her
original title be restored on final publication.

Elizabeth Gaskell remained convinced that Dickens had
acted in bad faith over the publication of *North and South*,
promising her twenty-two numbers instead of twenty. She
could count on Anna Jameson's sympathy, a writer of billow-
ing prose, when she complained: 'Every page was grudged
me, just at last, when I did certainly infringe all the bounds
& limits they set me as to quantity. Just at the very last I was
compelled to desperate compression' (G.L. 225). Unhappy
with Dickens's cavalier alteration of her title, she ironically
suggested: 'I think a better title than N. & S. would have
been "Death & Variations". There are 5 deaths, each beauti-
fully suited to the character of the individual' (G.L. 220).
Elizabeth Gaskell was often malicious, particularly when
angry, and this irony was directed at the butcher of Little
Nell, and the acknowledged master of the death scene. She
was discovering what all writers of independent spirit found
when they came under Dickens's editorial hand. Dickens had
once assured Douglas Jerrold that all contributions to his
journal would be anonymous, to which Jerrold replied 'reading aloud the words that appeared at the top of every page,
"Conducted by Charles Dickens", I see it is *mon*onymous
throughout'.[1] In 1855, when the first edition of *North and
South* appeared, the concluding chapter of the twenty-first

part in *Household Words* had been amplified to form chapters 44 to 48 of the final work. But Dickens complained that she was diffuse and wordy, that not enough happened, and then too slowly, and found confirmation of his criticism in the declining sales of *Household Words*. His final opinion of *North and South* was that it was 'wearisome in the last degree',[2] and proceeded to cultivate Wilkie Collins, whose narrative techniques were far better suited to serial publication than Elizabeth Gaskell's densely woven studies of middle- and working-class life.

Times had improved in Manchester by the early 1850s and there was no longer widespread depression throughout the city. The trades-unions had become stronger, developing their own social identity within the environment of industry and the city. George Howell, writing of the engineers' strike and lock-out in Manchester of 1851–52, could claim with some pride that the Amalgamated Society of Engineers 'keeps its own poor, sustains its sick, buries in decency its own deceased members and their wives, and maintains for its members a rate of wages which could not otherwise have been obtained and continued in this country'.[3] The power mule-spinners in the cotton-mills had formed their own unions, and there were looser and less well-organised associations amongst the carders and weavers. The working class could not be designated as a single group in society, for within it there were elite sections contending against each other, and determined to maintain their skill through systems of apprenticeship and closed shops. Unions had become an accepted part of industrial life, and strikes the means by which they achieved their goals. In *Mary Barton*, a union still has the nature of a conspiracy, but in *North and South*, the trades-union is acknowledged as the representative body for the workers. The novel completes certain themes in *Mary Barton*, analysing the reasons for middle-class involvement with working-class movements, the nature of social concern, in the changing attitudes of Margaret Hale and John Thornton's abdication from the role of master to that of employer in his factory.

It is not only unions that have assumed new dimensions in society through the efforts of the workers; middle-class people who disdained trade and had pity only for the rural poor are now drawn into new relationships with industrial society. Industry is recognised as the most profitable investment, and Margaret's loan to Thornton portends the Limited Liability Acts of 1855–56 that made shareholding, in the modern sense, a legally defined process. *North and South* was an inadequate and misleading title, as Elizabeth Gaskell knew, for the novel is not merely concerned with the contrast between a rural south of England and an industrial north, but shows Manchester as the heart of a new society, drawing London to it, as well as the south and even Oxford. Whereas *Mary Barton* saw Manchester assessing London. *North and South* makes Manchester the focus of attraction for the whole of England. Engels's and Carlyle's predicted revolutions never occurred in England, for reasons that are implicit in the Manchester of *North and South*. Here there is no simplistic division of society into Engels's bourgeoisie and proletariat or Disraeli's two nations; instead Elizabeth Gaskell traces the vital linkage of social communities, and the interaction as individuals move from one group to another. As early as 1825, this interlocking aspect of English life had been accurately expressed in an article, 'Mechanics' Combinations', in the *St James's Magazine*. The writer concluded that despite a spate of riots and disturbances there was no likelihood of revolution: 'The state of society in England is too complicated,—all classes are too much dove-tailed into each other, to allow us to entertain the least apprehension of any rising of one part against another.'[4] It is this complexity that Elizabeth Gaskell defines through the sensibility of her heroine, Margaret Hale, in *North and South*.

The novel begins in what most middle-class girls of that day would have selected as their natural and most becoming environment. If the workers of *Mary Barton* chose to linger in Green Heys Field, then surely a young, well-bred woman would wish to be in the drawing-room of a handsome house in Harley Street, surrounded by all the rustling excitement of a fashionable London wedding. Subtly it is suggested that this is a world like the enchanted palace of Sleeping Beauty, safely sheltered from all the problems of society, and almost dead. The bride is asleep, worn out with all the preparations for her wedding. It is as though Edith's whole purpose in life has come to an end now that she has found herself a husband. She sleeps so soundly that Margaret Hale, her cousin, is unable to wake her. There are no narrative disjunctions in *North and South*, for Margaret can be relied upon to express, initially at least, the feelings and opinions of her readers. What could be more pleasing to a young woman of taste than the refinement and gaiety of the final dinner party given to Edith's friends? Snatches of conversation drift towards Margaret as she recalls the ten years she has spent with Edith, who is now to marry a handsome young officer, Captain Lennox. ' "She is a lucky girl" '; ' "I have spared no expense with her trousseau" ' are phrases that float from the next room. Unable to rouse Edith, Margaret agrees to display the Indian shawls that were part of the legacy Aunt Shaw received from her late husband, the general. As she carries down the shawls, Margaret's thoughts are travelling back to her home, the parsonage at Helstone. Harley Street is to be a place of crisis and decision for her, since Henry Lennox, the barrister brother of the amiable captain, has already determined that Margaret shall be his wife. Having endured the hectic tumult of trivialities surrounding the wedding, Margaret finds herself speaking to Henry of the country village that she now regards as her real home. Ten years of living in London with Aunt Shaw and Edith have given Helstone all the charm of childhood memory for Margaret. She tells Henry that Helstone 'is like a village in a poem—in one of Tennyson's poems' (Ch. 1). Henry, shrewdly cross-examining her, imagines that within a fortnight he will appear as the most welcome rescuer in that rustic wilderness.

Elizabeth Gaskell's novel moves according to a narrative and sequential order of time, but the characters are constantly engaged in a recall of the past that is then adapted and made part of present consciousness. It is a game in which the past is dredged and stones miraculously become jewels. Elizabeth Gaskell is always aware of a fact that seems to elude most historians. It is not what has happened that is important, but what people believe has happened. Thus Aunt Shaw fabricates an image of devotion and sacrifice from what she now chooses to imagine as a loveless marriage forced upon her by a sense of duty. The marriage was, in fact, a deliberate choice that gave her every material comfort but denied her romance. However, by shuffling her memories, Aunt Shaw can justify every present indulgence by recalling past deprivations. It is even possible for her to envy her sister who married for love without regard for money. Love is, as Elizabeth Gaskell implies, what one most desires, and it is characteristic of a woman like Aunt Shaw to prefer possessions to passion while denying this fact to the whole world. Nevertheless, Aunt Shaw is not an isolated comic figure in the frivolity of Harley Street; her recall of time past is close to the pattern of Margaret's own mind at this time. But whereas Aunt Shaw's imagination can never be tested by reality, Margaret must return to her past and live in the village that always reminds her of a poem by Tennyson. Henry Lennox, a man of the world not given to dreaming, is justified in his confidence.

Helstone, like Harley Street, is not wholly to Margaret's taste. She rejoices in the long walks with her father, her sense of power and authority over the people and the place. The fern can be crushed down 'with a cruel glee, as she felt it yield under her light foot', and just as she 'took a pride in her forest', she knows that its 'people were her people' (Ch. 2). Despite the tedium of her home with a discontented, ailing mother and dispirited father, Margaret does not regret the life of London. In Helstone she feels that she has a responsible part to play in society, whereas in London she was always the poor relation who, it must be allowed, was not always reminded of her poverty. Her social attitudes are those of the country gentry and when her mother timidly embarks on a little prospective matchmaking with young Gorman, the son of a family of coachbuilders, Margaret can reply from the security of her acknowledged social rank: ' "I call mine a very comprehensive taste; I like all people whose occupations have to do with the land; I like soldiers and sailors, and the three learned professions, as they call them. I'm sure you don't want me to admire butchers and bakers, and candlestick-makers, do you, mamma?" ' (Ch. 2). Life within doors is becoming a monotony of small oppressive duties without alleviation because of her father's constant preoccupation.

When he calls, Henry Lennox has no doubt that Margaret will have had sufficient time to assess Tennyson's poetry by the actuality of village life. He loves Margaret with all the capacity of a heart strengthened by his perception that she would make an admirable wife for a rising young barrister, despite her lack of money. But when he offers marriage, Margaret refuses, and with him, forswears London, theatres, gay dinner parties and the wit of intelligent people. And as soon as Margaret has chosen Helstone and a life as guardian of the poor, and mistress of the forest, Mr Hale announces his decision to leave the church.

Weak, vacillating, but childishly stubborn in small things —as when the idea of pears takes possession of his mind after dinner and nothing will satisfy him until Margaret has plucked the last of the brown pears from the south wall—Mr Hale suddenly admits to the long crisis of conscience that has forced him to resign from the Church of England and to find a post as a tutor in a northern industrial town. Typically, it is Margaret who must break the news to her mother, and Margaret who must supervise the packing and departure. Hale is depicted as a man who has the courage of his convictions, but not the courage to defend or suffer their consequences. It was a common situation and one that Elizabeth Gaskell knew from her own family and immediate friends. Her father had resigned as a Unitarian minister because he could not accept money for preaching, and Froude left the church for reasons of conscience and became a tutor to the Darbishire children in Manchester. But it is not Hale who bears the responsibility for this decision, but Margaret. Helstone, dearer than ever now that she must leave it, must be put behind her as though she were a farmer's daughter sent off to the city to earn her living. She could look upon Helstone as her own small kingdom where deference was a traditional right accorded to the clergy. Milton-Northern represents all that is alien and repugnant to her. She knows and despises butchers and bakers, but cotton spinners and industrial workers are beyond her experience and comprehension. Slowly she becomes aware of the interlocking connections between Helstone and Milton. It is old Mr Bell, Hale's tutor at Oxford and best man at his wedding, who has advised Milton as a suitable place to find work. Bell has owned property in Milton from the days when it was a quiet country town; now he is the proprietor of city factories, including the land on which the Thornton mill stands. A man like Bell who had inherited family property in a city like Manchester could live in a university college and find his income as an absentee landlord increasing every year. Bell is not the fairy godfather of the novel, but the motive force in this society. Indirectly, he not only controls Hale's future and his family's, but that of Thornton as well. The ownership of land was still the criterion of wealth, particularly if that land was within reach of a growing city.

Margaret's life has been changed for a reason that she cannot fully comprehend: 'The hard reality was, that her father had so admitted tempting doubts into his mind as to become a schismatic—an outcast; all the changes consequent upon this grouped themselves around that one great blighting fact' (Ch. 5). She can neither accept her father's decision, nor refuse to accompany her family to a town that she already detests in imagination. Hale cannot even rationalise his doubts to Margaret, but his determination in this matter is as inflexible as his resolution to have pears for dessert. The source for each is emotional and beyond his capacity to formulate intellectually. Hale's mind is a diffuse wilderness of unresolved doubts and insecurities that he can only lose in the study of philosophy and the classics. He is not a Casaubon, that desiccated human coprolite, but a bewildered, sensitive man who has always been able to shield himself from the vicissitudes of life at the expense of others. At the moment of greatest crisis he shows less fortitude and commonsense than his wife. Self-indulgent, like most introspectives, his only contribution to the plans for departure is to question whether Dixon, his wife's devoted old servant, should accompany them to Milton. He has never cared for Dixon, a mutual dislike, and at this moment his avoidance of personal discomfort is such that he can justify dismissing Dixon for reasons of economy. Again, it is Margaret who decides and Margaret's will that prevails. In the novel there is a double for Mr Hale in Boucher, who takes his own life after betraying the union, just as Hale dies when the full recognition of what he has done to his wife and daughter is forced upon him. Mr Hale's crisis of conscience has not arisen from doctrinal doubts but from his inability to understand and minister to human suffering. At his wife's funeral he is like an automaton of grief, and when it is over, '. . . putting his hand on Margaret's arm, he mutely entreated to be led away, as if he were blind, and she his faithful guide' (Ch. 33). Suffering does not bring forth any strength in Hale, or even an awareness that for a Christian it can be the gate of resurrection. Unable to discriminate between metaphysical and social suffering, he is as helpless to aid and comfort his wife, dying of a lingering and painful disease, as he is to speak a few words of comfort to the bereaved Mrs Boucher. When she must be told of her husband's death, Higgins and Margaret naturally turn to Hale:

'Papa, do you go', said Margaret, in a low voice.
'If I could—if I had time to think of what I had better say; but all at once——' Margaret saw that her father was indeed unable. He was trembling from head to foot.
'I will go,' said she (Ch. 36).

As Margaret knows, to her infinite pity, her father has parted from his church not because of 'imaginary doubts' and 'uncertain fancies', as Henry Lennox maintains, but because of deep psychological inadequacies. A man who can accept neither the reality of suffering nor the inevitability of death cannot minister to others.

As Charlotte Brontë observed, one of the major themes of North and South is 'a defence of those who conscientiously differ from her [the Church], and feel it a duty to leave her fold'.[5] Elizabeth Gaskell believed that ministering to the needs of society was the most practical form of religious expression. It was no longer permissible in her opinion for a practising Christian to divorce his religious beliefs from an active commitment to social reform. It was because so many had been guilty of this failing in the past, that men like Higgins had lost all faith in Christianity and turned to militant socialism. Charles Kingsley wrote Christian Socialist tracts disguised as novels, but Elizabeth Gaskell defines the social and psychological implications of religion in society and to the individual.

Margaret Hale never questioned her church just as she never doubted her place in social life until she came to Milton. In Helstone her religion had always been expressed through her charity to others, a patronage that involved reading 'with slow distinctness to their old people', nursing the parishioners' babies and carrying 'dainty messes to their sick'. The poor were grateful, and she was comfortable in the knowledge of her own benevolence. They were, when all was said and done, 'her people' (Ch. 2). What startles and alarms Margaret in Milton is the lack of deference in the workers who jostle past her in the street, the factory girls who stop to enquire about the cut of her gown and its cost, and the working men who pay an open compliment on her appearance. She soon discovers that she cannot patronise the Milton workers as she did the villagers of Helstone. When she first meets Nicholas Higgins and his sickly daughter, Bessy, in the street near her home, her first feeling of compassion leads directly to a request for their name and address. She intends to visit them, possibly with soup, a gracious gesture on the part of a lady. But Higgins's reaction is one of sharp suspicion:

> ... at Helstone it would have been an understood thing, after the inquiries she had made, that she intended to come and call upon any poor neighbour whose name and habitation she had asked for. 'I thought—I meant to come and see you.' She suddenly felt rather shy of offering the visit, without having any reason to give for her wish to make it, beyond a kindly interest in a stranger. It seemed all at once to take the shape of an impertinence on her part; she read this meaning too in the man's eyes (Ch. 8).

It would have been inconceivable that Margaret should feel guilty of being impertinent to anyone in Helstone, but in Milton, charity was more insulting than a curse to a man like Higgins.

Margaret Hale's religion changes from an emphasis on charity and good works to active social reform, and Elizabeth Gaskell implies that she is the better Christian for it. Certainly she becomes the medium of reconciliation between men of widely divergent belief. Her brother Frederick is cheerfully contemplating becoming a Roman Catholic upon his marriage to a Spanish heiress, her father is unable to reconcile his faith with his life, and Nicholas Higgins has chosen to abandon all religious observance. Unlike John Barton who finds justification in the Bible for radical dissent and voices his rage against society in terms of prophecy, Nicholas Higgins has become a pragmatic socialist. For him, religion is a palliative, and the Methodism of his daughter something akin to Halévy's 'opiate of the masses'. His daughter yearns for a death that will robe her in gold and lead her to a kingdom of eternal glory, but Higgins has only contempt for a religion that denies men bread on earth but promises cake in heaven:

> '. . . a man mun speak out for the truth, and when I see the world going all wrong at this time o' day, bothering itself wi' things it knows nought about, and leaving undone all the things that lie in disorder close at its hand—why, I say, leave a' this talk about religion alone, and set to work on what yo' see and know. That's my creed. It's simple, and not far to fetch, nor hard to work' (Ch. 11).

A religion of tractarian disputes, of moral exhortation, and men and women like Honeythunder and Mrs Pardiggle dispensing charity, was producing a multitude like Nicholas Higgins of varying degrees of cynicism.

It is Bessy's wild rhapsodies that Margaret finds more alarming than her father's blunt secularism. Her illness and eventual death are the result of conditions in the mill where she worked—' "the fluff got into my lungs and poisoned me" ' (Ch. 13). Margaret is troubled and her father enraged when Bessy consoles herself with the belief that the measure of her suffering on earth will correspond precisely to the measure of her joys in heaven. The Book of Revelations has been her escape, and when Margaret advises her to read other parts of the Bible, Bessy replies in a frenzy: ' "I dare say it would be wiser; but where would I hear such grand words of promise —hear tell o' anything so far different fro' this dreary world, and this town above a', as in Revelations?" ' (Ch. 17). In

Bessy's faith there is no time or need for social action. It is her passionate conviction that all her pain and sorrow have been predicted in order that the promise of heavenly bliss might be fulfilled. Higgins is savagely bitter and Margaret disturbed when Bessy insists that her disease of byssinosis is a divine judgment that will entitle her to a glorious place in heaven. Both know that God had little hand in the dangerous economies of the factory-owner and the apathy of the workers. Margaret now understands that if she is to remain a Christian she cannot stand aside from the conflicts and divisions of social life in Milton. She must equate her religion with her desire for social change—indeed, one cannot exist without the other. For old Mr Bell of Oxford, whose every instinct is to conform with the past in religious practice and social behaviour, Margaret has become ' "a democrat, a red republican, a member of the Peace Society, a socialist—" ' (Ch. 40). But as Margaret reminds him, Mr Bell, although an Oxford don, is also a Milton man and the future does not rest in a denial of one in favour of the other, but in a reconciliation of both. It is not difficult for Bell to reach a compromise by leaving his entire fortune to his goddaughter, socialist and red republican though she may be.

John Thornton is at first acquaintance all that Margaret expected to dislike in Milton; the very mention of his name immediately brings to mind the offensively garish wall-paper in their new home. To her mother's query about her father's friend, whom she has already described as 'not quite a gentleman', she continues:

'I should not like to have to bargain with him; he looks very inflexible. Altogether a man who seems made for his niche, mamma; sagacious, and strong, as becomes a great tradesman.'
'Don't call the Milton manufacturers tradesmen, Margaret, said her father. 'They are different.'
'Are they? I apply the word to all who have something tangible to sell; but if you think the term is not correct, papa, I won't use it. But, oh mamma! speaking of vulgarity and commonness, you must prepare yourself for our drawing-room paper. Pink and blue roses, with yellow leaves! And such a heavy cornice round the room!' (Ch. 7).

Margaret is sustained by the certain knowledge that she is a lady, that she will always remain one despite her income, and this innate sense of superiority enables her to endure the new rich of Milton, and even be amused by them. Her attitude is quite inexplicable to Thornton, just as the servant girls who come to be interviewed by Dixon 'even went to the length of questioning her back again; having doubts and fears of their own, as to the solvency of a family who lived in a house on thirty pounds a-year, and yet gave themselves airs, and kept two servants, one of them so very high and mighty' (Ch. 9). Elizabeth Gaskell never denies the reality of status in English society and shows that it frequently operates by means of nuances of behaviour as unintelligible to the outsider as a Chinese opera to a European. Margaret Hale's awareness that she is a lady is not based upon wealth or even birth; it is derived from the sense of propriety that is best expressed as a consciousness of social responsibility. Wealth was not despised so long as it was not used as a means of oppressing others less fortunate. One of Margaret's difficulties in Milton is to find the means of demonstrating her instinctive need to give help without giving offence. If the cult of gentility had one great virtue, it was in its looseness of definition, and its ability to thrive on the most modest income. Thornton's dining-room is a mausoleum of ostentatious wealth and his dinner-party, a groaning display of food, but the Hales' drawing-room is warm with subdued light, books and baskets of embroidery and knitting (Ch. 10). The difference is essentially one between those who live in the full dimensions of their inherited culture and those who regard life as an acquisitive race for material goods and power.

Froude recognised the Hales' drawing-room as a mirror image of his own, and what he gave his employers in Manchester was the same traditional scholarship that Thornton and his friends were bent on acquiring from Hale. No two cities are made to seem more dissimilar than Oxford and Milton in *North and South*, but the two are already bound to each other economically through Mr Bell. Money has a way of making friends where society sees only strangers. The real sense of division is a cultural one, with Thornton believing that Oxford lives in the past of Greece and Rome while his problems are those of the present. There is no reconciliation of these differences, and if the way is clearly not open for social partnership then at least it is possible for an occasional greeting. Thornton's demand is for relevance:

'If we do not reverence the past as you do in Oxford, it is because we want something which can apply to the present more directly. It is fine when the study of the past leads to a prophecy of the future. But to men groping in new circumstances, it would be finer if the words of experience could direct us how to act in what concerns us most intimately and immediately; which is full of difficulties that must be encountered; and upon the mode in which they are met and conquered—not merely pushed aside for the time—depends our future. Out of the wisdom of the past, help us over the present. But no! People can speak of Utopia much more easily than of the next day's duty; and yet when that duty is all done by others, who so ready to cry, "Fie, for shame!"' (Ch. 40).

To which Bell replies with a question that has not been answered today: ' "And all this time I don't see what you are talking about. Would you Milton men condescend to send up your to-day's difficulty to Oxford? You have not tried us yet." '

Opinions change in *North and South* as people come to know each other, and often the most consistently held belief assumes a quite different aspect with experience. Margaret, who could first think of Thornton as a tradesman whose appearance immediately brings to mind the vulgar decoration of a room, is hurt and astonished when her brother Frederick later has exactly the same impression of him. He tells his sister that he took Thornton to be a person of no social consequence who had come to the house on an errand: ' "He looked like someone of that kind," said Frederick, carelessly. "I took him for a shopman, and he turns out a manufacturer" ' (Ch. 31). Understanding is dependent upon circumstance and individual vision, and what is reality for one is fiction for another. Frederick's shopman has become the maker of a new society in Margaret's eyes. To her father he has always been a captain of industry, but Higgins sees him as an old bulldog wearing jacket and breeches and making a pretence of being human. There is no settled mode of presentment in *North and South*, just as there are no definitive statements about faith and society. It is not a tract that is being preached but an experiential process in a situation where a number of variant and frequently contradictory opinions fluctuate and contend. Margaret is mediator, but she is also more subject to change of heart and mind than anyone else as she moves through all ranks of society.

Thornton is the epitome of the Manchester entrepreneur, a man who fulfils in his own person 'the functions of capitalist, financier, works manager, merchant and salesman'.[6] So close is his identification with the factory, that he chooses to live beside it where he can hear the hum of the machinery and be able to overlook his whole domain. His dislike of London is as great as John Barton's. In Thornton's opinion it is Westminster that regulates trade and imposes restrictions upon the owner's management of his affairs, it is parliament that is encroaching upon the rights of free men to conduct their business as they choose. Liberty and freedom of action are embodied in every theory Thornton has about the economy, but in Margaret's eyes, Thornton's libertarianism is founded upon an arrogant assumption of power. A generation from the early manufacturing squires like the first Sir Robert Peel, the Ashworth Brothers, and John Fielden, Thornton has no wish to impose his authority or his morality upon his workers in the hours that they are not actually in his employ. He justifies this as demonstrating his respect for the liberty of his employees, but Margaret sees beyond this 'wise despotism' to Thornton's application to life of his most cherished business principle, buying cheaply and selling dear. Translated into social terms Margaret defines this as an indifferent tyranny, and hardly the respect for independence that Thornton preaches with such vehemence. Margaret argues from a belief in the necessity for social responsibility that Ruskin and Kingsley were already putting into practice. In her opinion Thornton cannot refuse to be involved with his workers,

'. . . not in the least because of your labour and capital positions, whatever they are,' she says, 'but because you are a man, dealing with a set of men over whom you have, whether you reject the use of it or not, immense power, just because your lives and your welfare are so constantly and intimately interwoven. God has made us so that we must be mutually dependent. We may ignore our own dependence, or refuse to acknowledge that others depend upon us in more respects than the payment of weekly wages; but the thing must be, nevertheless' (Ch. 15).

And Thornton in the course of the debate is suddenly confounded by his confession:

'Cromwell would have made a capital mill-owner, Miss Hale. I wish we had him to put down this strike for us.'
'Cromwell is no hero of mine,' said she, coldly. 'But I am trying to reconcile your admiration of despotism with your respect for other men's independence of character' (Ch. 15).

It is only when circumstance and conviction force Thornton into a new relationship with his workers that he realises society's freedom inevitably necessitates some abridgement of personal liberty.

The contest between Margaret and Thornton is sharpened by the current of sexual feeling between them. They share a sense of physical vitality that makes those around them seem pallid and a trifle wan. Henry Lennox's attraction to Margaret is heightened by the list of Italian words she has copied from Dante's *Paradiso* that he finds on the parlour table in Helstone, but it is not her intellectual attributes that make Thornton want her as his wife. He assumes her opinions to be foolish and misguided, but he is fascinated by a bracelet on her arm 'which would fall down over her round wrist. Mr. Thornton watched the re-placing of this troublesome ornament with far more attention than he listened to her father' (Ch. 10). Elizabeth Gaskell presents the action of the bracelet as an image of overt sexuality, apparent to Thornton but not manifest to Margaret, busily pouring tea, or to anyone else in the room. It is the covert, personal nature of Thornton's perception that gives it such intensity. When Hale playfully uses Margaret's thumb and little finger to pick up a lump of sugar, Thornton becomes almost dizzy with his desire to use Margaret in the same way. Two trifling incidents precisely define the nature of Thornton's feeling.

Elizabeth Gaskell knew and acknowledged sexual passion and its power over human lives, but in men she saw it too often becoming an impulse to oppress, with the resulting obliteration of a woman's personality and sense of identity. As a form of enslavement, it was not romantic but cruelly destructive. Charlotte Brontë quarrelled with Harriet Martineau when the latter complained that the heroine of *Villette* was governed only by the passion of love, that the women of the novel lived, thought and dreamed of nothing but love. It was a criticism that touched closely the very source of Charlotte Brontë's creativity and one that she flinched from examining. For Elizabeth Gaskell, women loved, frequently unwisely, but love was not always the dominant force in their lives. Like men, they too knew, and frequently understood better, the meaning of duty. Mary Barton, though deeply in love, can turn away from Jem to nurse her father alone, and in *North and South* the violence of the riot at the factory is only equalled by Margaret's rage when she receives a proposal of marriage from Thornton, who believes that a woman who would step in front of him to face an angry mob must be infatuated with him. The scene at Marlborough Mills when Margaret goes out to stand beside Thornton has been misunderstood by many critics. It is not the selfishness of individualised love, but her awareness of a duty to others that prompts her action. Her shame and anger are aroused when her action is construed as that of a lover. For a man to stand by another's side in time of danger was natural, but for a woman to do the same implied that her inherent timidity had been overcome by a greater passion. Vehemently, Margaret rejects Thornton's statement that he owes everything to her, his pride in his work, his very sense of being, as irrational and blasphemous, and continues by refuting his claim that her public defence of him constituted an admission of love. With difficulty, she tries to explain that it was not because she was ' ". . . prompted by some particular feeling for you—you! Why, there was not a man—not a poor desperate man in all that crowd—for whom I had not more sympathy—for whom I should not have done what little I could more heartily" ' (Ch. 24). It is Margaret's pride that is so deeply wounded, her realisation that in Thornton's opinion a woman is only capable of a brave and generous action towards a man if she is in love with him. Charlotte Brontë always saw women defined by their sex, but Elizabeth Gaskell was aware that women, like men, shared common human responsibilities, and those responsibilities should not be made subject to passion.

It is Margaret who can rationally examine the emotional argument with Thornton, deciding that even though her action at the mill had aroused distress, she would do the same again if the need arose. Thornton has reproached Margaret with not understanding him, but Margaret's feeling is that Thornton has seen her not as an individual but as an extension of his life that may be transformed by his devotion into an image of worship. Margaret considers this to be idolatrous. Being a Christian, she cannot accept human love as a substitute for worship. The misunderstanding between them has not, she feels, been of her making: ' "I never thought of myself or him, so my manners must have shown the truth. All that yesterday, he might mistake. But that is his fault, not mine. I would do it again, if need were, though it does lead me into all this shame and trouble" ' (Ch. 24). Thornton is distraught after the rejection of his proposal and wanders off into the country to find some refuge from his humiliation. Elizabeth Gaskell was at her best in describing abnormal states of feeling and so it is not the incident at the mill that carries most dramatic import but its emotional and psychological outcome. Thornton is

... almost blinded by his baffled passion. He was as dizzy as if Margaret, instead of looking, and speaking, and moving like a tender graceful woman, had been a sturdy fish-wife, and given him a sound blow with her fists. He had positive bodily pain —a violent headache, and a throbbing intermittent pulse. He could not bear the noise, the garish light, the continued rumble and movement of the street. He called himself a fool for suffering so; and yet he could not, at the moment, recollect the cause of his suffering, and whether it was adequate to the consequences it had produced. It would have been a relief to him, if he could have sat down and cried on a door-step by a little child, who was raging and storming, through his passionate tears, at some injury he had received (Ch. 26).

And since he cannot bring himself to have strangers witnessing his grief, Thornton returns home and, like a child, tells his mother: ' "No one loves me,—no one cares for me, but you, mother" ' (Ch. 26).

Suffering, in Elizabeth Gaskell's psychology, brought people to the source of their being. It was a means whereby a person could either hide from himself or find himself and make a fresh beginning. Thornton returns to his mother, to the woman whose life and happiness had been dependent upon his. It is an emotional relationship he had hoped to duplicate with Margaret. Taught to love selfishly and exclusively by his mother, Thornton is broken when Margaret attributes quite another reason to an action that seemed to him such an open profession of devotion. Thornton discovers his common humanity with his workers when he makes peace with Nicholas Higgins, but he becomes a man when he sees Margaret as a woman and not as a chivalric symbol of love requiring the dedication of his life. As a Christian, Margaret understands that no human being can tolerate the love that is meant for God, and no one should be so presumptuous as to demand such a love. Moreover, for a woman this veneration was a means of effectively excluding her from the activities of everyday life since the language of exclusion in a social context can always utilise praise or abuse. Angels of the house, the Victorian ideal of femininity, could not go out seeking work and were entirely dependent upon the offerings of their devoted male worshippers. By defining women as spiritual beings they were effectively removed from competition with men at the workbench or in the factory. Women who were made objects of worship, or who sought this role, were confining themselves to the altar or the hearth. Nothing could be further from Margaret's angry rejection of Thornton's adoration than Lady Eleanor's smiling command to Alton Locke, in Kingsley's novel, that he is her servant 'by the laws of chivalry' and must in some way, never fully explained, find the solution to the ills of English society in Texas (*Alton Locke*, Ch. 40). It is a continuing theme in Elizabeth Gaskell's novels that love transformed to worship can only lead to futility and disappointment.

Sexuality in *North and South* is far more than a definition of human gender, it is a quality of mind and temperament. Margaret has the desire to govern, to show authority and have it respected, and she is startled when Milton does not show the same deference as Helstone. Her contest with Dixon is a tense struggle over Mrs Hale. It is not simply the desire to be a dutiful daughter serving her mother's needs that arouses Margaret to battle, but the challenge to her position as head of the house that is posed by Dixon. When Mrs Hale grows fearful that Margaret may become jealous of Dixon acting as her nurse as well as her servant, Margaret replies impetuously: ' "Let me be in the first place, mother—I am greedy of that" ' (Ch. 16). And she establishes herself as her mother's nurse with Dixon to assist her. Thornton and Margaret are remarkably similar in temperament, with Margaret demanding the same authority in her own home that Thornton has in his. When they are brought together at the conclusion of the novel it is not with any sense of inferiority on Margaret's part. Indeed, she is prepared to finance Thornton, to use the capital Mr Bell has left her to establish a partnership that will permit Marlborough Mills to open again. It was not without reason that Parthenope Nightingale, perhaps with her sister Florence in mind, remarked grimly to Elizabeth Gaskell that she doubted whether Margaret would ever be happy with Thornton, though she had no doubt as to his future bliss.[7] Margaret Hale was too much of a master at heart to want a Victorian husband, but Elizabeth Gaskell does provide the safeguard that her husband is also her debtor.

Margaret eventually learns to stand alone without parents or godfather. Her brother, whom she once thought would relieve her of some of the family burden, has chosen to live in Spain and marry an heiress. Margaret becomes the mainstay of her family, fulfilling a role that should by convention have belonged to her father or her brother. She is the hero of *North and South,* and if Frederick displays feminine characteristics—his willingness to sit by his mother's bed at night, the storm of weeping after her death—then it devolves upon Margaret to plan for his future as well as her own. All her efforts to clear Frederick's name and have him absolved of charges of mutiny end in failure. Frederick is confirmed in his bitterness towards England and all that is English, while Margaret is forced to lie in order to save him from possible arrest. It is not the rumoured suspicion that she has been seen in compromising circumstances with a young man that wounds Margaret, but the knowledge that she has fallen from her own moral standard of honesty. She is angry and hurt when Mrs Thornton warns her that her reputation may become tarnished, but she faints when she has lied to the detective about her presence at the railway station. Again, the incident in which Frederick escapes is theatrical and contrived, but its consequences are tense with psychological implication.

On her return to London, Margaret looks back from the same window where she had sat as a girl wondering about her future with her aunt and cousin. Time is recalled in a complex pattern of memory whereby the past is transformed by the realities of the present:

> But when night came—solemn night, and all the house was quiet, Margaret still sat watching the beauty of a London sky at such an hour, on such a summer evening; the faint pink reflection of earthly lights on the soft clouds that float tranquilly into the white moonlight, out of the warm gloom which lies motionless around the horizon. Margaret's room had been the day nursery of her childhood, just when it merged into girlhood, and when the feelings and conscience had been first awakened into full activity. On some such night as this she remembered promising to herself to live as brave and noble a life as any heroine she ever read or heard of in romance, a life sans peur et sans reproche; it had seemed to her then that she only had to will, and such a life would be accomplished (Ch. 48).

It is Margaret who is the most self-conscious character in the novel, but this consciousness continually moves from emotional response to rational understanding. She is not a static guide for men's behaviour, not an angel in the house; indeed it is stressed that when Edith, Mrs Shaw and Margaret take up residence together, it is Margaret who probably had 'the worst temper of the three, for her quick perceptions and over-lively imagination made her hasty, and her early isolation from sympathy had made her proud' (Ch. 49). Her standard of morality is not derived from the opinion of others but from her own self-realisation. Even as her aunt begs her not to be 'strong minded' whatever else she may choose to be, Margaret has decided that:

> If all the world spoke, acted, or kept silence with intent to deceive—if dearest interests were at stake, and dearest lives in peril—if no one should ever know of her truth or her falsehood to measure out their honour or contempt for her by, straight alone where she stood, in the presence of God, she prayed that she might have strength to speak and act the truth for evermore (Ch. 48).

This is not the voice of a Victorian heroine but a Christian hero. Again it is consistent with the dominance of sense over sensibility in Margaret that she does not rush to give her newly acquired wealth to Thornton when she hears of his financial collapse. Instead, she has an agreement drawn up by Henry Lennox and offers it to Thornton saying: ' ". . . if you would take some money of mine, eighteen thousand and fifty-seven pounds, lying just at this moment unused in the bank, and bringing me in only two and a half per cent.—you could pay me much better interest and might go on working Marlborough Mills" ' (Ch. 52). As a Unitarian, Elizabeth Gaskell distrusted blind faith, as a woman she knew that love could be a destructive force unless tempered by reason. Romance may have lost some of its glow in Manchester but it had gained immeasurably in substance.

If Margaret displays the accustomed masculine characteristics of rationality, strength and moral rectitude, it is her father who embodies all that is most feminine. A charmingly impractical aesthete, he is immediately drawn to Thornton, yielding to his assurance, finding spiritual solace with him after Mrs Hale's death, quoting his theories, recommending the books on economics that Thornton has advised him to read. There is no effort to disguise the quality of their relationship. Femininity is always the defining characteristic of Hale's nature, whether it is his impulse for pears or his shrinking from pain. When he returns timidly to Oxford as the guest of Mr Bell, he is touched by the kindness of those who would have felt indignation at his religious backsliding had he been a stronger man. Instead, he is greeted with the 'tender gravity' that was the approved attitude towards a widow, or a woman similarly bereft 'For Mr. Hale had not been known to many; he had belonged to one of the smaller colleges, and had always been shy and reserved, but those who in youth had cared to penetrate the delicacy of thought and feeling that lay below his silence and indecision, took him to their hearts, with something of the protecting kindness which they would have shown to a woman' (Ch. 41). Intellectually confused to the last, Hale is brought to an understanding of his own lack of rationality and moral strength but significantly, he makes no effort to define his doctrinal differences with the church. For Hale it is enough to know that he would still have left the church but that ' "I might have done differently, and acted more wisely, in all that I subsequently did for my family. But I don't think God endued me with over-much wisdom or strength" ' (Ch. 41). Margaret and her father are both brought to an understanding of themselves, but while Margaret's prayer is for renewed strength, her father begs to be excused his inadequacies.

One reason why Marxism later seemed so irrelevant as a force in English political and social life is made apparent by Margaret Hale, the middle-class Christian Socialist, working with Nicholas Higgins, the union delegate, and John Thornton, the mill-owner. Neither Marx nor Engels appreciated that capitalism was capable of modification and it was people like Margaret Hale who helped to civilise it. She is not a woman devoted to family duties alone, her kingdom is not the hearth where she can reign enshrined by the love of her family; in effect the whole reach of society is within her grasp. She moves from Marlborough Mill to Higgins's fireplace, she questions and challenges, annoying Higgins and angering Thornton. One of her complaints when she returns to London is

'. . . the strange sense of the contrast between the life there, and here. She was getting surfeited of the eventless ease in which no struggle or endeavour was required. She was afraid lest she should become sleepily deadened into forgetfulness of anything beyond the life which was lapping her round with luxury. There might be toilers and moilers there in London, but she never saw them; the very servants lived in an underground world of their own, of which she knew neither the hopes nor the fears; they only seemed to start into existence when some want or whim of their master and mistress needed them. There was a strange unsatisfied vacuum in Margaret's heart and mode of life . . .' (Ch. 44).

Margaret demands the right to be an active member of society, unconfined to any particular region or class. Nothing could have been less accurate than Engels's comment in 1844 on 'the utter ignorance of the whole middle-class of everything which concerns the workers'.[8] Doing good was a middle-class avocation and is one reason why England was not engulfed by social revolution in the nineteenth century. Just as Annie Besant took up the cause of the matchgirls and Samuel Plimsoll that of the seamen, Margaret Hale undertakes to defend the workers and is appalled when Thornton confuses social responsibility with personal infatuation.

Between John Thornton and Nicholas Higgins, the industrial conflict erupts with a violence that neither desires. Thornton justifies existing conditions by the fact that a number of poor men have made themselves owners and employers. To Margaret and her father he expounds the faith that sustains every self-made man from that day to this:

'It is one of the great beauties of our system, that a working-man may raise himself into the power and position of a master by his own exertions and behaviour; that, in fact, every one who rules himself to decency and sobriety of conduct, and attention to his duties, comes over to our ranks; it may not be always as a master, but as an overlooker, a cashier, a bookkeeper, a clerk, one on the side of authority and order.'
'You consider all who are unsuccessful in raising themselves in the world, from whatever cause, as your enemies, then, if I understand you rightly,' said Margaret, in a clear, cold voice (Ch. 10).

And Thornton finds he must recount the story of his own youth as a draper's assistant in order to counter Margaret's challenging question. In a passage that reveals far more to Margaret than he would wish, it is made evident that Thornton the master has been the accomplishment of his mother, 'a woman of strong power, and firm resolve'. Denying violent feelings of any kind towards the workers Thornton makes claim to obvious moral superiority:

> 'I believe that this suffering, which Miss Hale says is impressed on the countenances of the people of Milton, is but the natural punishment of dishonestly-enjoyed pleasure, at some former period of their lives. I do not look on self-indulgent, sensual people as worthy of my hatred; I simply look upon them with contempt for their poorness of character' (Ch. 10).

Poorness of character was, of course, most obvious inside any public house or gin shop. There has always been a social, and therefore a moral, difference between those who drink in public and those who can afford to drink at home.

Certainly Nicholas Higgins is not portrayed as an Alton Locke or a Tregarva, the Cornish gamekeeper of Kingsley's *Yeast*, both apostles of temperance. He drinks and frequently blunders home intoxicated. But this blatant evidence of moral weakness is interpreted quite differently by his daughter, Bessy, who suffers most from it. She sees drunkenness not as a disease in itself, but the symptom of a more insidious malady in an industrial society. Work had lost its sacramental quality, it had also been made subject to regular hours that were unknown in the country or in cottage manufacture. Samuel Greg complained of the 'restless and migratory spirit'[9] of his millworkers, their abiding resentment of factory labour that resembled the parish workhouses where overseers supervised every aspect of production, and, above all else, the deathly monotony of the work itself. In the first chapter of *Mary Barton* it is indicated that the workers may have spontaneously taken advantage of the fine weather to grant themselves a holiday, and in *North and South* Bessy explains why so many chose drink instead of Thornton's path of rectitude and self-denial:

> 'There are days wi' you as wi' other folk, I suppose, when yo' get up and go through th' hours, just longing for a bit of a change—a bit of a fillip, as it were. I know I ha' gone and bought a four-pounder out o' another baker's shop to common on such days, just because I sickened at the thought of going

on for ever wi' the same sight in my eyes, and the same sound in my ears, and the same taste i' my mouth, and the same thought (or no thought, for that matter) in my head, day after day, for ever. I've longed for to be a man to go spreeing, even if it were only a tramp to some new place in search o' work. And father—all men—have it stronger in 'em than me to get tired o' sameness and work for ever. And what is 'em to do? It's little blame to them if they do go into th' gin-shop for to make their blood flow quicker, and more lively, and see things they never see at no other time—pictures, and looking-glass, and such like. But father never was a drunkard, though maybe, he's got worse for drink, now and then' (Ch. 17).

One passage like this illuminates chapters of social history on the subject of alcoholism amongst the working class. There is an understanding of the nature of factory work and its effect on people in *North and South* that is crucial to an interpretation of the period. In many cases, the temperance movement was a refusal to admit social justice by denying the real cause. Bessy is quite prepared to admit her father drinks, but she knows why he drinks. And Margaret later makes clear to her father that she has brought Nicholas Higgins home after Bessy's death 'as a last expedient to keep him from the gin-shop'. When he has recovered from the shock of having a 'drunken infidel weaver' in his drawing-room, it is Mr Hale who brings out the best in Higgins by his natural courtesy and by calling him, a man who was never customarily addressed in that fashion, Mr Higgins. Living constantly with the contempt of others, denied a living wage for work that devours his life with unendurable monotony, it is little wonder that Higgins visits the gin shop for a moment of solace.

Unlike John Barton, who inveighs against society in the tones of Amos, Nicholas Higgins is a secular radical who is firmly of the opinion that those who need religion most should be converted first, and that did not require a mission to the working poor but to the rich. Higgins has never been handed a tract on religion by his employer, Hamper, who, instead, has been at some pains to convince him that wages are dependent upon trade and the open market. Nassau Senior and his wages fund theory derived from Malthus was the creed of the Manchester school of economics, and it is to this faith that Hamper desires to convert Higgins.

> It explicitly stated that the level of wages was determined by the means available for wage payments, divided by the number of employed workers. This, of course, was in a sense a self-evident statement. But by assuming or implying that the fund itself was fed by profits, it was possible to suggest that any attack on profits would diminish the source from which wages were paid. Beyond a certain point this was undoubtedly true —if all profits were dispersed as wages, there would be little hope of increasing wages in the long run through better machines and equipment.[10]

Had wages been solely determined by profits then Higgins would have been impressed, but he knew that, on the contrary, this principle was not practice when it came to the cotton industry. The wages fund theory had no meaning for working men who saw a cut in their wages as a reduction of their living standards, and when they were told they had to starve in order to conform to economic theory they were naturally inclined to damn the theory. However, Hamper is quite prepared to proselytise, and Higgins recalls being accosted by him when a strike was rumoured:

> 'Hamper met me one day in th' yard. He'd a thin book i' 'is hand, and says he, "Higgins, I'm told you're one of those damned fools that think you can get higher wages for asking for 'em; ay, and keep 'em up too, when you've forced 'em up. Now, I'll give yo' a chance, and try if yo've any sense in yo'. Here's a book written by a friend o' mine, and if yo'll read it yo'll see how wages find their own level; without either masters or men having aught to do with them; except the men cut their own throats wi' striking like the confounded noodles they are"'
> (Ch. 28).

When the level of payment demanded by the employers is justified by an appeal to political theory that disregards a man's right to a living wage, then Higgins feels justified in his contempt. In his opinion, Hamper's little book is a specious vindication of an older practice of the employers: buying labour cheaply, like buying cotton at the lowest market rate, meant increased profits. Economics had replaced religion as a means of diverting attention from the necessity of changing the capitalist system.

In the interval between *Mary Barton* and *North and South* there took place the collapse of the Chartist movement and the failure of that vaunted panacea for all social ills, the repeal of the Corn Laws. Job Legh in *Mary Barton* was as fervent a supporter of repeal as any city manufacturer, but the free trade that promised a penny loaf on every working man's table proved to be a dead sea fruit. There was no bulging granary of foreign grain to pour down onto the English market, and prices for bread remained as high after repeal as before. It is disillusion with Westminster and social and religious theory that has made Nicholas Higgins a confirmed trades-unionist. And the union in *North and South* is no longer a conspiracy, but an organisation reluctantly recognised by the owners and capable of imposing its authority upon its members. Again, it is Margaret who probes the weakness of the union as she has the economic theories of Thornton and his friends. When she enquires if the state of trade may not have made a reduction in wages necessary, Higgins replies with considerable force:

'State o' trade! That's just a piece o' masters' humbug. It's rate o' wages I was talking of. Th' masters keep th' state o' trade in their own hands; and just walk it forward like a black bug-a-boo, to frighten naughty children with into being good. I'll tell yo' it's their part—their cue, as some folks call it—to beat us down, to swell their fortunes; and it's ours to stand up and fight hard—not for ourselves alone, but for them round about us—for justice and fair play. We help to make their profits, and we ought to help spend 'em' (Ch. 17).

Kropotkin was right when he saw English Socialism as derived from Robert Owen[11] with only slight reference to European socialist movements. The Owenite tradition that alarmed Carson now sustains Higgins just as Nassau Senior provided an ethic of work for Thornton and Hamper.

In *Mary Barton*, the union delegates meet together and plan to murder Harry Carson, but in *North and South* Higgins is infuriated when Boucher defies a union order and leads a riot mob to Marlborough Mill. Higgins and his fellow delegates of the Spinners' Union have determined to eschew all violence, to compel public opinion to intervene on their behalf and to exist as best they can on a meagre strike fund. It is Thornton's importation of Irish labour that inflames Boucher and sends him to the mill at the head of a mob demanding vengeance. The effect of the riot is not to strengthen the union but to cripple it. All known trades-unionists like Higgins are barred from employment, and those that do work are compelled to sign a pledge that they will not provide funds for the union. When Higgins argues this point with Hale and Margaret, there is no question that Margaret's defence of Boucher carries less weight than Higgins's claim to speak for the greater number. Pledges reluctantly given by the workers to their employers only produce hypocrites and liars in Higgins's experience. He defines his loyalty to the union as that of a soldier to his country: ' "I just look forward to the chance of dying at my post sooner than yield. That's what folk call fine and honourable in a soldier, and why not in a poor weaver-chap?" ' (Ch. 17). Better than any writer of the period Elizabeth Gaskell understood that a trades-union was not a mere combination of workers confronting the employers, but a society in which men could find an identifiable place, a society that imposed its own standards of behaviour and loyalty. Indeed, if the choice had to be made between his country and the union, a man like Higgins would choose the union without a moment's hesitation. There are many men like him in England today, and their traditions of loyalty and solidarity are as strongly maintained as those of any regiment of the line. Higgins's proudest boast is: ' "I'm a member o' the Union; and I think it's the only thing to do the workmen any good. And I've been a turn-out, and known what it were to clem; so if I get a shilling, sixpence shall go them if they ax it from me" ' (Ch. 36). When Margaret declares that a coward like Boucher should be pitied and not forced into the union against his will, Higgins replies in language familiar to any shopsteward or delegate that the union is the only power the workers possess, it is a chain in which Boucher is a weak link —a link that must be severed and cast aside:

'I ha' read a bit o' poetry about a plough going o'er a daisy, as made tears come into my eyes, afore I'd other cause for crying. But the chap ne'er stopped driving the plough, I'se warrant, for all he were pitiful about the daisy. He'd too much mother-wit for that. The Union's the plough, making ready the land for harvest-time. Such as Boucher—'twould be settin' him up too much to liken him to a daisy; he's liker a weed lounging over the ground—mun just make up their mind to be put out o' the way. I'm sore vexed wi' him just now. So, m'appen, I dunnot speak him fair. I could go o'er him wi' a plough mysel', wi' a' the pleasure in life' (Ch. 36).

And Boucher, who has first defied the union and then sought work at Hamper's below the agreed rate, drowns himself in a shallow brook that carries waste from the dyeworks. In an industrial community a man who betrays his mates and cannot find refuge with the employers has nowhere to go.

There is a correlation in the novel between the attitudes of Thornton and Higgins. Just as the union has its defaulter in Boucher, the employers find Slickson a reluctant ally in the struggle. Thornton is convinced that Slickson has pre-cipitated the strike by initially seeming to comply with the union's demands. Higgins blames Boucher for his weakness, and Thornton charges Slickson with irresolution: ' "I believe it's Slickson's doing,—confound him and his dodges! He thought he was overstocked; so he seemed to yield at first, when their deputation came to him, and of course, he only confirmed them in their folly, as he meant to do. That's where it spread from" ' (Ch. 18). Higgins has little pity for the weakling and Thornton knows he will receive just as little from his fellow employers when his mill fails. Because Thornton refuses to speculate with his creditors' money, he is ruined, and Watson, his brother-in-law, who gambled and won, is praised as the wisest and most far-seeing of men. Thornton and Higgins look to individual men as culprits but the accumulating evidence of the novel implies that the troubled nature of the cotton industry itself, and the violence of the unions, are inherent defects in a society governed only by competition and gain.

The narrative movement of the novel is not conveyed by Margaret alone, although it is her changing vision of herself and society that is dominant. She is deliberately made imperfect both in character and opinion so that the reader may not be prejudiced in favour of one witness. The most awkwardly contrived incident in *North and South*, the return of Frederick to Milton, is Margaret's doing, and her plans to have him exculpated from charges of mutiny result in a delay that almost brings about his capture. The statements made in the novel are brought collectively to the tribunal of the reader's judgment. The force of each character's testimony, its truth or falsehood, and the reasons for rejecting or revising it, come from within the experiential process of the novel itself. Margaret, who has spent her first weeks in Milton yearning for Helstone, is still capable of seeing that a Milton workman's house is furnished more comfortably than any cottage in Helstone, and that the millworker has the means at hand to educate himself and his family. When, in his moment of greatest despair, Higgins speaks of going south, of finding work as a rural labourer, it is Margaret who tells him bluntly:

'You would not bear the dullness of the life; you don't know what it is; it would eat you away like rust. Those that have lived there all their lives, are used to soaking in the stagnant waters. They labour on, from day to day, in the great solitude of the steaming fields—never speaking or lifting up their poor, bent, downcast heads. The hard spadework robs their brain of life; the sameness of their toil deadens their imagination; they don't care to meet to talk over thoughts and speculations, even of the weakest, wildest kind, after their work is done; they go home brutishly tired, poor creatures! caring for nothing but food and rest' (Ch. 37).

The life of a working-man in Manchester was hard, but there were reading rooms and lectures; he could hear good music and help to make it. He was not cut off from the cultural life of the city. Neville Cardus is not untypical of many Mancunians of working-class origin.

Margaret returns to Helstone at the conclusion of the novel and sees not only the changes there, but how she is now a stranger to the young woman who had once gone back and called it home. The recall of the past is not simply through memory, it is made a physical reality for her. The improvements in Helstone are now jarringly repugnant to Margaret. There is a small school in which the children are taught by methods unknown to her, cottages have been pulled down and rebuilt more hygienically, and her father's successor is an ardent teetotaller bent on eradicating strong drink from the village. At first prepared to question these changes, Margaret is confronted with the past that she once accepted without thought. One of the women has burnt a neighbour's cat in the oven to counteract a gipsy charm, and Margaret is forced to look back on her position in Helstone as one of questionable authority over a group of semi-literate peasants. Like most people who have experienced the life of the city she now feels bound to its problems. There is to be no returning to find haven in an arcadian cottage in a country village.

The fabric of the novel is given density by continuing reference to conditions of work, prices and trading methods. Elizabeth Gaskell is acutely conscious of business, there is no blurring of detail when industry and money are discussed. Like Balzac she can account for a man's rise to success and provide the balance sheet of his failure. Thornton is bankrupted because he has overextended his capital buying new machinery to meet the challenge of American yarns entering a duty-free market. In turn, the trade was dependent upon seasonal fluctuations for success. The strike, and a cold spring following a bleak winter, produce little demand for cotton fabric and Thornton finds himself with raw cotton bought on credit and machinery that has cost him the last of his capital. Unlike the older mill-owners, longer established in Milton, he has not been able to invest his profits in land, and it is only Margaret's loan that enables him to survive as a manufacturer. Land had always been acquired by manufacturers for reasons of status, but it also provided the most convenient security for raising needed capital in time of industrial recession.

There is no solution to the problems of an industrial society in *North and South*, but a hint of compromise is given, with more to follow. Thornton ruefully tells Mr Bell how he decided to establish a canteen for his workers and had it refused point blank by Higgins on behalf of the men.

Later, when Thornton had abandoned the idea he is astonished when ' ". . . this Higgins came to me and graciously signified his approval of a scheme so nearly the same as mine, that I might fairly have claimed it; and, moreover, the approval of several of his fellow-workmen, to whom he had spoken" ' (Ch. 42). It is not the canteen itself that is significant, but the relationship established between employer and workers in the unspoken agreement that amenities within the factory are not privileges to be magnanimously conferred by the owner, but rights to be secured by the men. It is the beginning of collective bargaining that is being described in a situation where management and employees meet regularly for negotiation. And Thornton has no illusions that harmony will prevail in the cotton industry as a result of discussions with the union delegate over a lunch-room. In London, Colthurst, the parliamentarian, questions him closely as to the likelihood of his methods preventing further strikes. Thornton replies that strikes will continue to be a characteristic of the industry, but adds: ' "My utmost expectation only goes so far as this—that they may render strikes not the bitter, venomous sources of hatred they have hitherto been. A more hopeful man might imagine that a closer and more genial intercourse between classes might do away with strikes. But I am not a hopeful man" ' (Ch. 51). The pattern of industrial life in *North and South* is established as a series of compromises, makeshift procedures that patch the cart but do not mend it. Millenarian hopes have been abandoned together with plans for revolution, and people contrive to make the best of an inefficient system that still manages to preserve a small measure of freedom for the individual.

6
The Life of Charlotte Brontë: passion and creativity

Elizabeth Gaskell always had reservations about the novels of Charlotte Brontë. She was undecided about *Jane Eyre*, certain that *Shirley* had many weaknesses, and inclined to agree with Harriet Martineau's strictures on *Villette*. But she was convinced of Charlotte Brontë's genius and determined that the world should see the novels as her triumphant victory over misery, humiliation and death. There are few more sombre biographies than Elizabeth Gaskell's life of Charlotte Brontë, and yet it is resonant with the enormous vitality of the Brontean imagination. Cowan Bridge is transformed into Lowood School, the Taylor family become the Yorkes, and Brussels where she had loved Monsieur Heger so hopelessly is the Villette of kaleidoscopic nightmare and hallucination. The biography is not a 'life and works' in the traditional sense; there is no attempt to engage in a critical literary examination of the novels. That is a task Elizabeth Gaskell prefers the reader to undertake, finding it sufficient throughout to quote an occasional review and its effect on Charlotte Brontë, and referring critical judgments to received opinion. Considerations of structure and form in the novels have no place in the biography and have been the preoccupation of succeeding scholars. What does concern Elizabeth Gaskell is the creative process, the way in which reality is shaped by imagination into tangible works of art. Again and again, she speaks of questioning Charlotte Brontë about her methods of writing. It was a consuming interest for Elizabeth Gaskell, culminating in the reminiscence when she recalled a conversation on her last visit to see Charlotte Brontë at Haworth:

> I asked her whether she had ever taken opium, as the description given of its effects in 'Villette' was so exactly like what I had experienced—vivid and exaggerated presence of objects, of which the outlines were indistinct or lost in golden mist,

etc. She replied that she had never, to her knowledge, taken a grain of it in any shape, but that she had followed the process she always adopted when she had to describe anything which had not fallen within her own experience; she had thought intently on it for many and many a night before falling to sleep—wondering what it was like, or how it would be—till at length, sometimes after the progress of her story had been arrested at this one point for weeks, she wakened up in the morning with all clear before her, as if she had in reality gone through the experience, and then could describe it, word for word, as it had happened. I cannot account for this psychologically; I only am sure that it was so, because she said it (Ch. 27).

The Life of Charlotte Brontë is a study of the creative act seen through Charlotte Brontë's own testimony and the witness of the biographer, a complex and penetrating analysis of the literary artist and the first, and still one of the finest, psychological studies of the writer at work.

Sir James and Lady Kay-Shuttleworth enjoyed bringing artists and writers together, not wholly from a desire to bask in the company of literary lions, but because they believed that art flourished in the society of its own kind. Lady Kay-Shuttleworth did not hesitate to tell Elizabeth Gaskell that she hoped Charlotte Brontë would gain immeasurably from an association with her. The results were not quite what she anticipated. Charlotte Brontë found a friend and confidant for the last five years of her life. But Elizabeth Gaskell was given the life of Charlotte Brontë to render from the scattered chaos of letters and memories into the ordered reality of art. When Lady Kay-Shuttleworth invited Elizabeth Gaskell to meet Charlotte Brontë in 1850 at Briery Close, a rented house not far from Low-wood, Elizabeth Gaskell was already sparkling with enthusiastic anticipation. She could scarcely restrain her excitement in a letter accepting the proposed invitation: 'No! I never heard of Miss Brontë's visit; and I should like to hear a great deal more about her, as I have been so much interested in what she has written. I don't mean merely in the story and mode of narration, wonderful as that is, but in the glimpses one gets of *her*, and her modes of thought, and all unconsciously to herself, of the way in wh. she has suffered' (G.L. 72). The novels were always to assume a lesser interest for Elizabeth Gaskell beside the compelling drama of Charlotte Brontë's life. It was not a literary critic who wrote to Lady Kay-Shuttleworth, but the novelist who had found a subject. Already it was not what Charlotte Brontë had written, but what she had left unsaid that was capturing Elizabeth Gaskell's imagination. In her words to Lady Kay-Shuttleworth the brilliant paradox of the biography is enunciated. The *Life* is the study of a writer, but it is also the paradigm of the novelist engaged in the examination of her own technique while discussing the methods of another. There is no sense of stasis in the work, no point of final judgment as the two writers meet and talk, discussing every aspect of their craft from publishers to the sources of their inspiration. This is not the lesser spirit recording the work of genius, Boswell of Johnson, Lockhart of Scott, Forster of Dickens, but two writers of equal magnitude talking in the world of art that happily survives death. At their first meeting it seemed to Charlotte Brontë that she had never met anyone so congenial, a woman whose sympathy comforted the fears of her childhood and the suffering of recent years. They quarrelled about politics and literature. Charlotte Brontë called Elizabeth Gaskell a democrat and despised Tennyson, yet, when they had parted, Elizabeth Gaskell wrote to Charlotte Froude, 'but we like each other heartily I think & I hope we shall ripen into friends' (G.L. 78). If Elizabeth Gaskell had recognised her subject, Charlotte Brontë greeted her interpreter to the world.

Never had a meeting been more auspiciously arranged. Elizabeth Gaskell was already acquainted with a great many of Charlotte Brontë's friends, and it was possible for her to measure her own opinions against those of others who had known Charlotte Brontë longer and more intimately. They both understood Yorkshire, its unique characteristics, and Elizabeth Gaskell always took pains to note the differences between the people of Yorkshire and those of her own Lancashire. Unlike many critics then and since, she was not alarmed by the ferocity in the novels of the Brontë sisters, nor did she find Haworth unlike many small villages in the country. She was well acquainted with the violence of Yorkshire life from her own experience and her reading of *The*

Memoirs of the Life of the late Mrs Catharine Cappe (London, 1823). Catharine Harrison's life before her marriage was that of a young Unitarian woman engaged in good works at Long Preston in Craven and at Catterick. Throughout the story of her life she laments the barbarous cruelties of the Yorkshire country folk, and Elizabeth Gaskell did not find them much changed in her own day. Catharine Cappe had edited a volume of verses written by Charlotte Richardson, the worker poet, and Elizabeth Gaskell quoted from this work in the *Life*. The Brontë sisters were not the first Yorkshire women to record the life around them.

Elizabeth Gaskell could speak to Charlotte Brontë as a fellow countrywoman who understood what it meant to be torn between domestic duties and the creative urge to write. Elizabeth Gaskell always had the faculty of being able to lose herself in her characters to such an extent that the narrative voice becomes an echo to the voices of her fictional people, the transposition of reality from the narrator to the subject. In the *Life*, there are occasions when it seems as though she is writing and thinking in the manner of Charlotte Brontë, as if she had subconsciously assumed the moods and passions of her subject. At no point is this more apparent than in the treatment of Branwell Brontë, already dead and scarcely lamented when she heard the story from Charlotte and later from her father and the folk of Haworth. The description Elizabeth Gaskell gives of him is like Charlotte Brontë defining the character of a person by a moral disposition of certain features, rather in the manner of her assessment of Thackeray's portrait in a letter to George Smith: 'To me the broad brow seems to express intellect. Certain lines about the nose and cheek betray the satirist and cynic; the mouth indicates a childlike simplicity—perhaps even a degree of irresoluteness, inconsistency—weakness, in short, but a weakness not unamiable. The engraving seems to me very good' (Ch. 26). Now, it could be Charlotte Brontë speaking as Elizabeth Gaskell describes Branwell: 'I have seen Branwell's profile; it is what would be generally esteemed very handsome; the forehead is massive, the eye well set, and the expression of it fine and intellectual; the nose too is good; but there are coarse lines about the mouth, and the lips, though of handsome shape, are loose and thick, indicating self-indulgence, while the slightly retreating chin conveys an idea of weakness of will' (Ch. 9). The tone, the moral vision, are precisely Brontean and quite unlike Elizabeth Gaskell's usual scant regard for physical characteristics.

Indeed, while Charlotte is observed from the perspective of Elizabeth Gaskell's experience and understanding, the Brontë family, with one exception, that of Patrick Brontë, is seen through the eyes of Charlotte. This gives the biography its intensity, a concentration of vision that distorts even as it illuminates. Little can be learned or understood of Emily and Anne in the *Life*. Emily is a brooding recluse given to moments of savage passion, beating the old mastiff, Keeper, with her fists until his face is bloodied and his eyes swollen, or searing a bite from a rabid dog with a red hot iron. Anne is little more than a quiet presence fading gently from life into death. Neither could be regarded as an accurate portrait of the two sisters. There is nothing in the anecdotes of Emily to explicate *Wuthering Heights* or the fervent poetry of religious love that recalls Richard Rolle:

> What I love shall come like visitant of air,
> Safe in secret power from lurking human snare;
> What loves me, no word of mine shall e'er betray,
> Though for faith unstained my life must forfeit pay.
>   'The Visionary'

Instead, Emily seems another burden that Charlotte has to carry, a burden made all the heavier by her refusal to be nursed or receive medical attention in the last stages of her illness. It is not Emily's progress towards death that is recorded but Charlotte's torment of baffled love and anger, the anger at being repulsed, the grief at being excluded from Emily's solitary rituals of pain. Elizabeth Gaskell captures the cadence of anguish from Charlotte's lines: ' "In this state she resolutely refuses to see a doctor; she will give no explanation of her feelings; she will scarcely allow her feelings to be alluded to. Our position is, and has been for some weeks, exquisitely painful" ' (Ch. 16).

There is no explanation of why Emily chose to die as she

did, no intimation of Winifred Gérin's belief that Emily willed her own death as an act of daring resolve to gain the mystic's crown of everlasting life.[1] But one does know exactly how Charlotte felt. Elizabeth Gaskell's control never falters in this regard. It is Charlotte's life, not Emily's or Anne's, that is being analysed. It was a method she deliberately chose knowing its consequences. The danger was not merely one of antagonising those who were alive but of selecting her evidence so that it bore witness to Charlotte's mind and attitudes. As Elizabeth Gaskell noted, she wanted to describe Charlotte Brontë 'without mingling up with her life too much of the personal history of her nearest and most intimate friends' (Ch. 26). It was a method that revealed Charlotte Brontë but presented her family and friends as shadows, and, occasionally, as grotesque emanations of her own personality. Elizabeth Gaskell quotes without comment Charlotte Brontë's impression that George Henry Lewes's face reminded her of Emily (Ch. 20), and Julia Kavanagh was Martha Taylor 'in every lineament'. Martha was the sister of Mary Taylor, Charlotte's school friend, who had gone to New Zealand to make her fortune. No matter where she went or what she saw, Charlotte Brontë's standards were drawn from Haworth and her family. It was a unique and eccentric perception of reality that was as narrow as it was intense. Elizabeth Gaskell observed in the biography that Emily had always been regarded as the prettiest of the children, and since Lewes's engagingly simian countenance had been remarked by more people than Elizabeth Gaskell, there was no need to elaborate upon Charlotte Brontë's curious perception. It was an excellent example of her ability to see what she wanted, despite all visual evidence to the contrary.

It seems clear now that Elizabeth Gaskell had contemplated writing a biography of her friend before she received a letter from Patrick Brontë requesting that she compose a study of his daughter. John Geoffrey Sharps is of the opinion that the article 'A Few Words about "Jane Eyre"', which appeared in *Sharpe's London Magazine* (June 1855) was written, in part at least, by Elizabeth Gaskell herself.[2] Ellen Nussey was so provoked by the article that she immediately wrote to Mr Nicholls suggesting that Elizabeth Gaskell should be asked to undertake a biography. Nicholls was obdurate in his opposition, and no doubt it was his resistance that made Patrick Brontë the more determined that Charlotte Brontë's life should be recorded. She was his last surviving child, the witness that testified to the literary accomplishments he had bequeathed his family. He was not to permit her to be forgotten as Mrs Nicholls, the wife of an obscure country curate. Ellen Nussey too felt a proprietary right over Charlotte Brontë's memory; after all, she held the greatest number of letters from her friend. These were the letters that Nicholls had ordered her to destroy. Ellen Nussey was always to look upon herself as a joint author as the work progressed. Unfortunately there were others who cast themselves in the same role. The most helpful and unobtrusive of Elizabeth Gaskell's assistants was her husband.

William Gaskell was eager to help his wife in her research and made enquiries at the 'Black Bull' and amongst those who would have been hesitant to catalogue Branwell Brontë's shortcomings and misdoings to a lady. Elizabeth Gaskell knew from the first that she was stepping between the two men who were determined to take possession of Charlotte Brontë's memory. To the Reverend Arthur Nicholls she was always his late wife, Mrs Nicholls, but to Patrick Brontë, she was his daughter Charlotte, who had taken his name and made it famous amongst the rich and eminent. Knowing that she could never gain Nicholls's aid or assistance, and realising that he would refuse to relinquish any letters or documents belonging to Charlotte, Elizabeth Gaskell displayed remarkable diplomatic skill. She 'pulled rank' on Nicholls by asking Sir James Kay-Shuttleworth to come to her assistance. His tactics were those of British gunboat diplomacy, but immensely effective. To George Smith she wrote: 'I went from Gawthorp, accompanied by Sir J. P. K. Shuttleworth, to whom it is evident that both Mr Brontë and Mr Nicholls look up.—& who is not prevented by the fear of giving pain from asking in a peremptory manner for whatever he thinks desirable. He was extremely kind in forwarding all my objects; and coolly took actual possession of many things while Mr Nicholls was saying he could not possibly part with them' (G.L. 297). Shuttleworth, like Ellen Nussey, regarded himself as a joint author of the biography, seizing upon the unpublished manuscript of *The Professor* and supervising its editing and publication. The sullen resistance of Nicholls was only equalled by the exuberant enthusiasm of Charlotte Brontë's friends, all of whom offered their advice and help to Elizabeth Gaskell.

Ellen Nussey possessed letters from Charlotte's childhood to her death. Mary Taylor wrote from New Zealand and Harriet Martineau, overlooking her past difference with Charlotte, permitted Elizabeth Gaskell to see several letters and became embroiled with Nicholls as a result. Harriet Martineau never flinched from an argument and Nicholls found that his scruples were like flying chaff before Harriet Martineau's moral invective. Patrick Brontë wrote a reminiscence of the children that revealed more of himself than his family. It was an extraordinarily difficult task to placate those who felt hesitant about permitting her to read private letters, or who wanted to censor them before she read them. Rumour had to be sifted from fact, and Elizabeth Gaskell continually found herself mediating between opposing and often belligerently antagonistic interpretations of Charlotte Brontë's life and achievements. Above all others there was Patrick Brontë, who had not the slightest doubt that he had been a loving and inspiring father to Charlotte's genius, despite Elizabeth Gaskell's own impression of the old man. 'Queer', was the adjective she used to describe him after her first visit to Haworth, and a longer acquaintance did not alter her view. He ate alone with a gun on the table and had been known to indulge in wild fits of temper, destroying furniture and cutting up his wife's new gown because he disliked the style of the sleeves. It was not until the first edition of the biography had been published and his friends remarked the eccentricities that Patrick Brontë saw them as aberrations and asked for these passages to be amended in subsequent editions. At first reading he had been delighted with the portrait of himself as an original and unconventional father to genius. Mary Taylor, writing to Ellen Nussey, expressed herself with customary vigour on the subject:

I can never think without gloomy anger of Charlotte's sacrifices to the selfish old man. How well we know that, had she left him entirely and succeeded in gaining wealth, and name, and influence, she would have had all the world lauding her to the skies for any trivial act of generosity that would have cost her nothing! But how on earth is all this to be set straight! Mrs. Gaskell seems far too able a woman to put her head into such a wasps' nest, as she would raise about her by speaking the truth of living people. How she will get through with it I can't imagine.[3]

Elizabeth Gaskell's method was to permit Charlotte to speak for herself, making every effort to permit the reader to see and judge without the special pleading of an intrusive narrator. It also meant that critics had to contend with Charlotte Brontë's own testimony. Often it proved more difficult for Elizabeth Gaskell to defend her friend's opinions than her own interpretation. Where she could not reveal fully all details of Charlotte's life, Elizabeth Gaskell informs the reader plainly of the omissions. Brussels is an enigma unless read in conjunction with *The Professor* and *Villette*, the marriage to the Reverend Arthur Nicholls is briefly sketched, and Branwell's mysterious dismissal from the employ of the Robinson family is given in Charlotte Brontë's own words. The only way to present the truth about Charlotte Brontë was to allow her to speak for herself, and few biographers have placed greater reliance upon letters to reveal their subject. Elizabeth Gaskell's assiduous collection of correspondence from George Smith, Charlotte's school friends and the acquaintances of her brief period of fame, provided the bricks for the biography; the cement was a narrative reflecting Charlotte's own opinions.

There are few incidents in the biography that are more indicative of Elizabeth Gaskell's method than the notorious passage concerning Branwell Brontë and Mrs Robinson. There were tales in Haworth about Branwell's relationship with his employer, and there is little doubt that they had been spread by Branwell himself. There were also the accounts given by Charlotte and her father. Margaret Lane states that Elizabeth Gaskell 'took Mrs Robinson's misconduct for granted, and told the tale in such sepulchral tones that her readers were left without a possibility of doubt'.[4] Mrs Robinson, having become Lady Scott, was outraged when she read in the biography that she had seduced a lad half her age. She demanded a retraction, which Elizabeth Gaskell promptly supplied. The passage relating the subsequent fate of 'the wretched woman, who not only survives, but passes about in the gay circles of London society, as a vivacious, well-dressed, flourishing widow,' exists only in the first edition. And yet the tone of the passage vividly recalls Jane Eyre's opinion of Blanche Ingram; it is unlike Elizabeth Gaskell to voice moral indignation in tones of such shrill vehemence. There is no question that it was Charlotte's own opinion of what had befallen her brother in the Robinson household which Elizabeth Gaskell recorded, and it was Patrick Brontë's as well. He wrote to Elizabeth Gaskell warmly commending her denunciation of the 'diabolical woman' who had seduced his son. It is quite evident that Elizabeth Gaskell did not fully check the evidence purporting to support Branwell's account of the wretched business. The Reverend Mr Robinson did not stipulate in his will that his widow would be deprived of maintenance and inheritance if she married Branwell, although the incident no doubt provided George Eliot with the inspiration for Casaubon's treatment of his wife, Dorothea. The will, like so much else in the story, was a figment of Branwell's imagination concealing facts that were more sordid. It is Phyllis Bentley's belief that Branwell was dismissed because of his homosexual relations with the Robinsons' son, Edmund, or because of his corruption of the boy with drugs and alcohol.[5] Elizabeth Gaskell accepted the story that was told her by Patrick Brontë and Charlotte, and she related it in the tones of Charlotte Brontë. Few writers have denounced sexuality with such vehemence and been so attracted by all its manifestations, and it is this aspect of Charlotte's nature that is reflected throughout the whole suppressed passage. Elizabeth Gaskell was threatened with a libel suit by Lady Scott's solicitors when the first edition was published, but it was Charlotte and her father who were really culpable.

Today if a biographer cannot find evidence of his subject's parentage and childhood he is tempted to invent them, and the biographies of Shakespeare, each more fanciful than the next, bear eloquent testimony to this. The trampled countryside of Stratford-upon-Avon is visible and painful evidence of the belief in heredity and environment as defining influences upon the artist. But whereas the biographer of Shakespeare walks tightropes of attenuated scholarship to reach his subject, Elizabeth Gaskell was able to talk to those who had known Charlotte Brontë as a child. She had discussed those days with Charlotte herself, and then spoken to her father and the family servants. She had visited Haworth Parsonage and heard late at night the echoing steps of Charlotte Brontë pacing around the room below her bedroom. As she told John Forster: 'Tabby says since they were little bairns—Miss Brontë and Miss Emily and Miss Anne used to put away their sewing after prayers and walk all three one after the other round the table in the parlour till near eleven o'clock. Miss Emily walked as long as she could, and when she died Miss Anne and Miss Brontë took it up—and now my heart aches to hear Miss Brontë walking, walking, on alone' (G.L. 167). It was a story that Elizabeth Gaskell was able to confirm for herself. 'I found that after Miss Brontë had seen me to my room she did come down every night, and begin that slow monotonous incessant walk in which I am sure I should fancy I heard the steps of the dead following me. She says she could not sleep without it—that she and her sisters talked over the plans and projects of their whole lives at such times' (G.L. 167). It is this kind of direct confirmation of evidence that gives the *Life* its quality of veridical truth.

As a Unitarian, Elizabeth Gaskell had a sensitive regard for the special characteristics of childhood, and throughout her life she advocated education that stressed individuality, not conformity or competition. It was for this reason that she sent her four daughters to four different schools. Throughout the biography, it is the education of Charlotte both within and without the home that is emphasised. What she describes is a process in which the children taught each other, developing personalities that were separate and yet curiously interdependent. When one sister was ill the others hastened home to nurse her, and their writing, so different in its external form, has underlying unities that are bound to the family and Haworth. It was a pattern that Elizabeth Gaskell saw developing when Maria, the eldest daughter, was forced to become a mother to her sisters and brother. Maria read to them from the paper and commented upon the affairs of the day. 'Long before Maria Brontë died, at the age of eleven, her father used to say he could converse with her on any of the leading topics of the day with as much freedom and pleasure as with any grown-up person' (Ch. 3). It was Charlotte who took Maria's place and became the head of this family of children, organising the games that became the avocations of their adult life. Elizabeth Gaskell takes pains to note that Patrick Brontë had no particular affection for children, preferring to leave them to the servants and their own resources while he retired to his study. He was oblivious to the stories, the novels and poetry that were being written in the family kitchen by his children.

Elizabeth Gaskell did not explore at great length the little books and manuscripts that the children left as their treasure hoard from those years. But she was aware of their significance, and she did attempt to read as many as she could decipher. Her reluctance to pursue this area further is easily understood. Not blessed with perfect eyesight herself, Elizabeth Gaskell found the manuscripts impossible 'to decipher without the aid of a magnifying glass' (Ch. 5). Even the later works troubled her considerably and she noted of one piece that 'it is in too small a hand to be read without great fatigue to the eyes' (Ch. 9). Elizabeth Gaskell was quite convinced that Charlotte Brontë had ruined her own eyesight by an addiction to minuscule calligraphy and 'nimminy-pimminy' attempts to reproduce old line engravings in stipple work. Nothing could be more dissimilar from Elizabeth Gaskell's own bold flowing hand than Charlotte Brontë's cramped neat penmanship. Nonetheless, Elizabeth Gaskell insisted that in the Gondal and Angrian cycles, in the plays and magazines, lay the seeds that were to flower as the novels and poetry of later life. It was the intoxication of this imaginary world that sustained the children and kept them in a limbo between childhood and maturity. Subtly, Elizabeth Gaskell constantly speaks of Charlotte seeming half-grown in appearance, of being like a wise child among adults. The antithesis between the reality of the world and the life of the imagination is epitomised in one glowing scene in which she comments upon

the introduction of 'Tales of the Islanders', composed in
1829. The children were recalling the night two years previously when they had chosen their islands and those who
would live there. Elizabeth Gaskell writes:

> Two or three things strike me very much in this fragment; one
> is the graphic vividness with which the time of the year, the
> hour of the evening, the feeling of cold and darkness outside,
> the sound of the night winds sweeping over the desolate snow-
> covered moors, coming nearer and nearer, and at last shaking
> the very door of the room where they were sitting—for it
> opened out directly on that bleak, wide expanse—is contrasted
> with the glow and busy brightness of the cheerful kitchen
> where these remarkable children are grouped (Ch. 5).

It is an image that was to haunt their lives as it was to colour
their writing. In all the novels there are storms that rage
outside and a world that threatens to engulf a fragile and
happy island of refuge. Those days in which reality had been
kept at bay by the magic of art never quite vanished from
their lives. In Elizabeth Gaskell's own opinion no writer was
more dependent upon her childhood and a place for her
inspiration than Charlotte Brontë. Haworth was the talisman
that protected the Brontës from life by declaring the world
unreal.

The school at Cowan Bridge was portrayed in *Jane Eyre*
as Lowood and the Reverend Carus Wilson as that black
pillar of righteousness, Mr Brocklehurst. In repeating Charlotte Brontë's own version of her days there, confirmed by
her school friends Mary Taylor and Ellen Nussey, Elizabeth
Gaskell found herself caught up in another acrimonious and
bitter dispute. But in this case the retraction was marked by
a terse footnote. Charlotte was quoted as saying that the
school from which her two sisters Elizabeth and Maria were
taken home to die was like a charnel house. 'Typhus fever
decimated the school periodically; and consumption and
scrofula, in every variety of form bad air and water, bad and
insufficient diet can generate, preyed on the ill-fated pupils'
(Ch. 16). To which Elizabeth Gaskell appended the footnote:
'Mr. W. W. Carus Wilson wishes me to mention that this
statement is a mistake. He says they have only had typhus

fever twice in the school (either at Cowan Bridge or at Casterton) since its institution in 1823.' Prepared to retract a statement, given initially on the dubious evidence of Branwell Brontë, she was not willing to accommodate facts to placate the injured feelings of a man who had cast such a blight and desolation over Charlotte Brontë's childhood. It is not Haworth that seems solitary and isolated, but Cowan Bridge where Charlotte lost her sisters, where she could not play games because of her poor sight and awkwardness, and where she yearned for the 'glow and busy brightness' of the family kitchen, transformed into a gaudy island of adventure by the imagination of the four children. The girls at school were a poor substitute for that companionship of creative genius. Haworth customs were not only apparent in her manners and clothes; her very mind had been shaped by that place. Mary Taylor and Ellen Nussey both recalled her telling stories, and their urging her to 'make it' when the narrative faltered. All her life Charlotte Brontë was to make the world after the fashion of Haworth. Haworth was like a well from which she drew the water of her inspiration, and the well in which she ultimately drowned.

Few biographers have taken such pains to delineate a place as Elizabeth Gaskell did in the first chapters of the *Life*. For her Charlotte Brontë's works were as much a part of that particular area of Yorkshire as the grey rocks, and moors of bracken and heather. Thornfield, like Wildfell Hall and Wuthering Heights, was kin to 'the grey ancestral houses to be seen here and there in the dense hollows of the moors' (Ch. 2), houses as dark and secretive as those who lived behind the shuttered windows and heavy doors. The people of the West Riding were unlike any to be found in the rest of England. They were frank to the point of brutal contempt for the feelings of others, and in describing them, Elizabeth Gaskell drew not only upon her own knowledge, but Catherine Cappe's memoirs, and the reminiscences of those who had lived in Haworth when Charlotte Brontë was a child. The pleasures of the West Riding were no less robust than its other pursuits. If the rich delighted in cockfighting and bareknuckle bouts, there were sports in which the whole community shared:

The amusements of the lower classes could hardly be expected to be more humane than those of the wealthy and better educated. The gentleman who has kindly furnished me with some of the particulars I have given remembers the bull-baitings at Rochdale, not thirty years ago. The bull was fastened by a chain or rope to a post in the river. To increase the amount of water, as well as to give their workpeople the opportunity of savage delight, the masters were accustomed to stop their mills on the day when the sport took place. The bull would sometimes wheel suddenly round, so that the rope by which he was fastened swept those who had been careless enough to come within its range down into the water, and the good people of Rochdale had the excitement of seeing one or two of their neighbours drowned, as well as of witnessing the bull baited, and the dogs torn and tossed (Ch. 2).

It was a sport that Catherine Cappe had witnessed and deplored a generation earlier.

Beside the violence of the West Riding as the sisters had known it, the passions of their novels are temperate indeed. Their lives may have been sheltered but they knew the village of Haworth and neighbouring Keighley. If there were evidences of brutality all around them there were also some obvious social virtues. The exquisite cleanliness which Elizabeth Gaskell noticed in the parsonage was typical of the homes kept by Yorkshire women, remarkable for their domestic skills, 'diligent and active' in all their ways. Emily Brontë reading German while she made bread, and Charlotte cleaning the potatoes, differed from those 'notable Yorkshire housewives' only in their scholarship. Haworth Parsonage was not an outpost of cleanly civilisation in a wilderness of squalor. The violence of the West Riding was visible at every turn, but so was its relative affluence, its trim gardens and clean windows. The violence of the parsonage was withdrawn and secretive, symbolised by Patrick Brontë's pistol on the table and the bloody wars of Angria and Gondal. Patrick Brontë's eccentricities, his rages and sullen moods were not remarkable in this community and Elizabeth Gaskell notes them only to illustrate her subject. But she is careful to state:

I do not pretend to be able to harmonise points of character, and account for them, and bring them all into one consistent and intelligible whole. The family with whom I have now to do shot their roots down deeper than I can penetrate. I cannot measure them, much less is it for me to judge them. I have named these instances of eccentricity in the father because I hold the knowledge of them to be necessary for a right understanding of the life of his daughter (Ch. 3).

Not only was the life of Patrick Brontë related but that of the mother, who brought with her the legends of Penzance, and later of Aunt Branwell, who continued the Cornish traditions of ghostly tales, premonitions and spectral visitations. It was Aunt Branwell who deepened the sense of sin in the children with her Methodist emphasis upon hellfire and damnation, and told the shuddering stories of Penzance that she had heard as a child. Gradually from this web of childhood the novels are seen emerging as ordered forms.

When their mother lay dying, 'the six little creatures used to walk out, hand in hand, towards the glorious wild moors, which in after days they loved so passionately; the elder ones taking thoughtful care for the toddling wee things' (Ch. 3). The moors become a dominant presence in the biography as they were in the Brontës' lives and works. The moors provided Emily with a refuge and a sense of peace denied her by the world, and Charlotte later traced her dead sister's footsteps across them even as she walked in ghostly memory around the parlour table. There is the continuing sense of Charlotte living in and through her sisters and brother as they did through her. A recurring scene is the time when the four sat together, or paced the room, discussing 'past cares and troubles' (Ch. 8), and more pleasantly, the plots of their novels. Elizabeth Gaskell felt that the four surviving Brontës shared the same spiritual life, as if each were part of the one strange being. No critic has ever pointed more directly to the essential mystery in the life of the Brontës. She notes that Emily could not live away from Haworth, that Anne pined for the company of her sisters, and Charlotte was desperately unhappy away from home. Even Branwell, for so long regarded as the shining hope of the family, was extinguished when he left Haworth.

Charlotte, like her sisters, loved Branwell, but they recognised in him the painful corroboration of the general regard for educated women held by their father and the world at large. Their father had lavished time and money upon Branwell, he was to become an artist and a scholar, and yet he was the least talented of the four surviving children. With considerable perception Elizabeth Gaskell realised that while each child sustained the other, Branwell was the one most affected by the devotion and admiration of his sisters. 'There are always peculiar trials in the life of an only boy in a family of girls. He is expected to act a part in life; to *do* while they are only to *be*; and the necessity of their giving way to him in some things is too often exaggerated into their giving way to him in all, and thus rendering him utterly selfish' (Ch. 9). The sisters had the art of transforming reality into the fiction of their novels and poetry, but Branwell's attempts were clumsy imitations of his sisters'. The boy for whom so much had been sacrificed became the drunkard and drug addict whose creative faculty was expressed in fantasies wherein Mrs Robinson declared her ardent and undying love for him. From the most limited experience of life the sisters created passionate dramas, but Branwell reduced his life to maudlin and melodramatic apologies for his failure.

From Charlotte and her father, and from the village folk that William Gaskell questioned, Elizabeth Gaskell was able to draw the portrait of the brilliant boy whose future had once seemed to offer hope and security to his sisters. Her observation moves insensibly into the witness of Charlotte herself, and the cadence of Elizabeth Gaskell's voice becomes one of hysteria as the sisters watch Branwell commit himself to madness and death.

> For some time before his death he had attacks of delirium tremens of the most frightful character; he slept in his father's room, and he would sometimes declare that either he or his father would be dead before the morning. The trembling sisters, sick with fright, would implore their father not to expose himself to this danger; but Mr. Brontë is no timid man, and perhaps he felt that he could possibly influence his son to some self-restraint, more by showing trust in him than by showing fear. The sisters often listened for the report of a pistol in the dead of the night, till watchful eye and hearkening ear grew heavy and dull with the perpetual strain upon their nerves. In the mornings young Brontë would saunter out,

saying, with a drunkard's incontinence of speech, 'The poor old man and I have had a terrible night of it; he does his best —the poor old man! but it's all over with me' (Ch. 13).

It was not Branwell's life that was being destroyed but their own as well. It was for his sake that their education had been bought so cheaply, and with him 'all the great possibilities of their earthly lives snapped short' (Ch. 13). They had loved Branwell with an intensity that they could never again bestow upon any other man, and he had betrayed their love by wasting his talents and fornicating with a married woman. It is more than sisterly shame at a brother's degradation that is implied by Elizabeth Gaskell when she adopts Charlotte's shrill tones of moral indignation. It is not a sister disgraced but a woman scorned who gave voice to the passages that were so speedily excised from the first edition. But it was Emily who suffered most and Elizabeth Gaskell implies that she died of a broken heart when Branwell was laid to rest in the graveyard at Haworth. 'In fact, Emily never went out of doors after the Sunday succeeding Branwell's death. She made no complaint; she would not endure questioning; she rejected sympathy and help' (Ch. 16). Elizabeth Gaskell had no appreciation of Emily's mysticism; what she saw was a woman dying of rejection and loss, and reacting by casting aside the proffered love of her sisters.

It was largely because of Patrick Brontë's preoccupation with his son that Charlotte became morosely resentful of the status of women and the constant denigration of their talents. Her novels are a plea for the acknowledgment of women as passionate beings, her letters demand the right to be criticised as a writer, not as a lady novelist condemned to the prejudgment of sex. It was an aspect of a subject that was close to Elizabeth Gaskell's own experience and one that still troubles every woman who chooses to combine running a home with a career. 'Henceforward Charlotte Brontë's existence becomes divided into two parallel currents—her life as Currer Bell, the author; her life as Charlotte Brontë, the woman. There were separate duties belonging to each character—not opposing each other; not impossible, but difficult to be reconciled' (Ch. 16). When Charlotte Brontë wrote to George Henry Lewes it was with the anger of a woman who had been forced to assume a masculine pseudonym in order to be accorded serious attention: ' "I wish you did not think me a woman. I wish all reviewers believed 'Currer Bell' to be a man; they would be more just to him. You will, I know, keep measuring me by some standard of what you deem becoming to my sex; where I am not what you consider graceful you will condemn me" ' (Ch. 18). The *Life* is a feminist manifesto if only because Charlotte's personality and career were stunted by father, brother and husband, and a world that regarded her novels as the improper expression of femininity. Charlotte Brontë knew what it meant to write as a woman and be made subservient to what she chose to call 'femineity'. Elizabeth Gaskell assessed what this meant to Charlotte Brontë as a person.

Slowly, with compassion and understanding, Elizabeth Gaskell traces the neurosis that was to cripple the children emotionally even as it gave strength to their creativity. It was not from health that the Brontës wrote, but from sickness, a sickness of mind and body that would have driven weaker spirits to madness and despair. Branwell was the first to succumb, and his death was self-induced. But even Charlotte, as Elizabeth Gaskell records through the medium of her letters, suffered from bilious headaches that were her immediate response to stress, an inability to cope with strangers and at times a fear of meeting people that produced a mute paralysis. Elizabeth Gaskell was a shrewd observer of psychological conditions with a sympathy for the mentally disturbed that was unusual in her day. Her brother-in-law, Sam Gaskell, was regarded as one of the foremost authorities in England on mental illness and became a Commissioner in Lunacy in London. From the first pages of the biography she is bent on defining the symptoms of neurosis engendered by acute isolation. Charlotte Brontë's childhood had not been one devoid of all happiness; there was always the firelit kitchen and the company of her sisters and brother, but it was a childhood to which the outside world came only in the form of journals and newspapers. Elizabeth Gaskell knew the loneliness of the upland districts of Yorkshire where 'a solitary life cherishes mere fancies until they become manias' (Ch. 2). This solitude was reinforced after her mother's death, and by the years she spent at Cowan Bridge where her beloved elder sisters contracted the fever that inflamed an incipient tuberculosis. At an early age Charlotte Brontë learned to associate any departure from Haworth with suffering and death. The paradox which Elizabeth Gaskell stresses throughout the biography is that the parsonage at Haworth, epitomising desolation to visitors, was a haven of refuge for the Brontës. From Charlotte Brontë's letters it is not difficult to differentiate between the physical and psychological ailments that beset her. No one revealed herself more openly in her letters and novels than Charlotte Brontë because, as Elizabeth Gaskell observed, no one was more innocent and more unaware of her own real nature. The plain and passionate virgins of her novels are Charlotte yearning for an experience that she both desired and feared.

Harriet Martineau had complained that *Villette* was the morbid expression of women who were obsessed with the need for love, and continued her criticism by stating that in real life women were rather more than vehicles of sexual passion. It was a criticism that Charlotte Brontë resented even though she did not understand quite what Harriet Martineau had meant. Elizabeth Gaskell believed that Charlotte Brontë wrote as a desperate and compulsive release from frustrations that she did not consciously comprehend. In a letter to Lady Kay-Shuttleworth, Elizabeth Gaskell wrote in the coded English generally employed by Victorians when discussing sex, but her meaning was clear. Charlotte Brontë yearned for the orgasmic pleasure of physical passion, but, as Elizabeth Gaskell remarked, such pleasure is intermittent and the woman who makes it the object of her life is condemned to bitter disappointment. No one realised with more insight that the novels were symbolic fictions and, beginning almost playfully, Elizabeth Gaskell was soon probing the nature of Charlotte Brontë's creativity, and her own:

The difference between Miss Brontë and me is that she puts all her naughtiness into her books, and I put all my goodness. I am sure she works off a great deal that is morbid *into* her writing, and *out* of her life; and my books are so far better than I am that I often feel ashamed of having written them and as if I were a hypocrite. However I was not going to write of myself but of Villette. I don't agree with you that one cannot forget that it is a 'written book'. My interpretation of it is this. I believe it to be a very correct account of one part of her life; which is very vivid & distinct in her remembrance, with all the feelings that were called out at that period, forcibly present in her mind whenever she recurs to the recollection of it. I imagine she *could* not describe it in the manner in which she would pass through it *now,* as her present self; but in looking back upon it all the passions & suffering, & deep despondency of that old time come back upon her. Some of this notion of mine is founded entirely on imagination; but some of it rests on the fact that many times over I recognised incidents of which she had told me as connected with that visit to Brussels. Whatever truth there may be in this conjecture of mine there can be no doubt that the book is wonderfully clever; that it reveals depths in her mind, aye, and in her *heart* too which I doubt if ever any one has fathomed. What would have been her transcendent grandeur if she had been brought up in a healthy & happy atmosphere no one can tell . . . (G.L. 154).

Long before the death of her friend, Elizabeth Gaskell was analysing her and intimating her awareness of Charlotte Brontë's creative gifts. The theme of the biography was already apparent. If sexual sublimation was the source of creativity then sexual frustration produced neurosis, and throughout the *Life* both aspects of Charlotte Brontë's sexual nature are seen contending with each other. When finally she relinquished art for marriage, she paid for her choice with death.

Throughout the biography Elizabeth Gaskell is at pains to emphasise that Patrick Brontë's dislike of children was perpetuated in his own family. Anne was repelled by them, Emily's impatience with them made her an impossible teacher and Charlotte was disturbed by children to a degree that passed the bounds of rational dislike for noisy and intolerant small creatures demanding time and care. Elizabeth Gaskell was able to watch Charlotte with her own daughters and was amused when she insisted that they were prodigies of wit and decorum. Fond mother as she was, Elizabeth Gaskell never saw her children as being more than normal and reasonably well-behaved young people. It was

Charlotte Brontë's complete inability to communicate with children, or even to be at her ease with them, that most astonished Elizabeth Gaskell. This fear of children was the fear of death, and Elizabeth Gaskell quoted from a letter that referred directly to the 'baby-phantom' that haunted Jane Eyre.

> 'Charlotte was certainly afraid of death. Not only of dead bodies, or dying people. She dreaded it as something horrible. She thought we did not know how long the "moment of dissolution" might really be, or how terrible. This was just such a terror as only hypochondriacs can provide for themselves. She told me long ago that a misfortune was often preceded by the dream frequently repeated which she gives to "Jane Eyre", of carrying a little wailing child, and being unable to still it. She described herself as having the most painful sense of pity for the little thing, lying *inert*, as sick children do, while she walked about in some gloomy place with it, such as the aisle of Haworth church' (Ch. 7).

When she married her father's curate, Arthur Bell Nicholls, it was in the mood of passive despair similar to that Elizabeth Gaskell was to ascribe to Sylvia on her marriage to Philip Hepburn.

Elizabeth Gaskell is insistent that Charlotte Brontë never wrote another line of fiction after she became Mrs Nicholls, despite Thackeray's statement to the contrary and the opinion of Margaret Lane. There is no mention in the letters that Charlotte Brontë wrote after her marriage or that she was engaged in any kind of creative fiction. It was a subject she would have mentioned to Elizabeth Gaskell, who was already feeling a little awkward in her correspondence with her friend. She was well aware that Mr Nicholls was the Mr McCarthey of *Shirley*, for whom 'the circumstance of finding himself invited to tea with a dissenter would unhinge him for a week'. It would have given Charlotte Brontë no little pleasure to be able to inform her friend that she was engaged on a new novel and was writing with the same encouragement that William Gaskell gave his wife. Instead, she wrote of her life as

. . . more occupied than it used to be: I have not much time for thinking: I am obliged to be more practical, for my dear Arthur is a very practical as well as a very punctual and methodical man. Every morning he is in the National School by nine o'clock; he gives the children religious instruction till half-past ten. Almost every afternoon he pays visits amongst the poor parishioners. Of course he often finds a little work for his wife to do, and I hope she is not sorry to help him. I believe it is not bad for me that his bent should be so wholly towards matters of life and active usefulness, so little inclined to the literary and contemplative.[6]

The man who censored Charlotte Brontë's letters, and demanded that Ellen Nussey should destroy those his wife had sent her, was not likely to fire his wife's inspiration. Instead, Elizabeth Gaskell conveys the truth as delicately as possible—Charlotte Brontë succumbed to a severe chill after taking a long walk in the rain at her husband's insistence. As usual, his request came when she was about to write, and Elizabeth Gaskell quotes from Charlotte's letter to Ellen Nussey: ' "I intended to have written a line yesterday, but just as I was sitting down for the purpose Arthur called to me to take a walk" ' (Ch. 27).

Charlotte Brontë did not die from tuberculosis like her sisters but from a neurotic condition of pregnancy. Elizabeth Gaskell was convinced that if only she had known of her friend's illness she could have saved her. To John Greenwood, the stationer in Haworth from whom the Brontës bought paper and ink, she wrote: 'I do fancy that if I had come, I could have induced her,—even though they had all felt angry with me at first,—to do what was so absolutely necessary, for her very life. Poor poor creature!' (G.L. 233). From the first indication of pregnancy Charlotte had begun to vomit, and Elizabeth Gaskell describes the symptoms so clearly that more than one doctor has diagnosed hyperemesis gravidarum, the pernicious vomiting which denotes an unconscious desire to expel the foetus. As Philip Rhodes states, Elizabeth Gaskell's description is a classic diagnostic model.[7] Certainly, it was not challenged by those who had tended Charlotte Brontë in her last days. 'Long days and longer nights went by; still the same relentless nausea and faintness, and still borne on in patient trust. About the third week in March there was a change; a low, wandering delirium came on; and in it she begged constantly for food and even for stimulants. She swallowed eagerly now; but it was too late' (Ch. 27). Had Elizabeth Gaskell gone to Charlotte Brontë in those last months it is quite possible that she could have sustained her with her own comfort and strength. She had seen the links between the phantom child that Charlotte dreamed of carrying through Haworth church, and the baby that she now unconsciously wished to destroy, even at the cost of her own life. But, as Charlotte Brontë's most eminent dissenting friend, she was not informed of her illness, and only learned of her death from John Greenwood.

It was William Makepeace Thackeray who published the fragment 'Emma' in *Cornhill Magazine* in 1860 and intimated that it had been composed after her marriage. The preface was Thackeray at his most unctuous, referring to Charlotte Brontë by her married name and insisting on her eagerness to defer to her husband's literary judgment.

> One evening, at the close of 1854, as Charlotte Nicholls sat with her husband by the fire, listening to the howling of the wind about the house, she suddenly said to her husband, 'If you had not been with me, I must have been writing now.' She then ran upstairs, and brought down, and read aloud, the beginning of a new tale. When she had finished, her husband remarked, 'The critics will accuse you of repetition.' She replied, 'Oh! I shall alter that. I always begin two or three times before I can please myself.' But it was not to be. The trembling little hand was to write no more.[8]

It is quite contrary to Elizabeth Gaskell's evidence, and in the biography she made no mention of her friend being engrossed by anything more demanding than letters and the affairs of the parish. Charlotte had not married on a high tide of optimism but, as Elizabeth Gaskell stated: 'She felt what most thoughtful women do who marry when the first flush of careless youth is over, that there was a strange, half-sad feeling in making announcements of an engagement— for cares and fears came mingled inextricably with hopes' (Ch. 27). Her creative genius was to be consummated with a dead child, not the living fictions of her novels. The time of composition of 'Emma' is underlined in a letter from Elizabeth Gaskell to Emily Shaen, in which she describes her visit to Mr Nicholls accompanied by the redoubtable Sir James Kay-Shuttleworth. They then acquired a number of the minute juvenile books and 'the beginning (only about 20 pages) of a new novel which she had written at the end of 1854, *before* marriage; & I dare say when she was anxious enough' (G.L. 308). Elizabeth Gaskell had wanted to publish 'Emma' as an appendix to the third edition of the *Life* and, after relating the plot to George Smith, added 'it was begun a year or so before her marriage & Mr Nicholls always *groaned literally*—when she talked of continuing it' (G.L. 387). Later critics like Clement Shorter and Margaret Lane have chosen to adopt Thackeray's genial interpretation of a marriage combining art and domesticity, but this was not the truth as Elizabeth Gaskell had known it. One subject the two women had discussed at length from their first meeting was their writing. There was no longer any reason to discuss it after Charlotte's marriage.

The penultimate chapter of the *Life* is one of the most terrifying passages in English literature, a crisis of cold horror as father and husband began their struggle for the living memory of Charlotte Brontë. 'Early on Saturday morning, March 31, the solemn tolling of Haworth church bell spoke forth the fact of her death to the villagers who had known her from a child, and whose hearts shivered within them as they thought of the two sitting desolate and alone in the old grey house' (Ch. 27). Haworth was never so cold as the barren and wasted lives that surrounded Charlotte Brontë in her last days. The last friend to speak on behalf of Charlotte Brontë was Mary Taylor, and she included the public amongst those who had denied her the right to a full life:

'She thought much of her duty, and had loftier and clearer notions of it than most people, and held fast to them with more success. It was done, it seems to me, with much more difficulty than people have of stronger nerves and better fortunes. All her life was but labour and pain; and she never threw down the burden for the sake of present pleasure. I don't know what use you can make of all I have said. I have written it with the strong desire to obtain appreciation for her. Yet what does it matter? She herself appealed to the world's judgment for her use of some of the faculties she had—not the best, but still the only ones she could turn to strangers' benefit. They heartily, greedily enjoyed the fruits of her labours, and then found out she was much to be blamed for possessing such faculties. Why ask for a judgment on her from such a world?' (Ch. 28).

The world was not as heartless as Mary Taylor believed, and Elizabeth Gaskell knew she could appeal to a public that would honour and praise their friend. The *Life* is a challenge and a victory won by two women, one living, one dead, who had known friendship and shared the secrets of their literary craft together.

Few biographies have ever been written under the searching gaze of so many interested and critical participants. Charlotte Brontë's friends had outlived her, and all desired their own opinion of her to be preserved. Moreover, most of these friends disliked each other and Elizabeth Gaskell learned to walk warily between them. Charlotte Brontë's own letters form the greater part of the *Life*, but Elizabeth Gaskell did not use them as a veridical statement of their writer's intentions. As she commented in a letter to W. S. Williams, who had once proposed to Charlotte Brontë and permitted her to read the letters she had sent him, 'I have read them hastily over and I like the tone of them very much; it is curious how much the spirit in which she wrote varies according to the correspondent whom she was addressing, I imagine' (G.L. 274). This is a delicate observation too often disregarded by historians, who tend to use letters as blunt observations of fact, ignoring the wider reality of a letter as part of an implied dialogue. Elizabeth Gaskell was conscious of this in the biography, but she could not designate those to whom the letters were addressed. She had to use oblique methods to reveal the relationship, even so the 'Mary' of the letters is soon defined by her own characteristic style, and the freedom with which Charlotte wrote to her is evident. The facility with which people read themselves into the biography is a tribute to Elizabeth Gaskell's skill at revelation without recourse to precise definition. In effect, it was not the biographer who was challenged after the first edition was published, but Charlotte Brontë herself.

Legally, as she soon found, she was not free to publish letters received by Charlotte Brontë, despite the writers having given their permission. They had become part of the Brontë estate and Mr Nicholls was executor. It seemed that he could even extend his legal authority over the hundreds of letters Charlotte Brontë had sent to Ellen Nussey. Almost distraught, Elizabeth Gaskell wrote to George Smith: 'I am *most* careful to put nothing in from Miss Brontë's letters that can in any way implicate others. I conceal in some cases the name of the persons she is writing to. But what shall I do if Mr N were to prohibit all I have written from appearing?' (G.L. 318). She disliked Sir James Kay-Shuttleworth's bullying methods, and felt remorseful at using him to browbeat Nicholls but she had no alternative. It was possible to placate Patrick Brontë with a few subsequent emendations, but the *Life* stirred up the hornets' nest of public and private acrimony that Mary Taylor had predicted.

It would have been easy for Elizabeth Gaskell to stress Charlotte Brontë's life of introverted sexuality by dwelling upon the Brussels incident, but she was at pains to avoid direct reference to the passionate love that had inspired *Villette*. The delicacy and restraint Elizabeth Gaskell employed at various moments in the biography permitted the creative sublimation of Currer Bell to comprehend the frustrations of Charlotte Brontë's quest for love. Unlike many modern biographies it is not a sex-and-works study of a writer. Elizabeth Gaskell quotes many of the French compositions that Charlotte Brontë wrote in Brussels, and the description of the pension points directly to the dormitory of Madame Beck's school in *Villette*. But she does not provide a glossary of sources. By continually leading the reader back to the novels, Elizabeth Gaskell states a theme in which the novels provide a tonal dimension to the events of Charlotte Brontë's life, a fictional counterpoint to historical fact. It is typical of Elizabeth Gaskell's own literary technique that the reader is called upon to play such an active role. There is only one work of Charlotte Brontë's that receives the biographer's unqualified approval and that is, perhaps surprisingly, the biographical notice that Charlotte prefixed to the edition of *Wuthering Heights* and *Agnes Grey* published in 1850. This she describes as 'unique in its pathos and power' (Ch. 14). The *Life* can well be expressed in those terms, the pathos of deprivation and the power of the human spirit surmounting every obstacle.

Within the biography certain themes are sounded and echoed in related passages, even as Charlotte's life resonates through the novels. It is, in a quite extraordinary sense, a musical work, a study of sound patterns, the wind from the moors, the crackling fire, the rain on the gravestones outside the parsonage, the tolling bell, the footsteps of the living and the dead pacing round the table downstairs. It was in writing of her friend that Elizabeth Gaskell unconsciously acquired motifs that were to figure in *Sylvia's Lovers* and *Wives and Daughters*. And each in death sustained the other in a work that reflects Elizabeth Gaskell's fervent belief that men and women could conquer physical extinction with the creation of art. Charlotte Brontë was buried at Haworth but her spirit roamed free in the universe of fiction. It was Elizabeth Gaskell who helped to make that release possible.

7
Sylvia's Lovers: the Puritan ethic and sexual need

Elizabeth Gaskell's religious tolerance did not extend to Calvinists, as she confessed once to Charles Bosanquet in Germany (G.L. 405). She always found herself depressed by the exacting certitudes of Calvinism and the inclement temperament it induced in its followers. The quality she found most disquieting in Carlyle was precisely that Calvinist vision of the universe as a midnight landscape of peaks and precipices lit erratically by lightning flash. She had been grateful for Carlyle's praise of *Mary Barton* but later admitted to Lady Kay-Shuttleworth, 'I never cd enter in *Sartor Resartus*' (G.L. 72). The Unitarian regretted his exclusion from the main body of Christian belief, accepting it as a consequence of his faith, but the Calvinist rejoiced in his isolation and saw it as visible witness to his virtue in a world of sinners. Even to claim special privilege as a reward for public and private virtue was in itself questionable, Elizabeth Gaskell thought, and the translation of God into a divine accountant with his finger on the ledger was a concept alien to all forms of Unitarian thought. Humanity was innately good, not evil, and the human passions governed by reason could become the source of personal fulfilment. To regard sexual desire as inherently evil, the mark of the old Adam, was to defile the whole personality. Those who railed most against sex were those most attracted to it, and Elizabeth Gaskell was not slow to remark a very curious aberration in the first bishop of Manchester, James Prince Lee. Over his study door he had a painting of a baby, 'deathly livid, and with the most woeful expression of pain on its little wan face' (G.L. 70). Lee told his guests that it was a child who had been burnt, and then lingered for two days before dying. In those two days its portrait had been painted. It was, he assured the company, his favourite picture, and then proceeded to chat playfully with the eight-year-old Florence Gaskell. As Elizabeth Gaskell observed tersely to Eliza Fox: 'He's got something wrong with his heart.' Her meaning was explicit but a modern psychologist would doubtless have reached the same conclusion employing different terms.

She had found ample confirmation of her belief that the Calvinist's religious ethic was often a frustrated sexuality by her long acquaintance with the Brontës, and the Reverend Mr Nicholls. His mute suffering, his anguish before Charlotte Brontë agreed to be his wife, and his consuming possession of her afterwards were all portrayed in Philip Hepburn, the anti-hero of *Sylvia's Lovers*. Elizabeth Gaskell had traced the relationship between religion and an obsessive sexuality in 'Lois the Witch', the study of the Salem witch trials that appeared in *All the Year Round* in October 1859. When Lois comes to Salem she finds herself in a household where various psychotic conditions are sanctioned by a form of religion that is itself aberrant in practice and belief. Ralph Hickson, Lois's uncle, is senile and dying when she arrives, 'age and sickness had now rendered him almost childish at times' (Ch. 1), but he is a model of commonsense in comparison with his wife and children. The youngest daughter, Prudence, 'played all manner of impish antics, unheeded by them, as if it were her accustomed habit to peep about, now under their arms, now at this side, now at that, making grimaces all the while'. While Prudence engages in displays of manic activity her sister Faith suffers from acute depression. 'Faith grew sadder and duller, as the autumn drew on. She lost her appetite; her brown complexion became sallow and colourless, her dark eyes looked hollow and wild' (Ch. 2). Their brother Manasseh has escaped from reality to live in dreams and prophecy, and Lois is deeply troubled when he tells her that he has chosen her as his future wife, a choice ordained by God. Breathlessly he tells her that 'The visions come thick upon me, and my sight grows clearer and clearer. Only this last night, camping out in the woods, I saw in my soul, between sleeping and waking, the spirit come and offer thee two lots; and the colour of the one was white, like a bride's, and the other was black and red, which is, being interpreted, a violent death' (Ch. 2).

Manasseh is mentally disturbed, as his mother, Grace Hickson, is aware, 'and, if Lois had been a physician of modern times, she might have traced somewhat of the same temperament in his sisters as well—in Prudence's lack of natural feeling and impish delight in mischief, in Faith's vehemence of unrequited love' (Ch. 2). But there is no physician of the mind in Salem, only those who minister to the soul. For them, as for Grace Hickson, Manasseh's raving visions are proof of his election by God. In his prayers he sees Lois as a sacrifice, Lois as a bride of the Lamb, and his torments are increased by his longing for her and his awareness of the diabolical origin of carnal lust. The madness of the Hickson family spreads, and when Lois is accused of being a witch at the meeting-house, 'girls, women, uttering strange cries, and apparently suffering from the same kind of convulsive fits as that which had attacked Prudence, were centres of agitated friends, who muttered much and savagely of witchcraft'. The conclusion is foretold as religion is invoked to justify corporate madness and Lois, the one sane member of the community, is hanged.

> The stillness and silence were broken by one crazed and mad, who came rushing up the steps of the ladder, and caught Lois's body in his arms, and kissed her lips with wild passion. And then, as if it were true what people believed, that he was possessed of a demon, he sprang down, and rushed through the crowd, out of the bounds of the city, and into the dark dense forest; and Manasseh Hickson was no more seen of Christian man (Ch. 3).

The congregation of Salem repent of their violence but the conclusion is obvious. Religion as practised in Salem has not only fomented madness but instigated murder. Manasseh's visions of sexual desire and religious ecstasy are only particular symptoms of a 'strong and general delusion' at work in the community. It was Elizabeth Gaskell's first examination of Calvinism as a morbid social phenomenon, and her basic attitudes were not changed by her acquaintance with the Brontë family.

Calvinism in Salem was a more tortured and extreme manifestation of what Elizabeth Gaskell had found in the Haworth parsonage. She was fascinated by the withdrawn isolation of the Brontës, the underlying tensions of violence and sexual passion that were the fulcrum of genius not madness, as in the Hickson family. When Charlotte was dead, Elizabeth Gaskell found herself trying to appease the Reverend Arthur Nicholls, curate of Haworth and custodian of the relics of Charlotte Brontë. He always referred to his late wife as Mrs Nicholls and his possession of her in death, as in life, appalled Elizabeth Gaskell. But there was no doubting the depth of his love for her, and the torment he endured as a result of it. He had been Patrick Brontë's curate for almost eight years before he finally acknowledged his love. Charlotte Brontë describes how one evening, when she was waiting to hear the front door slam as he left the parsonage for the night, '. . . he tapped: like lightning it flashed on me what was coming. He entered—he stood before me. What his words were you can guess; his manner—you can hardly realise—never can I forget it. Shaking from head to foot, looking deadly pale, speaking low, vehemently yet with difficulty—he made me for the first time feel what it costs a man to declare affection where he doubts response.'[1] When she refused his proposal, he became physically ill and even contemplated emigrating to Australia as a missionary—the last resort of a desperate man. Torn between the raging anger of her father and the anguished strain of Mr Nicholls, Charlotte became as she wrote, 'entirely passive', and it was in that mood she married her ardent lover.

Even though she found Mr Nicholls a baulky and sullen man to interview, Elizabeth Gaskell pitied him for his long devotion and the ardour that had consumed so great a part of his life. But she could not forget that it was this love that had destroyed Charlotte Brontë. There is a creative link in Elizabeth Gaskell's writing between Manasseh Hickson, Mr Nicholls and Philip Hepburn of Sylvia's Lovers. In each, love was destructive because it was obsessive, a concentration of feeling that was partially induced by a narrow and enclosed faith. Not without reason had Mr Nicholls provided the model for Mr Macarthey in Shirley, a man who was 'decent, decorous and conscientious', but who would have had a fit if forced to sit at the same table as Dissenters. There had been times when Charlotte Brontë felt imprisoned by his jealousy, becoming alarmed and then fondly amused by his censorship of her letters and every detail of her life. In Elizabeth Gaskell's opinion a love like this was not rational; it partook of the nature of worship, and the object of worship as she never ceased to reiterate should be God, not man or woman. One of her projected titles for *Sylvia's Lovers* had been *Philip's Idol*, but she was aware of its equivocal nature when spoken, and abandoned it for *The Specksioneer*, the local term for a harpooner. This became *Sylvia's Lovers*, the title under which the work was published in three volumes by Smith and Elder in February 1863. Yet *Philip's Idol* expresses the main theme of the novel more closely than the others. As Philip Hepburn says as he lies dying in Widow Dobson's bed: ' "Child . . . I ha' made thee my idol; and if I could live my life o'er again I would love my God more, and thee less; and then I wouldn't have sinned this sin against thee" ' (Ch. 45). In the Reverend Mr Nicholls and Hepburn, Elizabeth Gaskell saw sexual frustration contending for possession of the man against every dictate of religion. The more Calvinism inveighed against the sins of the flesh, the more the demon shrieked defiance. All too often the spirit took refuge in madness and death.

George Eliot, like Charles Kingsley, regarded 1832 and the passing of the first Reform Bill as the foundation of modern democratic society in England. But Dissenters took a longer view and saw industry, commerce and social conscience taking new directions in the period of the Napoleonic wars. Thus Elizabeth Gaskell chose the turn of the century as the nexus of later historical developments. English society, she felt, would not have assumed the shape it did without the external pressure of war leading to the persecution of social and religious radicals, and the widespread imposition of arbitrary regulations. It was the penal laws that made revolt seem an Englishman's natural right and duty. *Sylvia's Lovers* is in many ways a necessary preface to *Mary Barton* and *North and South*. The nature of public protest, the role of religious observance and the relationship of Puritan ethical values to commerce, all provide a prelude to the discussion of an industrial society in the earlier novels. Whitby, the Monkshaven of the novel, was at the turn of the century a prosperous whaling port, but when Elizabeth Gaskell stayed there for a fortnight in 1859, it was a sleepy fishing town, depending as much on its holiday visitors as it did on its fishing smacks. The industry of whaling had long since passed to the North Atlantic and the New England ships, just as the cotton magnates of Manchester in *North and South* were being challenged by the United States. The novel concentrates on a particular society that embodies the changes that were taking place in Yorkshire.

Unlike many Unitarians, Elizabeth Gaskell's view of society was not atomistic, although she never failed to stress the role of the individual in effecting change. Heredity and environment both determined human personality, but free will could operate to modify inherited nature and a given society. She was also certain that people of the period and place she had chosen to describe were psychologically different from her contemporaries. The self-consciousness that she saw characterising her own age was a significant alteration in the human personality. So, the characters in *Sylvia's Lovers* are typified by their lack of introspection and their inability to examine motives and intentions. It was a subtle and most acute observation, and one that influenced the narrative method of the novel. The inhabitants of Monkshaven and the surrounding farms are neither scholars nor deeply thoughtful people. They frequently act without thinking and are often puzzled at the consequences of those actions. It is incongruous when a workhouse boy like Oliver Twist speaks with the fluency of a little Lord Fauntleroy and shows a sense of morality that would not shame Tom Brown, but it is also a form of social patronage on the part of the writer and an attempt to conciliate middle-class readers. Lack of education, poverty and a brutal environment do affect people, and the results are apparent in a minimal use of language to express their needs, and frequently an indifference to suffering. The writers of the great depression in the United States tried to magnify the worker by giving him a vocabulary and emotional responses in accord with those of the prospective reading audience. It is very doubtful if the panegyrics to the poor composed then did more than provide crude appeals to public sympathy. Between the subject and the reader, the reality of the worker and his psychological integrity was lost. Elizabeth Gaskell does not commit this error, and she is at pains to note that the frequent misunderstandings between her characters arise as much from their inarticulateness as it does from circumstance. The narrative commentary is that of the historian recording events that were overtaking a part of society known as the 'common people'. The techniques employed at a later date by social historians were already being utilised by Elizabeth Gaskell in her novel of a time and a people not given to self-analysis and rationalisation.

With quiet irony, the pervading tone of the narrative, Elizabeth Gaskell observes:

> In the agricultural counties, and among the class to which these four persons belonged, there is little analysis of motive or comparison of characters and actions, even at this present day of enlightenment. Sixty or seventy years ago there was still less. I do not mean that amongst thoughtful and serious people there was not much reading of such books as Mason *On Self-Knowledge*, and Law's *Serious Call*, or that there were not the experiences of the Wesleyans, that were related at class-meeting for the edification of the hearers. But, taken as a general rule, it may be said that few knew what manner of men they were, compared to the numbers now who are fully conscious of their virtues, qualities, failings, and weaknesses, and who go about comparing others with themselves—not in a spirit of Pharisaism and arrogance, but with a vivid self-consciousness that more than anything else deprives characters of freshness and originality (Ch. 7).

The social observation is an interesting one, for Elizabeth Gaskell felt that self-awareness arose from a process of comparison with others, and the result was not a heightened feeling of personal identity, but a loss. A man watching himself and using those around him as a mirror to reflect his actions will move more cautiously than the man who is oblivious of the opinions of others. She develops this theory in her discussion of the crowd that serves to reduce individual differences, just as a continuous appeal to a social consensus of opinion will produce a competition in conformity. Sylvia is a creature of incandescent emotions because her whole world is bound by feeling, and there are many like her in the novel. She seldom thinks and never prays, reading and writing are a dreary business to her, but love and hate are passions that she knows without any restraint imposed by reason.

It is in passages of social commentary that Elizabeth Gaskell reveals her refusal to subscribe to notions that the past was necessarily worse, or better, than the present. The past is never used to furnish values by which the present may be judged. Instead, she points to differences, and permits the reader to draw his own conclusions. To say a time was different is not to pass a moral verdict upon it. Far more important is the necessity to accept the past as it was to those who lived then, not to tramp through it like a tourist in a peasant village, wondering how on earth the people can live without flushing lavatories and air conditioning. She had lived in two historical periods herself—the little town of Knutsford was as far removed from Manchester as her fictional Monkshaven was from the drowsy port of Whitby. Her historical sense dominates the work by constant reference to the fact that it is possible to find a number of societies, common to varying historical periods, existing at the same time. Travelling from Manchester back to Knutsford was not just a journey of distance but a trip to the past.

The function of the novelist as historian is more complex and responsible than the narrator of fiction. The obligation to record the past faithfully is extended to the reader who must not be permitted to imagine that he stands at a fixed point in time watching all things change around him. Even as he reads, the society of the reader is assuming new forms, and by his recall of the past the historian is himself affecting the process of change. The past, as Elizabeth Gaskell continually states in the novel, is a part of present life. Some parts of it are visible like mountain peaks, others have been obscured by the drift of events. By the historian's recall of the past the terrain of contemporary society is made explicable for those who do not choose to follow the common practice of walking blindfold down a strange road. The past was not a box of curiosities to be examined in idle moments, but a living force directing current events. She expressed the theme with considerable wit in a lengthy passage discussing the vagaries of the vicar of Monkshaven:

> In looking back to the last century, it appears curious to see how little our ancestors had the power of putting things together, and perceiving either the discord or harmony thus produced. Is it because we are farther off from those times, and have, consequently, a greater range of vision? Will our descendants have a wonder about us, such as we have about the inconsistency of our forefathers, or a surprise at our blindness that we do not perceive that, holding such and such opinions, our course of action must be so and so, or that the logical consequence of particular opinions must be convictions which at present we hold in abhorrence? It seems puzzling to look back on men such as our vicar, who almost held the doctrine that the king could do no wrong, yet were ever ready to talk of the glorious Revolution, and to abuse the Stuarts for having entertained the same doctrine, and tried to put it in practice. It is well for us that we live at the present time, when everybody is logical and consistent (Ch. 6).

So much attention has been paid to Elizabeth Gaskell's charm that little attention has been accorded her gift of irony, frequently exercised at the expense of the reader.

For Elizabeth Gaskell as an historian, the most important aspect of her task was not the recreation of tangible evidence in the form of dress and behaviour, but the definition of psychological differences between her own age and that of the Napoleonic wars. She saw in her own society a greater homogeneity, which had been achieved by a corresponding loss of individuality. Crowds, mass movements, the growing emphasis upon democratic organisation were all means of enforcing uniformity. Eccentricity had become socially unacceptable. Quite bluntly, she found there were more 'characters' in Knutsford and in the world of the past because fewer people then were forced to work together in large groups, abiding by imposed restrictions on time and behaviour. Religious dissent was one means of asserting the right of the individual in a society that demanded general compliance with traditional forms, and social dissent was simply another aspect of the same libertarian principle. This process had been accelerated by the intolerable regulations imposed upon people as a result of the Napoleonic wars. By contesting the right of the press-gang to operate in Monkshaven, the people had learned to cooperate and to challenge the authority of the law and local government. Daniel Robson is hanged as a felon for calling on the crowd to burn down the 'Randyvow', where the impressed seamen are being held, but the town remembers him as a martyr and a hero. Similarly, the working class were to retaliate against the owners at a later date, and those who were arrested and convicted became the martyrs of their day, like the farm labourers of Tolpuddle. What is gradually taking shape in the port of Monkshaven is a social movement that will produce a conscious awareness and exploitation of class, to the amelioration of many injustices, but, and this point is crucial to Elizabeth Gaskell's thesis, with the inevitable loss of personal liberty.

In order to pursue a common cause, the individual must become part of the crowd. When John Barton joins the trades-union he becomes not only its agent for vengeance but its victim. At first the union seemed to be a group where men could assert their individuality in a class-ridden society, but eventually the union became as oppressive as the society from which it had emerged. The crowd in *Sylvia's Lovers* does achieve its purpose by rescuing the impressed seamen, but Daniel Robson, his last vestige of caution swept aside by a general call for destruction, finds himself marked down as a despoiler of property and is hanged for the crime committed by the crowd.

Although the Greenland whalers were protected against impressment during the Napoleonic wars, their vessels and crews were constantly being raided by the Royal Navy. Whalers were all competent seamen who could be relied upon to assume their places in the middle ranks of any naval ship. It was in the northern ports that the opposition to the press-gangs was most violent. In the south they inspired fear, but in the north there was rage and hatred. The Whitby men knew the value of solidarity:

For with them the chances of profit beyond their wages in the whaling or Greenland trade extended to the lowest description of sailor. He might rise by daring and saving to be a ship-owner himself. Numbers around him had done so; and this very fact made the distinction between class and class less apparent; and the common ventures and dangers, the universal interest felt in one pursuit, bound the inhabitants of that line of coast together with a strong tie, the severance of which by any violent extraneous measure, gave rise to passionate anger and thirst for vengeance (Ch. 1).

Between the rural gentry and the town there was a considerable amount of ill-feeling prompted by the prosperity of the whaling trade and the poverty of the country. The antagonism felt by the country gentry at a later date towards the manufacturers in the towns was presaged by the social conditions of Whitby and its environs.

Where the landed possessions of gentlemen of ancient family but limited income surround a centre of any kind of profitable trade or manufacture, there is a sort of latent ill-will on the part of the squires to the tradesman, be he manufacturer, merchant, or ship-owner, in whose hands is held a power of money-making, which no hereditary pride, or gentlemanly love of doing nothing, prevents him from using. This ill-will, to be sure, is mostly of a negative kind; its most common form of manifestation is in absence of speech or action, a sort of torpid and genteel ignoring all unpleasant neighbours; but really the whale-fisheries of Monkshaven had become so impertinently and obtrusively prosperous of late years at the time of which I write, the Monkshaven ship-owners were growing so wealthy and consequential that the squires, who lived at home at ease in the old stone manor-houses scattered up and down the surrounding moorland, felt that the check upon the Monkshaven trade likely to be inflicted by the press-gang, was wisely ordained by the higher powers (how high they placed these powers I will not venture to say), to prevent over-haste in getting rich, which was a scriptural fault, and they also thought that they were only doing their duty in backing up the admiralty warrants by all the civil power at their disposal, whenever they were called upon ... (Ch. 1).

The concision with which Elizabeth Gaskell analyses conflicting groups in society could well provide a model for most historians.

Irony, the traditional historical mode, is implicit in the

narrative technique. The novelist observes the past with sympathetic detachment while referring the reader to analogous conditions in the present. Whitby was not a town isolated in past time but a social prototype for any manufacturing centre at variance with a rural society that still controlled the machinery of local government and judicial authority. The sense of change, the movement of events, is not implied simply by the narrative flow of events in the novel, but by the historian as narrator linking the present with the past and pointing to the future.

Nevertheless, the future of Whitby does not lie in the surging ventures to the Greenland seas and the harvest of whales, but with the Foster brothers, Quaker by faith, shopkeepers and bankers by trade. Defoe had praised the Quakers for their honesty in business and general reliability as traders. (He knew of a Quaker pirate, but regarded him as a distinct anomaly.) Quakers were the first to set marked prices on the goods in their shops, one means of avoiding the barter and haggling of the market-place and fair-ground. In the Foster brothers and their two assistants, William Coulson and Philip Hepburn, Elizabeth Gaskell delineates the Puritan ethic that was later defined in sociological terms by Weber and Tawney. It is one of the most perceptive themes of social analysis in the novel, and surpasses George Eliot's depiction of the banker Bulstrode in *Middlemarch*. The Foster brothers, John and Jeremiah, had inherited a small shop in Monkshaven and because of a meticulous attention to business they had grown rich. Their lives were regulated by their faith, but this faith did not prevent them smuggling, like the rest of the town. Christian ceremony could always be accommodated to the needs of business. 'They would not for the world have had any sign of festivity at Christmas, and scrupulously kept their shop open at that holy festival, ready themselves to serve sooner than tax the consciences of any of their assistants' (Ch. 3).

Unlike the seamen and farmers they regulated their time as a matter of course, keeping set hours and taking an inventory of their stock at certain periods of the year. The ability to live according to fixed hours of work was one of the great difficulties faced by a modern industrial society. People accustomed to working sporadically and impulsively were only too ready to find any excuse to break the monotony of daily labour, like those who had taken themselves to Green Heys Fields at the beginning of *Mary Barton*. But the Quaker had acquired self-discipline, a faculty cultivated by Philip Hepburn, who regarded 'frugal self-denial' as a virtue, and had learned to live by a 'methodical appropriation of the few hours he could call his own' (Ch. 11). Defoe had been conscious of this aspect of Puritan business life when he wrote:

> It is the duty of every Christian to worship God, to pay his homage morning and evening to his Maker, and at all other proper seasons to behave as becomes a sincere worshipper of God; nor must any avocation, however necessary, interfere with this duty, either in public or in private. Nor, on the other hand, must a man be so intent upon religious duties, as to neglect the proper times and seasons of business. There is a medium to be observed in everything.[2]

It was their religion that inspired the Foster brothers to capitalist enterprise, and its inherent discipline that ensured its success.

The Quakers had first taken up banking as an adjunct to their trading, and the procedures they followed arose naturally in the course of business, without any appeal to the methods of Lombard Street. In *Sylvia's Lovers* the transition from shopkeeper to banker is given with astonishing accuracy.

> They had certainly begun to have a kind of primitive bank in connection with their shop, receiving and taking care of such money as people did not wish to retain in their houses for fear of burglars. No one asked them for interest on the money thus deposited, nor did they give any; but, on the other hand, if any of their customers, on whose character they could depend, wanted a little advance, the Fosters, after due enquiries made, and in some cases due security given, were not unwilling to lend a moderate sum without charging a penny for the use of their money (Ch. 3).

This practice had been extended to certain manufacturers on the surety of their supplying goods, and in the course of the novel, the Fosters' range as bankers has been extended to

Spitalfields and London. It is not long before the shop is transferred to Hepburn and Coulson, to be paid for on a yearly basis at a diminishing rate of interest, while the Fosters occupy themselves entirely with the banking house. The Puritan ethic may have entailed the repression of the individual personality, as Elizabeth Gaskell maintains in *Sylvia's Lovers*, but there was often the compensation of financial success. Before Philip Hepburn's life is destroyed by the return of Kinraid he has combined prosperity in business with the church's recognition of his personal virtues. It was no small thing for a young shopkeeper to aspire to the rank of churchwarden.

The narrow rigidity of business life personified by Philip Hepburn is alien and repellant to his cousin Sylvia, who has been raised on the seafaring tales of her father. His pride is, that when he was taken by the press-gang during the American War of Independence, he had cut off two fingers to secure his release from the navy. Bell, his wife, comes from the gentry, a Preston of Slaideburn, and desires nothing more than a match between Philip and Sylvia. She recalls how her heart was won by a gallant young sailor who told her that he once rode a whale's back. ' "Eh dear a' me!" said Bell, "how well I mind your telling me that tale! It were twenty-four year ago come October. I thought I never could think enough on a man as had rode on a whale's back!" "Yo' may learn t' way of winning t' women", said Daniel, winking at the specksioneer' (Ch. 9). Love is not subservient to any demand for social harmony. It is the embodiment of social dissent, a wild, irrational spirit that mocks at propriety. Philip loves Sylvia despite every dictate of his mind and commonsense. He is a shopkeeper and Sylvia can neither count nor write. She is deficient in every talent he requires in a wife. It is Hester Rose who loves Philip for the very qualities that Sylvia finds most unappealing. As a Quaker and an assistant in the shop she has learned to love Philip but has prudently abjured all notion of romantic passion.

Love was a vanity, a worldliness not to be spoken about, or even thought about. Once or twice before the Robsons came into the neighbourhood, an idea had crossed her mind that

169

possibly the quiet, habitual way in which she and Philip lived together, might drift them into matrimony at some distant period, and she could not bear the humble advances which Coulson, Philip's fellow-lodger, sometimes made. They seemed to disgust her with him (Ch. 11).

Yet Hester Rose and William Coulson seem ideally suited by temperament and faith, it is only the irrational force of sexual antipathy that makes her reject him.

Only the calamity of circumstance can overcome the physical disgust Sylvia feels for Philip and force her to become his wife. Elizabeth Gaskell was always conscious of the power of sexuality in life, and the overwhelming force it could become when frustrated or denied. Philip Hepburn is devoured by his passion for Sylvia, the private and public restraints of his life are torn apart by his longing for her. '. . . he had been brought up among the Quakers, and shared in their austere distrust of a self-seeking spirit; yet what else but self-seeking was his passionate prayer, "Give me Sylvia, or else I die" ' (Ch. 11). His love brings him no joy, it is a torment of the flesh that is not assuaged when he marries her. It then becomes a source of fresh pain. It is only when Sylvia is stunned by her father's death and her mother's senility that she can bring herself to share Philip's bed, a bed that seems like a coffin haunted by the presence of Charlie Kinraid. Nothing is more explicit than the depth of sexual attraction between Kinraid and Sylvia, and the loathing she feels whenever Philip touches her. At the Corneys' New Year's Eve party, the games are bawdy and ribald with forfeits paid and won that symbolise sexual play. Thus, when Sylvia's ribbon is held up by Mrs Corney, the call is that the owner should 'blow out t' candle and kiss t' candlestick' (Ch. 12). The inference is plain to everyone as Kinraid holds out the candle towards Sylvia, who slowly comes towards him and blows out the flame. It is a scene vital with the passions of love and tormented fury, as Philip stands in the shadows, watching Sylvia and Kinraid engage in the ritual of courtship.

Heroes and their like did not interest Elizabeth Gaskell, but ordinary people did. For her, the famous had lives that were open to public speculation, but men like John Barton and women like Sylvia Robson could provide themes for tragic poems for those with the discernment to appreciate the nature of their existence. She was deeply indebted to Scott for his use of environment as a narrative presence in the novel, but she also engaged in lengthy research to ensure a factual accuracy, writing to men who could recall the days of the press-gangs, and checking dates and events in local newspapers and the *Annual Register*. Charlotte Brontë had followed the same methods when writing *Shirley*, but that work is a disjointed failure while *Sylvia's Lovers* is an astonishing work of art and history. Charlotte Brontë failed because her characters spoke with one voice, her own, and their emotions and thoughts came from the same source. The men, as in all her novels, were cardboard stereotypes unless cast beyond the range of passion and desire. Hiram Yorke succeeds whereas Robert and Louis Moore are like puppets moving in response to the narrator's feverish imagination. But it is the men who dominate *Sylvia's Lovers* and each is as much an individual as he is expressive of a certain cultural and social milieu.

Daniel Robson is a man whose life came to an end when he left the sea and took to the land. With Charlie Kinraid on the other side of the fire, he travels back to the days of the whaling ships, one story leading to another more stirring until it seems to Sylvia that the Greenland seas contain more wonders than Brendon's Isles or misty Avalon. Philip Hepburn lives with the facts and figures of the present, his only dream is a longing for Sylvia, but Kinraid and Robson have the ability of children to roam beyond the bounds of the commonplace into worlds of vision and high romance. As a harpooner on a whaler, Kinraid is like a knight of chivalry to Sylvia. Through him she feels that it is possible to reach out and touch the fire of life itself. It is the passionate simplicity of Robson and Kinraid that stands in such effective contrasts to the prim conformities of Hepburn.

In fact, Daniel was very like a child in all the parts of his character. He was strongly affected by whatever was present, and apt to forget the absent. He acted on impulse, and too often had reason to be sorry for it; but he hated his sorrow too much to let it teach him wisdom for the future. With all his many faults, however, he had something in him which made him be dearly loved, both by the daughter whom he indulged, and the wife who was in fact superior to him, but whom he imagined that he ruled with a wise and absolute sway (Ch. 12).

Inconsistent, argumentative and cheerful, Robson's moods become darker and more obsessive after Charlie Kinraid's disappearance. In his own way, Robson had been as fond of the young harpooner as Sylvia. Yarning with him, he had relived his finest days, so that when news of the press-gang is carried up and down the coast, he becomes like a man possessed, tormented with the fear that Kinraid may have been impressed and not drowned after all. Uncertainty to a man of Robson's nature is more corrosive than a slow poison. His anxieties explode when the press-gang lures out the men of Monkshaven by ringing the fire-bell in the middle of the night. Half-drunk in the public house Robson calls for a counterattack against the 'Randyvow' to rescue the men who had rushed to the market-place at the sound of the bell. Robson finds himself leading the mob that burns down the dockside pub and, although a hero in the opinion of the town, he is a felon in the eyes of the law. To the end, even to the gallows, Robson remains stubbornly proud of his action, and the town is of the same mind.

> The rescue of the sailors was a distinctly popular movement; the subsequent violence (which had, indeed, gone much further than has been described, after Daniel left it) was, in general, considered as only a kind of due punishment inflicted in wild justice on the press-gang and their abettors. The feeling of the Monkshaven people was, therefore, in decided opposition to the vigorous steps taken by the county magistrates, who, in consequence of an appeal from the naval officers in charge of the impressment service, had called out the militia (Ch. 15).

It was the same kind of arbitrary and oppressive justice that the workers of Manchester were to suffer from throughout the early years of the nineteenth century. But in *Sylvia's Lovers* it is clear that the strikes and riots of the industrial city had long traditions that went back to days before machinery and factory. When individual men could not prevail against authority, the disaffected became an armed crowd, and a man who became its leader, like Daniel Robson, was remembered as a hero.

Passion dominates Sylvia's whole being, and her love can change to an implacable hatred that is animal-like in its ferocity. Untroubled by any sense of moral alternatives, she lives in a world of elemental contrasts, resisting any kind of change, whether it comes in the form of education or ethics. She is the most contented illiterate, despite Philip's efforts to teach her. The old church of St Nicholas is no more than a dreaming presence in the town, a place where reality drifts into vague assurances of comfort and peace. Sylvia, like most of her friends, is a pagan by instinct as well as by training, and when she goes to hear the funeral sermon for the murdered seaman, Darley, she is moved, not by any words spoken by the vicar, but by the concentrated feeling of the crowd. 'Sylvia's tears rained down her face, and her distress became so evident that it attracted the attention of many in that inner circle' (Ch. 6). It is across a grave that she first sees Charlie Kinraid, come to mourn his dead mate. He stares at Sylvia as the sprigs of rosemary are cast down on the coffin.

It is Sylvia's pride that her love is only matched in strength by her capacity to hate. When she hears that Dick Simpson, who gave evidence against her father, is dying in miserable squalor, she rejoices. ' "Them as was friends o' father's I'll love for iver and iver; them as helped for t' hang him" (she shuddered from head to foot—a sharp irrepressible shudder!) "I'll niver forgive—niver!" ' (Ch. 28). Sylvia responds physically to events, and speech is always accompanied by a corresponding gesture. The only way she can endure marriage with Philip is to become physically numb, and take refuge in a withdrawal from all feeling. With Philip, it always seems as though she is 'absent in thought of some kind' (Ch. 29), as though he has married someone in a trance. The bitterness he endures is the knowledge that he can neither arouse Sylvia to any sexual response nor find any satisfaction in a woman who is like a breathing corpse. The revulsion that has been overcome, but not conquered, is made clear in the passage where Kester warns Sylvia against marrying a man that she cannot love. Few writers have been able to convey with such clarity and concision a disgust inherent in a passionate sexuality that is undesired:

> Just as she was in this miserable state, wishing that the grave lay open before her, and that she could lie down, and be covered up by the soft green turf from all the bitter sorrows and carking cares and weary bewilderments of this life; wishing that her father was alive, that Charlie was once more here; that she had not repeated the solemn words by which she promised herself to Philip only the evening before, she heard a soft, low whistle, and, looking round unconsciously, there was her lover and affianced husband, leaning on the gate, and gazing into the field with passionate eyes, devouring the fair face and figure of her, his future wife.
> 'Oh, Kester', said she once more. 'What mun I do? I'm pledged to him as strong as words can make it, and mother blessed us both wi' more sense than she's had for weeks. Kester, man, speak! Shall I go and break it all off? say!'
> 'Nay, it's noon for me t' say; m'appen thou's gone too far. Them above only knows what is best.'
> Again that long, cooing whistle. 'Sylvia!'
> 'He's been very kind to us all,' said Sylvia, laying her rake down with slow care, 'and I'll try t' make him happy' (Ch. 28).

The cadence of the passage, moving from an urgent fretful rhythm to the flat banality of the last words signifies Sylvia's withdrawal from the reality of her emotions. The platitudes of her final utterance are her escape from the obscene command of that 'long, cooing whistle'.

Marriage has been forced upon Sylvia by the desperation of her circumstances. She is penniless, and burdened with a mother suffering from premature senility, when Philip proposes. When she accepts she knows that her life will be an emotional and social prison. She misses Haytersbank and the tasks of the farm at which she excelled, the animals who were in her care and the feeling of life burgeoning on every side. Her parlour in Philip's house represents a 'comfortable imprisonment' (Ch. 30), and her sentence there is confirmed by the arrival of a gaoler whom she both resents and loves. '. . . by and by, the time came when she was a prisoner in the house; a prisoner in her room, lying in bed with a little baby by her side—her child, Philip's child' (Ch. 30). The birth of a child was never an occasion for an outpouring of sentimental rhapsodies in Elizabeth Gaskell's novels. Every woman regarded the birth of a child differently, some welcomed it with joy, others like Hyacinth in *Wives and Daughters* saw it as an intolerable burden. It could, as in Sylvia's case, provide a tighter bond to the man she still finds physically repellant. Even her love for the child cannot dispel her resentment for 'the duties and chains of matrimony' (Ch. 33).

It is at Haytersbank, where she has gone to pick some leaves from a bush of balm to make tea for her mother, that Sylvia sees the figure of a man against the sky and knows instinctively that it is either Charlie or his ghost. She has dreamed of Charlie throughout her marriage, and now, when he returns, it is as though she is restored to life. It is not melodrama when Charlie confronts Sylvia and Philip, the feelings are too stark and anguished. Despite Philip's despairing plea for understanding, for compassion as a man who has been driven to madness by his love, Sylvia is about to leave with Charlie, who assures her: ' "I can get your pretence of a marriage set aside. I am in favour with my admiral, and he will do a deal for me, and will back me out. Come with me; your marriage shall be set aside, and we'll be married again, all square and above board" ' (Ch. 33). But even as she prepares to go with him, the baby cries, and Sylvia is reminded of her bondage. She kisses Charlie goodbye, and then turns the full passion of her hatred against Philip: ' "I'll niver forgive yon man, nor live with him as his wife again. All that's done and ended. He's spoilt my life, —he's spoilt it for as long as iver I live on this earth" ' (Ch. 33). The sense of something spoilt conveys all Sylvia's feelings of ravage, of flesh that is tainted. It is a physical sense of outrage at having been legally ravished by a man who evokes only sexual disgust in her. Yet, even as she rages against him, there is the awareness of Philip's kindness, of his consideration for her mother. In the past there had been moments when she was grateful for his friendship even when she could not tolerate his touch. She has never been indiffer-

175

ent to his goodness but she knows that in marriage it is the bed not the board that provides the measure of domestic happiness.

Sylvia learns to understand Philip when he is gone from her life, with each day bringing a fresh remembrance of his faithful love and watchful care. It is the arrival of the young and dazzling Mrs Kinraid, the heiress that Charlie has married, who confirms Sylvia in the conviction that Philip's love was of a more enduring nature than her sailor lover's. As her daughter grows from a baby to a toddling child, Sylvia's life dwindles. For a time, after her mother's death and Philip's mysterious departure, she has a 'green, breezy vision' of returning to Haytersbank and living at the farm again with old Kester (Ch. 37). But her days are now planned for her by Jeremiah Foster, who has asked Hester and her mother, Alice Rose, to live in the house behind the shop. Jeremiah has chosen to adopt the little girl, Bella, and Hester is as devoted to her as is her own mother. For Sylvia, there is no longer reason or purpose in her life. Her recollection of Philip's kindness does not alter her awareness of what he did to her. It is Sylvia's nature that she must always remain faithful to her emotions. To Jeremiah, she repeats her curse upon Philip and refuses to retract a syllable, saying:

'I daresay you think I'm very wicked, sir, not to be sorry. Perhaps I am. I can't think o' that for remembering how I have suffered; and he knew how miserable I was, and might ha' cleared my misery away wi' a word; and he held his peace, and now it's too late! I'm sick o' men and their cruel, deceitful ways. I wish that I were dead' (Ch. 36).

When Philip drags his way back from the wars to Monkshaven, Sylvia has to endure the grief of seeing her curse fulfilled to the point of death. She has indirectly assisted Philip to his grave by advising Kester's sister to turn out her starving lodger, to let him fend for himself. Yet only death can reconcile Sylvia and Philip, and bring them to an understanding of each other.

If Charlie Kinraid swaggers through the novel, gay, resolute and daring, Philip Hepburn darkens every page with his brooding presence. He is in so many ways the most admirable of men, compassionate and sensitive, but curiously repellent with a prim disapproval of the world around him that barely conceals his smouldering passion for Sylvia. When he stares at her, his gaze is scopophiliac, and so disturbing that Sylvia moves the candle so she may be decently concealed in shadow. It is the devouring, obsessive nature of his love for her that makes him both pitiful and repugnant. His feeling, and Sylvia's response, are defined with an accuracy that goes to the heart of the whole enigma of sexual attraction. He is a Quaker by training and instinct, conscientious, reliable and truthful, but perhaps because of these qualities he arouses more dislike than affection in the town. He talks of the duty a subject must pay the nation and Daniel Robson erupts with fury: ' "Nation here! nation there! I'm a man and you're another, but nation's nowhere" ' (Ch. 4). His reference to abstract principle arouses immediate suspicion in men who live their lives without theory. Even Kester distrusts him with an unconscious dislike, 'a kind of natural antipathy such as has existed in all ages between the dwellers in a town and those in the country, between agriculture and trade' (Ch. 15). Hepburn never visits the public-house in a town where every man, and a good many of the women, think nothing of getting drunk on occasion. His speech is always cautious, as precise as his book-keeping, and his accent and vocabulary are more refined than Sylvia's and her family. It is his continual self-consciousness, his watchful guard upon his actions that makes his passion for Sylvia the more violent in consequence.

Charlie Kinraid loves Sylvia truly, but he has loved and left other women before her, and when he finds her married with a child, he soon finds himself a wife. But Hepburn's love is irrational, and because of it he loses all sense of morality. To speak the truth is instinctive with Hepburn, but after he has seen Kinraid taken by the press-gang he says nothing, and his silence confirms the belief of the town that Kinraid was drowned by a surging wave. It is a lie told for the most selfish of reasons, hardly justified by his conviction that Kinraid is a philanderer bent on breaking Sylvia's heart, as he has broken so many others. The lie is to haunt him and eventually lead to his destruction. When Thurston Benson lied, it was to save Ruth and her child, and it entailed a considerable danger to his name and conscience. But Hepburn's lie arises from a spirit as troubled as Manasseh Hickson's. As Jeremiah says to Sylvia: ' "It was a self-seeking lie; putting thee to pain to get his own ends. And the end of it has been that he is driven forth like Cain" ' (Ch. 36). It is emphasised that the Calvinist insistence upon calm, the abnegation of anger and emotion, cannot be achieved without a distortion of the whole personality. For Kinraid, love is a part of his life, and after he has kissed Sylvia at the Corneys' party, and she has left with her father, he dances cheerfully with another pretty girl. In Hepburn's eyes, this is wanton lust, and his intolerance is sharpened by the narrow confines of his religion. His enlistment as a soldier, a wild and irrational act, is prompted by guilt and passion. If Kinraid is the man Sylvia loves, then he will become like Kinraid, and hope that the uniform will make her respond to him. His determination to seek atonement is compounded of lust and the desire to do penance, motives that war with each other even as he has always been torn by passion and restraint.

The novel echoes to the whisper of portent and fable. The Greenland seas, London and the campaigns against the French are all translated into stories that belong to legend. The whalers, returning each year from the Arctic seas, are living witness to the marvels that lie just beyond the verge of reality. Bell Robson, who had once been captivated herself by a sailor's yarns, takes refuge in a dour refusal to be influenced by anything more than the practical affairs of the farm and the town. She 'knew so little as to be afraid of believing too much' (Ch. 10). The account of the siege of Acre in which Philip Hepburn saves Kinraid's life is recorded in the same tone of fable as the marvels of the sea. Sylvia and Bella have been walking with Hester along the valley of a nearby river when Hester's silence becomes almost trancelike. When Sylvia speaks to her, Hester complains of a headache: ' "It has been bad all day; but since I came out it has felt just as if there were great guns booming, till I could almost pray them to be quiet. I am so weary of the sound" ' (Ch. 37). And the chapter describing the siege itself begins with the traditional invocation to fairy-tale and romance: 'Far away, over sea and land, over sunny sea again, great guns were booming on that 7th of May, 1799' (Ch. 38). This is another world from Monkshaven, belonging to the same order of imaginative reality as the Greenland seas and the men who rode whales' backs. To emphasise this quality there is the recounting of a Dartmoor ghost-story, when the wounded Kinraid swears that it was Philip Hepburn who carried him to the ship under French fire. A sailor assures him:

'Maybe it was a spirit. It's not the first time as I've heard of a spirit coming upon earth to save a man's life in time of need. My father had an uncle, a west-country grazier. He was a coming over Dartmoor in Devonshire one moonlight night with a power of money as he had got for his sheep at the fair. It was stowed in leather bags under the seat of the gig. It was a rough kind of road, both as a road and in character, for there had been many robberies there of late, and the great rocks stood convenient for hiding-places. All at once father's uncle feels as if some one were sitting beside him on the empty seat; and he turns his head and looks, and there he sees his brother sitting—his brother as had been dead twelve year and more. So he turns his head back again, eyes right, and never says a word, but wonders what it all means. All of a sudden two fellows come out upon the white road from some black shadow, and they look, and they let the gig go past, father's uncle driving hard, I'll warrant him. But for all that he heard one say to the other, "By—, there's *two* of them!" Straight on he drove faster than ever, till he saw the far lights of some town or other. I forget its name, though I've heard it many a time; and then he drew a long breath, and turned his head to look at his brother, and ask him how he'd managed to come out of his grave in Barum churchyard; and the seat was as empty as it had been when he set out; and then he knew that it were a spirit come to help him against the men who thought to rob him, and would likely enough have murdered him' (Ch. 38).

This extraordinary interpolation is the climax to the siege of Acre, and Elizabeth Gaskell's intentions are obvious. The focus of the novel is Monkshaven, all that surrounds it is coloured by imagination and dream. Thus, deliberately, Elizabeth Gaskell sets the events of the war and Philip's ordeal as a marine into the same formal pattern of romance. There is an account of the battle, but told after the fashion of a story recounted by a warm hearth in Monkshaven to the wondering amazement of the listeners. These were people who thought of London as a Babylon looming 'so magnificent through the mist of men's imaginations' (Ch. 17). The significance of Monkshaven is emphasised by casting the narrative events beyond it into an alternating fictional form. Acre is a blur of colour and exotic names suddenly transformed into a ghost-story from Dartmoor, just as Kinraid and Robson's stories ranged from the mouth of hell to shipwreck and tempest.

The contrast between imagination and reality is stressed again when Philip, on his return to England, is made bedesman at St Sepulchre's and finds there an old volume of the *Seven Champions of Christendom*.

> In it he read how Sir Guy, Earl of Warwick, went to fight the Paynim in his own country, and was away for seven long years; and when he came back his own wife Phillis, the countess in her castle, did not know the poor travel-worn hermit, who came daily to seek his dole of bread at her hands along with many beggars and much poor. But at last, when he lay a-dying in his cave in the rock, he sent for her by a secret sign known but to them twain. And she came with great speed, for she knew it was her lord who had sent for her; and they had many sweet and holy words together before he gave up the ghost, his head lying on her bosom' (Ch. 42).

It is this romance that begins to shape his thoughts until, in his own mind, he is that same Sir Guy who must find his way back to his lady. The reality of the spare room and the truckle bed in Widow Dobson's cottage where Hepburn is slowly starving is the world of Monkshaven.

The conclusion of the novel could well be taken as a study in the interaction of historical fact, myth and popular tradition. Philip and Sylvia meet again and are reconciled at his death, a reconciliation on Philip's part that is based upon his awareness of the blasphemy in his idolatrous love for Sylvia. But the town does not remember the old legend that has been re-enacted in its midst. It creates a new legend that is told to the historian as narrator when she questions some of the older residents of Monkshaven. 'But the memory of man fades away. A few old people can still tell you the tradition of the man who died in a cottage somewhere about this spot, died of starvation while his wife lived in hard-hearted plenty not two good stone's-throw away. This is the form into which popular feeling, and ignorance of the real facts, have moulded the story' (Ch. 45). The past has a reality that can only be justly assessed by the historian, but even then, his vision will be limited by the temporal dislocation between his own person and that of his subject. It is not enough to know the facts alone. They were, as the old people said, that a man died of hunger while his wife lived nearby in comfort. Historical truth must go beyond fact to the psychological interpretation of events. And this task rightly belongs to the novelist, who provides a subjective delineation of a period by means of fictional types that can speak for the essential nature of their time. The last words of *Sylvia's Lovers* not only introduce the narrator but provide the key to her method throughout the work.

Acre, the Greenland seas, even the Monkshaven of the whaling days have become part of a legendary past, but the Fosters have survived the town's decline into a popular sea-side resort. Bella becomes the heiress to the old brothers' great wealth 'and she were married to a distant cousin of theirs, and went off to settle in America many and many a year ago' (Ch. 45). Again, there is reference to the present and an intimation of the future. Manchester had been the marvel of the world, but when Elizabeth Gaskell wrote *Sylvia's Lovers*, the cotton-spinning monopoly had been broken by American manufacturers, just as the Whitby whalers were to be outsailed by New England clippers when the Greenland seas were fished out. The reader is warned that his own world is changing, but the past may cast light on the future. What Whitby had become in Elizabeth Gaskell's time, Detroit may be in our children's lives.

8
Wives and Daughters: the economic landscape

It has become fashionable in recent literary criticism to regard *Wives and Daughters* as a comedy of manners, a work set apart in style and content from the rest of Elizabeth Gaskell's novels. *Mary Barton, Ruth* and *North and South* are considered to be social problem novels, while *Wives and Daughters* is seen as a pleasant excursion by Elizabeth Gaskell to the faraway world of her childhood with Jane Austen as her travelling companion. And yet this novel embodies the crisis in English life that endures to the present day. Industry still functions in a fashion reminiscent of a country estate, as though Melton Mowbray had quietly imposed its standards upon a city like Manchester. Nothing would have seemed more absurd to the Victorian observer than to state that the industrial city was being run like a rural village, but this was the case. What worked inefficiently in the country failed to work at all in the city. Industrial managers thought of themselves as country squires in a landscape of machines instead of cows, and while poets mourned the loss of rural values, it was precisely these values, translated to the city, that were to shackle the new society to the past. It was a process assisted by the long tradition of finding peace in the country and problems in the town. Men who had forgotten the Rebecca Riots and Captain Swing now felt that if only the methods of the farm could be applied to the factory then concord and harmony would prevail. Only recently have social historians stated that the Manchester of Victorian England can only be properly defined when it is seen as part of an agricultural community belonging to the eighteenth century.

Elizabeth Gaskell had always been aware of these temporal dislocations in contemporary society. She knew that while Nicholas Higgins was declaring his faith in the trades-union in Milton, and defying the owners, old Silas, the gamekeeper at Hamley, could not die at peace until he had fulfilled the term of his duty to the squire. Deference to the squire in Hamley, or to Lord Cumnor in Hollingford, was visible witness to the power of the aristocracy to maintain the traditions of the past, but when this same type of social subservience was demanded in Manchester, men responded with the trades-union and the strike. Prophetically, in *North and South*, Elizabeth Gaskell had seen the union ranged against the authority of management and government. In *Wives and Daughters* she examined the nature and source of that authority.

The period is never precisely defined in *Wives and Daughters* and there are numerous anachronisms that have been annotated by Kathleen Tillotson.[1] It is set before the First Reform Bill of 1832 and the railroads, but the society it represents still existed in 1864 when the first instalment of the novel appeared in the August edition of the *Cornhill Magazine* and may yet be found in isolated areas of England today. Lord Cumnor is a social dinosaur but his kin still browse in the higher ranks of government and on boards of directors, and Squire Hamley may be heard preaching the moral virtues of the foxhunt at any agricultural fair. A. W. Ward was correct when he wrote in his preface to *Wives and Daughters* in the Knutsford Edition: 'I see no reason and feel no desire for dividing her work into periods or drawing a hard and fast line between her earlier and her later "manner"; and, from this point of view, her last and greatest novel, "Wives and Daughters," may be regarded as representative of the whole of her work as a writer' (Vol. 8, p. xxx). Not only was it stylistically in a direct line of descent from *Mary Barton* and *Ruth*, but it dealt with the major social problem of Victorian England. In the most industrialised country of the world, it was still felt necessary to observe and to demand the rights and privileges of a feudal age.

Wives and Daughters spans the range of rural society during one of the more prosperous periods of English agriculture and in the favoured area of the north. The so-called 'golden age' of English agriculture in the third quarter of the century, when Elizabeth Gaskell was writing, hardly affected the depressed southern counties. But in the north and north-west, where livestock and mixed farming composed the main agricultural interests, prices were high and the rural worker did not suffer to the same degree as his counterpart in the south. There is no threat of insurrection or rick-burning from the placid servants and tenant farmers in *Wives and Daughters*. Indeed, those who worry most are the gentry, finding that they are not receiving an adequate return for their expenditure on improved farm buildings and drainage. The outstanding example of the time was the Duke of Northumberland, who laid out half a million pounds for a yield of about two-and-a-half per cent. Profits like these were far less than investors would have gained in commerce or industry. E. L. Jones quotes an anecdote that could have been voiced by Lord Cumnor: 'It is said that the Duke of Bedford inspected his farms after a thorough replanning and observed gravely to a tenant named Jonathan Bodger, "great improvements, Jonathan", to which Jonathan replied, "great alterations, your Grace". Although he nearly lost his farm for it, the tenant had shrewdly summed up much contemporary landowner investment.'[2]

Lord Cumnor could well afford to maintain his estates, but a man like Squire Hamley was becoming anomalous in English agricultural life. He was unable to dispose of his property because of entails and family sentiment. It was only by means of money borrowed from his son Roger that he was able to keep his land in production. If land had not been the standard of social prestige in England, few would have invested in it. But the man who did not carry the mud of his ancestral acres on his bootsoles could never quite command the rank of a gentleman. The industrialist buying an estate was not a phenomenon of the Victorian age. Those who made money in trade had always bought land as a preliminary step towards a title. As Lady Harriet informed her mother, Lady Cumnor, with singular perception and lack of tact: ' ". . . papa was saying that the Hamleys have been on their land since before the Conquest; while we only came into the county a century ago; and there is a tale that the first Cumnor began his fortune through selling tobacco in King James's reign" ' (Ch. 57). But whereas the Hamley estate was small and heavily in debt, Cumnor owned property in two counties. By the 1870s, about twenty-four per cent of the agricultural land of England was owned by men who held properties of more than ten thousand acres. Just as industry was developing larger units, small farms were being absorbed by the great estates, and a man like Hamley lived in dread of a neighbour like Cumnor.

The agent for the landowner played the same role that the manager did in business, and Elizabeth Gaskell in her own work marked the change from the family solicitor who served this function in the time of 'My Lady Ludlow', set at the turn of the century, to Preston, an acute and capable executive in *Wives and Daughters*. Dispute between old Squire Hamley and Preston was inevitable, and typically it arose over a question of drainage and fox covers. The draining of clay soil had been made possible when John Reade's invention of the clay pipe in 1843 was mass-produced. Government loans were first granted by Peel in 1846 to those farmers who wanted to reclaim their land. Hamley, whose one gesture to progress has been his interest in drainage, eagerly took up a loan from the government. But the work had not gone forward, partly because of his own apathy after his elder son's failure at Cambridge, and partly from lack of finance. It was salt in old wounds when he rode down to visit his dying gamekeeper and found that Preston was engaged in draining land that was close to his property. In a brilliantly modulated passage Hamley's chagrin and envy goad him into finding some reason for arguing with Preston.

As he drew near the spot, he thought he heard the sound of tools and the hum of many voices, just as he used to hear them once, a year or two before. He listened with surprise. Yes! Instead of the still solitude he had expected, there was the clink of iron, the heavy gradual thud of the fall of barrowsful of soil—the cry and shout of labourers. But not on his land— better worth expense and trouble by far than the reedy clay common on which the men were, in fact, employed. He knew it was Lord Cumnor's property; and he knew Lord Cumnor and his family had gone up in the world ('the Whig rascals!'), both in wealth and in station, as the Hamleys had gone down. But all the same—in spite of long-known facts, and in spite of reason—the Squire's ready anger rose high at the sight of his neighbour doing what he had been unable to do, and the fellow a Whig, and his family only in the county since Queen Anne's time (Ch. 30).

When he learns that Preston's navvies have been pulling up gorse to light their fires from his spinney where there had always been fox covers, Hamley has the excuse for an argument.

Everything about Preston grates upon the squire, his fine horse and finer clothes, and his lack of deference to a Hamley of Hamley. That Lord Cumnor can afford a servant dressed and mounted better than a Hamley is intolerable to the old man. Anger is aggravated to passion when Preston casually offers him half a crown for the despoliation of his fox covers. It is barely possible for Roger to make peace between Preston and his father by forcibly taking the reins of his horse and leading him away. Nonetheless, the squire is powerless to improve his financial position without the money earned by Roger on his scientific venture. And Roger knows that the money is lost like the money he had lent his brother, Osborne.

Elizabeth Gaskell rightly saw land conferring status but not wealth, and one without the other was like a cart with a missing wheel. Preston working so close to Hamley's property, pressing to the very boundary, was a portent of the future when yet another small estate would be bought up by the county magnate, or sold to a city industrialist. With no other source of income than his property, Hamley knows only one way of safeguarding the estate, and that too was a traditional one. The eldest son had to marry money, and preferably money and a title. Always conscious of the nuances of class in English society, Elizabeth Gaskell knew that the best of men regarded marriage as a transaction in which rank and capital comfortably changed hands, with the whole procedure sanctified by 'The rentroll Cupid of our rainy isles', as Tennyson expressed it in *Edwin Morris*. The squire, for example, had definite ideas on the subject that could be expressed in round figures. The elder son had to marry wealth and rank, but Roger, the younger, could settle for money—within reason. As the squire exclaims with all the honesty of his own contradictions: ' "I don't say but what if

Roger is gaining five hundred a year by the time he's thirty, he shall not choose a wife with ten thousand pounds down; but I do say, if a boy of mine, with only two hundred a year —which is all Roger will have from us, and that not for a long time—goes and marries a woman with fifty thousand to her portion, I'll disown him—it would be just disgusting' " (Ch. 5). Hamley had married the daughter of a merchant in the Russian trade and he could never quite forget her lack of antecedents, even though she had brought him a handsome marriage portion. It was his intention that his son Osborne should marry into a family like the Cumnors, certainly no lower in the social scale. Ironically, Osborne fulfils his father's hopes by marrying a French Catholic nursemaid.

Money, the lack of it, and the abuse of it, runs like a tarnished thread through the novel. When Hyacinth Kirkpatrick moves through the softly carpeted halls of the Towers she can smell the Cumnor money and feel it under her feet, and when her daughter accepts a compromising loan of £20 from Preston it is because she does not have a penny to her name. It is the middle-class women of this country society who are most affected because they have neither the means nor the opportunity to engage in trade, or undertake a profession. Hyacinth drags herself wearily and ineptly from one post as governess to another, never quite able to make ends meet, and yearning only for the day when a man will have to keep her in the state of matrimony. However, it can be just as difficult for a gentleman like Osborne Hamley, trained for nothing except to wait for his father's death so that he can inherit the estate. Gentility must be sustained by inherited wealth, but to live only in the expectation of an inheritance is in itself a form of death. Long before he has succumbed to heart disease, young Osborne Hamley is thrust into the limbo of an eldest son who knows that he cannot acknowledge his marriage, cannot even train for a career, until his father dies. When he is bankrupt, John Thornton knows that he can look for another job, and it is likely that he will find one. Certainly it is of no concern to him that he may endanger his status as a gentleman by finding employment. But the heir of an old county family like the Hamleys is bound by the custom of centuries as well as by the deficiencies of his own character. In order to maintain the property, and be regarded as a gentleman in county society, he must marry money. The need was even greater for women. Hyacinth collapses into marriage with Dr Gibson with hysterical relief while her daughter, more shrewd by temperament and better placed to make a choice, casts around her many suitors until she captures the richest and most refined. Her 'scrapes', as she chooses to call them, have marked a steady progression from Mr Preston to Mr Henderson, the young lawyer of good family and private means. As for Osborne Hamley there is no refuge for him except death after he has committed the unforgivable blunder of marrying a servant. It is a society that for all its outward grace and good humour is inflexible in demanding that money and rank should receive their due homage. Manchester, with its emphasis on money alone, was less demanding.

The Cumnors are the local fount of prestige, the pinnacle of county society confirmed by rank and wealth. And in the tradition of the very wealthy, they pay less for goods and service than the middle class because they can bestow prestige upon all those associated with them. Working for the merely rich was an exchange of labour for money, but serving the aristocracy was a privilege. Mrs Gibson cannot rest until she has hired a maid from the Towers, while her husband knows to the last penny the value of having Lady Cumnor as a patient:

> For the good doctor's business grew upon him. He thought that this increase was owing to his greater skill and experience, and he would probably have been mortified if he could have known how many of his patients were solely biassed in sending for him, by the fact that he was employed at the Towers. Something of this sort must have been contemplated in the low scale of payment adopted long ago by the Cumnor family. Of itself the money he received for going to the Towers would hardly have paid him for horse-flesh; but then, as Lady Cumnor in her younger days worded it—'It is such a thing for a man just setting up in practice for himself to be able to say he attends at this house!'
> So the prestige was tacitly sold and paid for; but neither buyer nor seller defined the nature of the bargain (Ch. 29).

A certain degree of moderation has to be observed between indifference to these unspoken rules of society and a grovelling subservience. Lady Harriet has nothing but contempt for Mr Preston when he presumes to speak in familiar terms to her; equally so, she despises the Browning sisters for their worshipful admiration in her presence. Nothing quite equals the disappointment of the Hollingford folk when the Duchess of Menteith arrives at the local ball without her diamonds. There were, and are, certain social obligations that the aristocracy must render to the public. One of the most important is the provision of entertainment, a constant display of spectacle to amuse the lower classes. Everyone at the charity ball, a synthesis of social observances, has expected to see and admire the famous Menteith jewels, the fame of which 'had trickled down . . . through the medium of ladies'-maids and housekeepers' (Ch. 26). Knowing that the duchess and her daughter are guests at the Towers, everyone has expected a magnificent display of ducal finery. Instead, the duchess arrives in a sprigged muslin wearing flowers in her hair and looking just like a buxom farmgirl. Lady Cumnor assumes the demeanour of Lady Macbeth at this affront to social proprieties, made even more embarrassing when an election is due. It is Lady Harriet who assesses the situation with great perspicacity and seeks to explain the social debacle of a duchess without diamonds to her unobservant brother, Lord Hollingford:

'. . . you don't know how these good people here have been hurt and disappointed without our being so late, and with the duchess's ridiculous simplicity of dress.'

'Why should they mind it?' asked he, taking advantage of her being out of breath with eagerness.

'Oh, don't be so wise and stupid; don't you see, we're a show and a spectacle—it's like having a pantomime with a harlequin and columbine in plain clothes.

'I don't understand how—' he began.

'Then take it upon trust. They really are a little disappointed, whether they are logical or not in being so, and we must try and make it up to them; for one thing, because I can't bear our vassals to look dissatisfied and disloyal, and then there's the election in June' (Ch. 26).

When an aristocracy combines genuine benevolence with such alert self-interest, it is impossible that it should not survive and flourish. Typically, the narrator casts Lady Cumnor in the role of a Shakespearean heroine, but Lady Harriet sees herself in the lowest and most popular form of public entertainment. It is not that Lady Harriet disdains the social system that endows her with rank and privilege, but she sees that it is sustained by the innate snobbery of the Hollingford locals. Her few democratic sentiments are personal, not general in nature. Only to Molly, who has the courage and commonsense to question the inconsistencies of her attitude, does Lady Harriet extend her friendship. The whole system of social privilege is based upon illogicalities that yet contrive to function. While aware of all the absurdities, Lady Harriet sees no reason to replace them or to refrain from profiting by them. But she never fails to be aware of the traditional duty of the English aristocracy to entertain people while exploiting them.

The society that is generated from the Towers and moves down by degrees to the old gamekeeper's cottage has cast the landscape into patterns that reflect its particular interests. Far from being a romantic breezy novel of the countryside, *Wives and Daughters* never looks at scenery without seeing economic value. Nature does not provide a sense of release but entails responsibilities and financial rewards. Squire Hamley loves the old trees under which he played as a boy, but he never forgets their worth as timber. There is a sense of constriction in the novel as great as that of the narrow streets of Manchester. Those who live in the country and by it, never cease to be aware of its worth in cash terms. Appropriately enough, the novel begins with Molly's visit to the Towers, the long-awaited day of the year when the school visitors are invited to admire the mansion gardens. It is a landscape that is planted with money and flourishes accordingly. 'Green velvet lawns, bathed in sunshine, stretched away on every side into the finely wooded park; if there were divisions and hahas between the soft sunny sweeps of grass, and the dark gloom of the forest-trees beyond, Molly did not see them' (Ch. 2). Lawns and flower-beds lead to hot-houses where attendant gardeners are waiting to admit the guests.

The whole day takes on the atmosphere of a fairy-tale, the flowers too bright, the scents too heavy, and Molly falls asleep under a tree where she is awakened by her future stepmother. The poor child, bewildered and sick, sits and watches while Hyacinth gorges on the chicken and jelly that Lady Cuxhaven has provided for her. Molly has found little pleasure in the palatial grounds of the Cumnor estate; she finds even less delight in watching the family eat and engage in the ponderous rallies that pass among them for humour and conversation. At the age of twelve, Molly Gibson has been released from the feudal allegiance that Hollingford people rendered the Cumnors. She has seen them as a child and disliked them, and it is her shrewd evaluation of them that affects her attitude to them afterwards. It requires a rare degree of magnanimity, unknown to any child, to be grateful for a day's visit to a flower-garden, denied at all other times, or to derive any satisfaction from watching others eat food that one could never afford oneself. Molly's disillusionment after the feverishly awaited visit is a social as well as a personal one. It was, after all, a child who saw that the emperor was naked.

Next in rank to the Cumnors were the Hamleys, although Squire Hamley never ceased to remind people that his family dated from the Heptarchy while the Cumnors were unknown in the county before the reign of Queen Anne. The constant appeal to tradition and family is always evidence of the absence of money, and Hamley's conversation moves diagonally from the one point of status to the other of money, without ever making them meet. When Molly visits the Hamleys she rides through another economic landscape where the income of the squire is implied in a few descriptive images: 'They swung in at the gates of the park in a few minutes, and drove up through meadow-grass, ripening for hay—it was no grand aristocratic deer-park this—to the old red-brick hall; not three hundred yards from the highroad' (Ch. 6). Squire Hamley has neither the income nor the inclination to landscape his property with the enthusiasm that Mr Rushworth devoted to Sotherton in *Mansfield Park*, or which occupied the attention of so many gardeners at the Towers. Inside the house, Hamley rejoices in the oak flooring joined so closely that not a speck of dust could filter down between the boards, but then he could never afford to buy the carpets that cushion every stair and hall at the Towers.

Furniture and clothes, trees and flower-beds, all have a price that is never far from the minds of the Hollingford people. When Hyacinth sits in a reverie before the dainty dressing table of her room at the Towers, her appreciation of its charm immediately devolves into the awareness of its cost:

'One would think it was an easy enough thing to deck a looking-glass like that with muslin and pink ribbons; and yet how hard it is to keep it up! People don't know how hard it is, till they've tried as I have. I made my own glass just as pretty when I first went to Ashcombe; but the muslin got dirty, and the pink ribbons faded, and it is so difficult to earn money to renew them; and, when one has got the money, one hasn't the heart to spend it all at once. One thinks and one thinks how one can get the most good out of it; and a new gown, or a day's pleasure, or some hot-house fruit, or some piece of elegance that can be seen and noticed in one's drawing-room, carries the day—and good-bye to prettily-decked glasses! Now here, money is like the air they breathe' (Ch. 9).

Far from being unaware of money, Lady Cumnor's most gracious gesture to Cynthia on the occasion of her marriage is to provide her with a set of account books '... at the beginning of which Lady Cumnor wrote down with her own hand the proper weekly allowance of bread, butter, eggs, meat, and groceries per head, with the London prices of the articles, so that the most inexperienced housekeeper might ascertain whether her expenditure exceeded her means' (Ch. 57). Unlike the romantic's vision of the country where people live untroubled by the pettifogging cares of commerce, Elizabeth Gaskell sees a town like Hollingford and the countryside around it presided over by a spirit that is more mercenary than arcadian. Lady Cumnor and old Mrs Thornton had more in common than they would ever have cared to acknowledge, and the standards of Hollingford were not so alien to the attitudes of the Manchester manufacturers as men might imagine.

It is true there are romantics in the novel who see the land primarily as an inspiration for poetry. Mrs Hamley has taught Osborne to be oblivious to the material aspects of the countryside and to devote himself to its aesthetic qualities. The result is an enfeebled sense of reality and quantities of flaccid verse that Molly, as a young girl, finds most affecting. Osborne professes to care nothing for the pursuit of agriculture, but he cannot support himself without the allowance derived from the estate. In many ways his attitude to the country is less appealing than that of Sheepshanks and Preston, who make no pretence of despising the source of their income.

There is one man who sees the country around him in quite a different fashion from the farmers and county gentry. Roger Hamley is a scientist, a naturalist bent on exploring a world in which his fellows stumble like blind and deaf cripples. For Squire Hamley, Osborne was always 'a bit of a genius' as a boy, with his gifts for poetry and painting, while Roger was never seen as more than a slow and steady lad. Mrs Hamley seriously doubted whether Roger should follow his brother to Cambridge, where his chances of achieving scholarly honours seemed remote. Hamley never ceased to wonder at Roger's interests, and never quite understood them. To Molly he confided:

'Roger knows a deal of natural history, and finds out queer things sometimes. He'd have been off a dozen times during this walk of ours, if he'd been here: his eyes are always wandering about, and see twenty things where I only see one. Why! I've known him bolt into a copse because he saw something fifteen yards off—some plant, maybe, which he'd tell me was very rare, though I should say I'd seen its marrow at every turn in the woods' (Ch. 6).

Roger not only loves the country, but he understands it, and he teaches Molly to have the same awareness of the life around her. The Miss Brownings seriously question Roger's sanity after they have prompted Molly to tell them all she knows of the young man. Artlessly Molly replies:

'Oh, he told me what books to read; and one day he made me notice how many bees I saw—'

'Bees, child! What do you mean? Either you or he must have been crazy!'

'No, not at all. There are more than two hundred kinds of bees in England, and he wanted me to notice the difference between them and flies' (Ch. 13).

Nature existed in its own right for Roger Hamley and he saw it without the acquisitive and predatory gaze of country folk. It was an attitude that bemused his father and convinced others of his inherent stupidity or lack of sensitivity. For romantics, nature existed to complement or arouse human emotions; for farmers, it was a source of income. The scientist is the intruder into this settled rural society, disturbing customary values, and subtly changing people's vision of the world, just as Roger teaches Molly to see a different landscape. Roger Hamley, in appearance and vocation, was Elizabeth Gaskell's close friend and relative Charles Darwin. Like Darwin, who used to come home at dawn with the foxes from his long nocturnal rambles, Roger neither exploits nor abuses nature. His greatest joy is to explore it.

For Unitarians, Darwin's perception of the evolutionary processes of life did not come as a blow to their faith, but as further confirmation of their belief in the power of human reason. Alone among the Christian sects the Unitarians rejoiced as they saw the plan of nature being unfolded without recourse to marvel or mystery. Having no faith in miracles the thesis of man arising from the slime of primeval nature seemed both rational and further proof of man's affinity with all living things. The great chain of being that Priestley had commended was changed from a fixed stair to an escalator on which man was being hurtled towards the stars, guided by his reason and providence. Charles Lyell, a Unitarian, had inspired Darwin in his work and provided visible evidence that religious faith need not require the abnegation of reason. Despite Elizabeth Gaskell's initial historical perspective of a time before railroads and the First Reform Bill, Roger Hamley, like Darwin, speaks from her own day and to the immediate concerns of her readers. When giving the outline of her novel to George Smith, she wrote: 'Roger is rough, & unpolished—but works out for himself a certain name in Natural Science,—is tempted by a large offer to go round the world (like Charles Darwin) as naturalist' (G.L. 550).

It was unusual for Elizabeth Gaskell to signify the immediate source of a character, but with most Unitarians she felt that Charles Darwin was the apostle of the age. An agnostic in his later years, Darwin had attended the Unitarian Chapel in Shrewsbury as a boy and always remained part of the Unitarian circle. His sister travelled in Europe with Meta Gaskell and he was a frequent guest at the Gaskell home in Plymouth Grove. She was not unconscious of Darwin's eccentricities of behaviour, and a clumsiness that was the bane of ladies conducting tea parties among the bric-à-brac and objets d'art of the Victorian drawing-room, but she never forgot his genius even in the middle of the broken china. So, despite all his deficiencies of manner and appearance, it is Roger's fame that brings Lord Hollingford to Hamley and finally Lady Cumnor herself to the Gibsons' drawing-room, requesting that the doctor should use his influence with Roger to secure his attendance at the Towers' house-party. It was obvious to Elizabeth Gaskell that all those who prided themselves on trimming their sails to the winds of change were taking note of Charles Darwin. Thus Lady Cumnor buries her pride and acknowledges a new allegiance: ' "You know me well enough to be aware that I am not the person, nor is the Towers the house, to go about soliciting guests. But in this instance I bend my head; high rank should always be the first to honour those who have distinguished themselves by art or science" ' (Ch. 57). Part, of course, of the Cumnors' genius for survival is precisely the recognition that a work like *On the Origin of Species* and its author may possibly be of more significance than *Burke's Peerage*, in print and in the flesh.

Mrs Gibson and Squire Hamley remain as unconscious as ever to the force of change that Roger Hamley represents in science and society. But the Cumnors are more astute and Lord Hollingford, the Cumnor heir, is already a friend and associate of Roger Hamley. Unlike Osborne who dies dreaming of making a name for himself as a lyric poet, Hollingford contemplates leaving politics for science. It is a question of survival, and there is little doubt in the novel that the process of natural selection has operated in favour of Hollingford and Roger Hamley. Evolutionary theories are implicit in *Wives and Daughters* as heredity and individual will struggle to produce a human being with the strength to survive in society and ultimately change it. Osborne Hamley is rendered unfit both by his physical ailment and his parents' doting affection, which saps any latent energy he may have possessed. Like many another mother in Elizabeth Gaskell's novels, Mrs Hamley realises too late that she has made an idol of her son. Roger Hamley does not conform to any accepted definition of a gentleman either in appearance or manner, but he enjoys perfect physical health and a lucid and thoughtful mind. Neither attribute has been spoilt by parental indulgence. It is an indication of Molly's own emotional maturity when she abandons her adolescent admiration of Osborne, the poet, for Roger, the man of science.

Hollingford is a curiously secular society that seems to have outlived one faith and be awaiting the advent of another. Certainly, *Wives and Daughters* is the least religious of Elizabeth Gaskell's novels in a traditional Christian sense. Ashton, the vicar, a kind and fatuous clergyman of private means, plays little part in the lives of his parishioners. They regard their vicar as a social institution and Easter less as a religious ceremony than a time for buying new clothes or refurbishing old ones. The doctor, Molly's father, has replaced the vicar as the confidant of the troubled and the comforter of the sick. In this decorous and quiet country-town there is less religion than would be found in Manchester. Elizabeth Gaskell sees English society as being inherently secular with a considerably higher number of the godless living in the country than in the town. Old Squire Hamley prays at night with his servants from a sense of duty, but thinks nothing of amusing himself at cards until they are all assembled. The institution of communal prayer is less a religious occasion than a time for asserting traditional values and the authority of the squire. There is nothing in the religious life of Hollingford or Hamley to incline Osborne or Roger towards a career in the church. Indeed, it is Roger who speaks with the new prophetic voice of science.

Like her husband, Elizabeth Gaskell saw materialist and

scientific doctrines triumphing in consequence of the failings of established religion. Mr Ashton, indolent and amiable, and so incapable of intellectual discussion that Mr Gibson could always lead him into a 'bog of heretical bewilderment', typified the more tolerant of those clergymen who maintained their belief in the Trinity despite every appeal to reason. Lady Cumnor believes in prayer books and Bibles as wedding presents but she never shows the slightest inclination to read them. They are guides for the conduct of her social inferiors, but as a Cumnor she has implicit faith in her own reason while admitting the necessity for an established church as a means of keeping people content with their station in life. Religion in the country is not a liberating force but a means of reinforcing established authority.

Dr Gibson sees the shape of the future in the discoveries of Roger Hamley, and for the first time regrets his age: ' "So many new views seem to be opened in science, that I should like, if it were possible, to live till their reality was ascertained, and one saw what they led to" ' (Ch. 60). Throughout the novel he makes no reference to religion or the life after death, that consuming interest of so many Victorian Christians. There is no mention of him attending church, yet he is the secular priest of this society. When Lady Cumnor is ill she allows herself to be temporarily governed by the doctor, not by the vicar. Even Squire Hamley, for whom a wet Sunday requiring church-going and family prayer is the most miserable day of the week, seeks Dr Gibson's help when his wife and son die. When troubled, Molly does not turn automatically to prayer like Ruth Denbigh, but sits and reasons her way through to the solution of a problem. It is only in her moment of deepest anguish that she seeks guidance from God. There is little question in the novel that people are managing to live decent and moral lives without the assistance of the local clergy.

It is Molly who brings both her father and Roger Hamley to a better understanding of human nature through the recognition of herself as a unique and very remarkable young woman. Dr Gibson was reluctant to have his daughter taught more than the mere rudiments of reading and writing, and he discourages all her efforts to study. His contempt for the intelligence of women is only comparable with his own ignorance of their talents. A solitary intellectual in a village of patients, for none is really a friend, he married first in conformity to social expectation. The grandniece of the resident doctor had made him a good wife but died when Molly was a child of four. However, it is not this wife who drifts through his mind whenever thoughts of love and marriage occur to him, but the Jeanie he had loved long ago in Scotland. Gibson prides himself on being a man of pure reason. 'He deceived himself into believing that still his reason was lord of all, because he had never fallen into the habit of expression on any other than purely intellectual subjects. Molly, however, had her own intuitions to guide her' (Ch. 3).

Now Elizabeth Gaskell never saw reason and passion as alien and antipathetic concepts, and here her attitude was very close to David Hume's. When he spoke of 'calm passion', he was arguing that reason can affect the feelings because emotions are to a certain extent cognitive. Molly has sensed that Hyacinth Kirkpatrick is a disturbing threat long before she learns that the softly spoken stranger in the garden at the Towers is to be her future stepmother. Molly feels strongly, and she apprehends the world first through her emotions. Later, a native commonsense and the trained rationality of men like Roger and her father teach her to balance her emotions with reasons. But neither of these teachers possesses her innate ability to estimate people by means of affective sympathy. Dr Gibson marries a shallow, vapid and amoral widow and Roger falls violently in love with the widow's daughter, a more refined and astute version of the mother. Because both men have learned to live too much in the company of reason their emotional nature is stunted. With Gibson, it is because of a love that he had put aside for the purpose of his career. With Roger, it was the constant denial of any token of love by his mother and the casual disregard of his father. It is Molly who teaches both men to find a harmony between love and reason.

Molly's nature has grown emotionally strong in the love of her father and the old family servants. She can also look back in time and catch glimpses of herself being caressed by her mother, her wet hair twisted around soft fingers, even as

Hyacinth deplores her profusion of curls. There is the comfort of love that does not require a traditional family group to sustain it. When Dr Gibson tries to create such a family he brings endless dissatisfaction into his own life and a great measure of grief into his daughter's. There is a delicate point here that recurs in many of Elizabeth Gaskell's works. A child requires love, but the adult remaining a child, like Phillis Holman, will always be an emotional cripple incapable of overcoming the crises of life. Dr Gibson states explicitly to Miss Eyre, the governess, that he wants Molly to remain a child, and a child she remains in her father's eyes until he intercepts the love-letter that young Mr Coxe has meant for her. Then he decides that Molly needs a mother, another way of restraining her growth, and, with a house in disarray, that he requires the services of a wife.

Molly's reaction to the news of her father's forthcoming marriage is less that of a daughter than a lover or a wife.

> She did not answer. She could not tell what words to use. She was afraid of saying anything, lest the passion of anger, dislike, indignation—whatever it was that was boiling up in her breast —should find vent in cries and screams, or worse, in raging words that could never be forgotten. It was as if the piece of solid ground on which she stood had broken from the shore, and she was drifting out to the infinite sea alone (Ch. 10).

And when Roger seeks to console her with the thought that her father may have found himself a pleasant companion, Molly replies in bewilderment, ' "He had me. You don't know what we were to each other—at least, what he was to me," she added humbly' (Ch. 10). This is the moment when Molly ceases to be the eternal daughter, her father's child, and becomes something more. And it is made plain that no girl can become a woman and eventually a wife until she has ceased to be a daughter. The stages of growth are often agonisingly painful, but the time is coming when she not only loves but understands her father, seeing him as a good and harassed man who has married foolishly and lived to regret it. As a result of her father's efforts to create a family with a readymade stepmother and a sister for his daughter, Molly lives in a state of tension that is unendurable. She pities Hyacinth for her stupidity—and no writer except Flaubert has made a stupid woman so interesting—but Molly also winces as her father's biting sarcasm disturbs Hyacinth without making her aware of the reason for his complaints.

Watching Cynthia, Molly discovers the insecurity and fear which produce the charming flirt who is compelled to fascinate every man who comes her way. Cynthia's charm is not an attribute but an obsession. Molly has to grope to the farthest reaches of her memory to recall an image of her mother, but that image is always one of comfort and love.

The sight of her father's bedroom redecorated for his new wife brings back the day when she was taken in to see her dying mother for the last time. Even this memory is one that Molly can cherish: 'She could see the white linen, surrounding the pale, wan, wistful face, with the large, longing eyes, yearning for one more touch of the little warm child, whom she was too feeble to clasp in her arms, already growing numb in death' (Ch. 13). But between Cynthia and her mother there is the hatred of two women who have been rivals in love for the same man. The enmity between them expresses itself more often in silence than in spoken words. In the flurry of millinery and dressmaking, for which both women possess a talent amounting to genius, there are sudden, incongruous pauses, an instant in which each takes the measure of the other, and the mother flinches. Both had once been rivals for the same man, Lord Cumnor's agent, Mr Preston, and Cynthia had triumphed.

At the charity ball Miss Hornblower confides a little of the story to the Browning sisters and Molly later learns more from Cynthia herself. But never the whole story, never the precise equation of fact and feeling that would enable her to know Cynthia better. Cynthia tells Molly openly that she cares nothing for her mother and in one chilling exchange between the two, the nature of their relationship is revealed. As usual, Hyacinth is ferreting her way through the probability of Osborne dying and his brother Roger becoming the Hamley heir. When Molly reproaches her, Hyacinth replies in plaintive explanation:

'I like everybody to have an opinion of their own; only, one else; but I should think myself wanting in strength of mind, if I could not look forward to the consequences of death. I really think we're commanded to do so, somewhere in the Bible or the Prayer-book.'

'Do you look forward to the consequences of my death, mamma?' asked Cynthia (Ch. 39).

Cynthia has always been an encumbrance to her mother, packed off to boarding-schools, hidden from sight when a prospective suitor came to call. She learns to despise the desperate game of snaring a husband, but soon acquires the art of 'calculating chances'. The essence of the game is never to be committed emotionally, to remember at all times that money and social position last longer than love. From Preston to Roger Hamley and Coxe, to her final acceptance of Mr Henderson, that paragon of good nature, prestige and private income, Cynthia's methods are a more polished version of her mother's. And after her marriage, Hyacinth can only envy her daughter, as a defeated rival does the victor. When Mr Gibson expresses the wish to be twenty or thirty years younger in order to see the new world of science, his wife replies with genuine regret:

'I only said I should like to belong to this generation. To tell the truth, I was thinking of Cynthia. Without vanity, I believe I was as pretty as she is—when I was a girl, I mean; I had not her dark eyelashes, but then my nose was straighter. And now—look at the difference! I have to live in a little country-town with three servants, and no carriage; and she, with her inferior good looks, will live in Sussex Place, and keep a man and a brougham, and I don't know what. But the fact is, in this generation there are so many more rich young men than there were when I was a girl' (Ch. 60).

Mrs Gibson always found Cynthia an obstacle in her pursuit of a second husband, knowing that with youth so prized in the marital marketplace, her daughter would always be preferred.

Cynthia has no objection to marrying for money but she cannot tolerate the thought that once she was bought for twenty pounds by Mr Preston in a situation where she confided her sorrows to him. For Preston, his love has been faithful and 'as sincere and unworldly a passion as ever man felt'. After all, as he takes pains to assure Molly, it must have been a sincere love that would make him choose a penniless girl for his wife when he could have married any number with private fortunes. Cynthia had written to Preston, and in those letters there were mocking references to her mother presuming to fancy herself as the future wife of the young agent. It is these letters that torment her. They reveal too much, not only of her mother, but of herself. She is quite aware that Preston understands her better than most, having been the first victim of her emotional duplicity. Cynthia cannot tolerate being observed in quite this fashion, or to be held accountable for her actions. She demands admiration without judgment because Cynthia, unlike her mother, knows what she is and can find refuge from herself only in the reflected approval of others. Cynthia uses people like mirrors, warmly flattering and commending mirrors that allow her to see an image that conceals the sordid loneliness and poverty of her youth. Everyone must love her, because unconsciously she demands consolation for the one love that she felt was her natural right, and which her mother denied her. Mrs Gibson constantly regretted that Cynthia was not born a boy, since boys were so much less trouble and could conceivably grow up to support their mothers.

It is not only men who are captivated by Cynthia, women also fall ready victim to her charm which is, as Elizabeth Gaskell defines it, the art of being whatever the other person desires. But those who venture to look beyond the glitter of that charm to the hunger that inspires it, meet the full force of Cynthia's hatred. And yet even her hatred is a show concealing a spiritual and emotional void. When Molly has sacrificed her reputation for Cynthia by demanding that Preston return the letters, and after Cynthia has confided something of the story of her life, Molly becomes a knowledgeable witness who must be thrust aside and ignored. Sheltered by her own stupidity Mrs Gibson never ceases to bask in the reflection of her own beauty and self-esteem, but Cynthia is intelligent, and her intelligence does not permit her this protection. Mrs Gibson trickles from one platitude to the next, guided only by a certain basic sense of self-preservation that saves her from any reckless social catastrophe, but Cynthia has learned to gamble with more verve and greater success.

Elizabeth Gaskell believed that heredity and environment shared equal functions in the development of character, and Cynthia is as much her mother's daughter as Roger is his father's son and Osborne, his mother's. But whereas Molly can always remember her mother's love and knows that her father will always cherish her, Cynthia has to play the coquette to win affection from strangers. Like Osborne Hamley, she has always had to play a part, and soon the part becomes the person. Dressed in black velvet, the idol of his parents, Osborne is the aesthetic creation of his mother, the young poet who consoles her for the rustic uncouthness of her husband. Less fortunate, Cynthia has not been the creation of one person, but of many. By reflecting the required mood of every company in which she is placed, Cynthia loses the integrity of her own personality. When she goes in search of her deepest feelings she finds only the phrases of trite romance—a heart like Faithful John's bursting with grief, Mr Preston frightening her with his tigerish skin. They are images like coloured screens hastily thrown up to conceal real meaning.

Cynthia's elusive charm, the mystery of her character, are masks concealing emptiness, but Molly, shrewd, passionate and sensitive, becomes a woman of infinite resource and compassion. The balance between the two 'daughters' is subtly altered in the novel. At the beginning, Cynthia bursts upon the reader in a dazzle of gaiety sharpened by the realisation of her past sufferings and her mother's dislike. Molly is the lumpish agglomeration of confused emotions that compose most immature girls. But, at the conclusion of the story, it is Cynthia who is beginning to irritate the reader with her constant evasions and inconsequential chatter. Like Osborne, planning to emigrate to Australia in his moods of despair, Cynthia plans to become a governess in Russia even when she has accepted Walter Henderson as her future husband. Molly grows and changes in the novel, and her strength sustains more people than Cynthia. She is adopted by the Hamleys as their lost Fanny, the daughter who died as a child. She comforts the squire in his grief, she is the confidant of Osborne's secret marriage, and finally she has to watch her new-found sister gathering up Roger Hamley even as she does young Coxe. It is Molly who sees clearly and speaks plainly, her goodness is not passive, a denial of action, but the positive force in the novel. It is she who struggles actively against her stepmother's stupidity and selfishness, and the stupidity troubles her most. She learns very quickly that fools are not susceptible to reason on the first evening she spends alone with her stepmother.

> Molly hastily finished her meal, and went upstairs again.
> 'I feel so lonely, darling, in this strange house; do come and be with me, and help me to unpack. I think your dear papa might have put off his visit to Mr. Craven Smith for just this one evening.'
> 'Mr. Craven Smith couldn't put off his dying', said Molly bluntly.
> 'You droll girl!' said Mrs. Gibson with a faint laugh. 'But, if this Mr. Smith is dying, as you say, what's the use of your father's going to him in such a hurry? Does he expect any legacy, or anything of that kind?'
> Molly bit her lips, to prevent herself from saying something disagreeable (Ch. 15).

Molly has sufficient courage to assure Preston that unless he returns Cynthia's letters she will inform Lady Harriet of the whole story. And Preston, worldly and sharp, knows that Molly is more quick-witted and clever than he. It is not only her intelligence that arouses his unwilling admiration but something else—'. . . he perceived that Molly was . . . unconscious that he was a young man, and she a young woman' (Ch. 44). Molly has overcome the sense of being a woman and become an individual in her own right. She argues with Preston not from feminine weakness, but from the strength of her own perception of what is right and proper. It is an insight of remarkable illumination, expressed lightly and without the didactic voice of a narrator. Too often the *bildungsroman* is assembled with such clattering of comment and directions to the reader that the novel's central character emerges in the last chapter as a miracle of authorial intent. But this is not Elizabeth Gaskell's method, and the most penetrating observations of character come in dialogue or the sudden apprehension of Preston that his discussion with Molly Gibson cannot be conducted by the socially defined rituals of implicit sexuality.

Wives and Daughters is a panorama of English rural society, but its narrative method employs little that is overtly visual. Squire Hamley's stream of consciousness occasionally flows into speech, but more often it is a subterranean commentary on the past, on the state of his feelings and all that has been denied him through lack of a worthy heir and the need for money. He is undoubtedly one of the most fully realised characters in fiction. Thoughts blur as anguish and rage transform the most trivial incident and give it significance beyond its immediate import. When Roger and his father sit and smoke together they say very little, but when they finally rise to go to bed, the squire confesses:

> 'Well, we've had a pleasant evening—at least, I have. But perhaps you haven't; for I'm but poor company now, I know.'
> 'I don't know when I've passed a happier evening, father', said Roger. And he spoke truly, though he did not trouble himself to find out the cause of his happiness (Ch. 23).

It is a scene handled with exquisite restraint, for it is at this moment that Roger no longer feels himself the second son, the clumsy shadow accentuating Osborne's grace and refinement. And with this awareness comes the knowledge that his father loves him.

Evidence is seldom given in direct comment, the narrative voice is quietly ironic, as though an older Lady Harriet were relating the events of her domain. But the point of view in the novel continually shifts from one character to another, and Gibson and Squire Hamley are defined as clearly in their thoughts and language as Mrs Gibson and Molly are by theirs. Character shifts according to situation and Mrs Gibson in the company of her daughter is not quite the same woman who purrs gently with Osborne Hamley. It is the meticulous analysis of motive and intent in Mrs Gibson that makes an essentially dull woman a character of extraordinary individuality. Any decision she makes is always reduced to a consideration of her own comfort, but this is never done

directly. Thus, when Lady Harriet suggests that the con-
valescent Molly should spend a few days at the Towers while
the family go to London for Cynthia's wedding, there is a
tumult of conflicting thought in her mind. Having admon-
ished Molly to submit in silence to the wisdom of her elders,
she begins tortuously to scheme:

> Meanwhile, Mrs. Gibson was rapidly balancing advantages and
> disadvantages. Amongst the latter, jealousy came in predomin-
> ant. Amongst the former—it would sound well; Maria could
> then accompany Cynthia and herself as 'their' maid; Mr.
> Gibson would stay longer with her, and it was always desirable
> to have a man at her beck and call in such a place as London;
> besides that, this identical man was gentlemanly and good-
> looking, and a favourite with her prosperous brother-in-law.
> The 'ayes' had it.
> 'What a charming plan! I cannot think of anything kinder
> or pleasanter for this poor darling' (Ch. 57).

Mrs Gibson functions like a slightly inefficient calculating
machine, continually counting and measuring, whether it is
the stitches in her worsted work, or the exact price a woman
should charge for a straight nose and a perfect French accent
with a corresponding reduction in the price for light eyelashes. Like most computers, she functions best with a multitude of trifles rather than with ethical or moral problems.
Her values can always be reduced to money and status,
beyond which she is ignorant to the point of complete
vacuity. It is not so much that she has deliberately eaves-
dropped on Dr Nicholls's consultation with her husband
over Osborne's health, but her inability to see it was wrong
both to do this and to attempt to benefit from it that enrages
and crushes her husband. With this awareness comes the full
recognition of his own folly in having married her, and the
irony of having chosen a woman like this to be a moral
guardian for his daughter. Fortunately Dr Gibson never
learns of the contents of Cynthia's letters to Preston, which
would compromise his wife even further in his eyes.

It is Lady Harriet who speaks both for and against the
feudal standards of this society. As a young woman of title
and great wealth, she feels no necessity to stand in the marital market place, and chooses instead to enjoy a single life

while arranging the lives of those around her. In a novel of consistent irony she is the one who confounds scandal and gossip by exploiting the traditions of social deference in the community. Whoever she visits feels privileged, and if she chooses to walk up Hollingford main street with Molly Gibson, then Molly's reputation is unsullied. It is a sour moment for Dr Gibson when he discovers that his marriage to Hyacinth has been arranged by the Cumnors, but at the conclusion of the novel, it is Lady Harriet who brings Roger and Molly together again at the Towers. Lord Hollingford and his sister, wagering on the prospects of the young people marrying, are reminiscent of Lord and Lady Cumnor devising the match between Gibson and Hyacinth.

The novel is incomplete. Like Charles Dickens, Elizabeth Gaskell died before she had completed the final chapters of her current work. But whereas the resolution of *The Mystery of Edwin Drood* has remained a puzzle for readers and critics, the end was clearly in sight for *Wives and Daughters*. Moreover, Elizabeth Gaskell had left clear indications that Roger would return from his scientific expedition in Ethiopia to marry Molly. Their future life would be led in London, not Hollingford or Hamley. Mr Gibson takes a partner and frequently travels to the city to enjoy the company of his daughter and scientific scholars, and 'to get a little rest from Mrs. Gibson'. It is a conclusion that recalls the final scenes of *Mary Barton*, where Jem and Mary decide to emigrate to Canada knowing that there is no future for them in Manchester. Similarly, Roger has long decided to leave, and his father accepts the fact that his son will never live and work at Hamley.

By the end of the novel, Hollingford and Hamley are worlds of the past that will never change because they provide a great deal of satisfaction for people like Mrs Goodenough, the Brownings, the Hamleys and the Cumnors—especially the Cumnors. A benevolent despotism can be quite agreeable, particularly when the despot is Lady Cumnor. With perfect sincerity she says to her daughter:

'I like everybody to have an opinion of their own; only, when my opinions are based on thought and experience, which few people have had equal opportunities of acquiring,

I think it is but proper deference in others to allow themselves to be convinced. In fact, I think it is only obstinacy which keeps them from acknowledging that they are. I am not a despot, I hope?' she asked, with some anxiety.

'If you are, dear mamma,' said Lady Harriet, kissing the stern uplifted face very fondly, 'I like a despotism better than a republic' (Ch. 57).

It was because so many people agreed with Lady Harriet that Hollingford and Hamley were to retain all the characteristics of a past age. The most liberal residents of the town continued to vote for the Cumnors, and the poorest pledged their allegiance to the lord like medieval vassals. Carlyle predicted mob rule and revolution if the suffrage were extended, but Elizabeth Gaskell was more percipient. She saw that the future of England would not be one of radical and violent change, but a long series of social compromises presided over by the Cumnors. Hollingford, governed by Lord Cumnor, was a happy relic of the eighteenth century, but, when applied to the city, the Cumnor methods guaranteed inefficiency with the possibility of social violence. A benevolent despotism satisfied the Browning sisters, but it was intolerable to people like John Barton, Nicholas Higgins and Margaret Hale. The compromise has yet to be effected that will produce a harmonious relationship between the industrial city and the country village. But Elizabeth Gaskell was quite certain of one thing: the traditions of Hollingford and the authority of the Cumnors would not work in Manchester.

9
Conclusion

Cranford was read and depreciated pleasantly by critics for whom Elizabeth Gaskell had become Lord David Cecil's 'gentle dove' in a literary aviary where peacocks and eagles were preferred. When George Orwell wrote, 'If you look for the working classes in fiction, and especially English fiction, all you find is a hole,[1] it is plain that he had not read Elizabeth Gaskell's industrial novels. P. J. Keating follows suit and declares Kipling to be the first Victorian writer who was not scared of the working class,[2] and Gissing as 'the first Victorian novelist, whose efforts can be traced through a series of novels, to struggle seriously with the artistic problems involved in the presentation of the working classes in fiction'.[3] It should, of course, be recognised that critics, like Dr Johnson reading *Lycidas*, have often been inclined to examine a book in the light of their own predilections, and find in it what they want to discover. Indeed, the discovery often precedes the search, a failing common to other than literary critics. Too often Elizabeth Gaskell has been misread, not read, or the critic has listened to the bland narrative voice in the novels and not to the urgent claims of the fictional characters.

Elizabeth Gaskell assumed many narrative voices in her work, from the ingenuous youth of *Cousin Phillis* to the invalid gentleman of 'Six Weeks at Heppenheim'. She had a curious faculty for writing letters to close friends like Eliza Fox in which she posed questions and then answered them for her reader. One of the main characteristics of her letters is the way in which many of them fall naturally into the form of a dialogue—with Elizabeth Gaskell playing both parts. The letter she dictated to her daughter Meta for Herbert Grey, (G.L. 420), advocating a tight plot, concise language and realistic description in a novel, has been widely quoted. But Elizabeth Gaskell's interest in narrative technique went far beyond this, as we can discover from her conversations with Charlotte Brontë. She frequently wrote hurriedly, but she was not an artless writer, creating without thought of structure and language. Her concern as a novelist was as much with form as it was with subject, a quality of her work that has long been observed by French critics.[4] This is indicated in a letter Mary Mohl wrote to her in 1860, obviously part of a discussion on narrative technique: 'I agree with you that a thing should be always *let seen*, and not shown. I wish that the animal who writes to be as invisible as the mechanism of our bodies.'[5] All too often the narrative voice in Elizabeth Gaskell's novels has been regarded as her own. Yet frequently it is a contrived persona that could best be described as Elizabeth Gaskell's impersonation of her average middle-class reader. It was this reader who was inclined to burn books he thought offensive and to censor the volumes at the lending library. In consequence, it is the narrator, as in *Mary Barton,* for example, who is the least credible and engaging character in the work.

P. N. Furbank quotes Sartre's apothegm that: 'Fictional beings have their laws, the most rigorous of which is the following: the novelist may be either their witness or their accomplice, but never both at the same time.'[6] Laws are as difficult to assert and maintain in literature as they are in history. The cautious critic generally prefers to speak of principles. But Furbank, taking Sartre as his guide, concludes his essay with the challenging comment: 'Mrs Gaskell is the poet of deceit; she knows the country of shams better than anyone. Only the trouble is, Miss Matty seems to have taken a hand in writing *North and South*.'[7] This is questionable, if only because Sartre's statement of authorial intent is not all-encompassing. It is possible, as Elizabeth Gaskell did, for the novelist deliberately to assume the role of the reader, or to cast the narrator into a fictional and fallible form, permitting the characters to assume a veridical reality in consequence.

Certainly, Elizabeth Gaskell's deficiencies as a writer were accentuated in her own day by Dickens's genius for visual metaphor. It is difficult to recall the appearance of her characters, but their feelings are unforgettable. People are described in phrases that are as trite and repetitive as their names. The profusion of Marys in her novels does not point to a casual or careless attitude, so much as to her lack of response to the external realisation of character. The name of a character will change in the course of a single work, but the descriptive development of personality never falters. There is a blurring of effect when action is observed, but that same action becomes vivid and intense as soon as it is made a process of thought and feeling. *Cranford* is the most visual of her works, and one reason for its popularity was its resemblance to the fictional modes of Charles Dickens. In France, it was always considered the least of her novels, never receiving general critical commendation.

Elizabeth Gaskell's characters are never less than complex human beings, beset with conflicting emotions and ideas. She never claimed to be anything else herself, and to Eliza Fox she wrote of the 'mes' in her nature that so often were at war with each other:

> One of my mes is, I do believe, a true Christian (only people call her socialist and communist), another of my mes is a wife and mother, and highly delighted at the delight of everyone else in the house, Meta and William most especially who are in full ecstasy [the family had just moved into their new home at Plymouth Grove]. Now, that's my 'social' self I suppose. Then again I've another self with a full taste for beauty and convenience whh is pleased on its own account. How am I to reconcile all these warring members? (G.L. 69).

Her awareness of this psychological complexity inclined her to an androgynous view of human nature. Thus she presents many feminine men like Mr Hale and a great number of masculine women like Margaret Hale and Faith Benson.

In 'The Grey Woman', there is a study of love between two women that could be defined as lesbian, and it is given in simple and explicit terms. There is no doubt at the conclusion of the story that a woman can love as deeply and passionately in a homosexual as in a heterosexual relationship. It is even possible for two women to form a family and care for a child as Anna and Amante do. Outwardly, 'The Grey Woman' is a traditional Gothic tale of terror, but the whole import of the story is changed by the relationship between the two women. Just as passionate love was possible between the elderly, so it was conceivable between members of the same sex. It was a dimension of character that was determined by Elizabeth Gaskell's religious awareness. With her fervent affirmation of the unique nature of every human being, it followed that people could only come to self-understanding, like Mr Hale, when their emotional needs were satisfied by their own appropriate objects of worship. Only through self-knowledge and psychological insight could people become truly religious. Anna and Amante in 'The Grey Woman' are aware of their own nature, and because they are faithful to themselves and each other, their relationship is essentially virtuous. Unconsciously echoing Pierre Bayle, Elizabeth Gaskell had written: 'My idea of Heaven . . . is a place where we shan't have any consciences,—and Hell vice versa' (G.L. 69). As a Unitarian of independent opinion Elizabeth Gaskell was more tolerant, because more realistic, than many psychologists and moralists today.

It was in her delineation of the working class and the social structure of English life that Elizabeth Gaskell best revealed her strength as a novelist. She knew and understood working-class life in Manchester, and appreciated its cultural vitality when her contemporaries were bewailing its blighted ignorance. Marx's concept of working-class alienation was derived from a theoretic economic model rather than from actual experience. Elizabeth Gaskell knew the meaning and function of solidarity and saw the trades-union as the new force in English social and political life. It was never to be Carlyle's England, or Marx's for that matter, but it was to be Elizabeth Gaskell's. A reflection of what she recorded in *Mary Barton* and *North and South* can be seen in a trades-union congress or in men whose first loyalty is to the union, not to class, Queen or country.

She also saw the Cumnors reaching into the future and claiming it as their demesne, and Lady Ludlow could still be heard in the twentieth century lamenting the rise of the mob and a working class grown articulate and powerful. V. Sackville-West was not voicing an unpopular sentiment abhorrent to her class when she wrote: 'I hate democracy. I hate *la populace*. I wish education had never been introduced. I don't like tyranny, but I like an intelligent oligarchy. I wish *la populace* had never been encouraged to emerge from its rightful place. I should like to see them as well fed and well houses as T.T. cows, but no more articulate than that.'[8] The intelligent oligarchy was to endure beyond the Ludlows and the Cumnors, and even Victoria Sackville-West. But in *Wives and Daughters*, Elizabeth Gaskell indicated the Cumnors' resilience, and chameleon quality of taking on the colour of the time without losing their identity and purpose in the process. The trades-union and an astute oligarchy are still evenly matched in English life. Elizabeth Gaskell did not minimise the dangers in such a confrontation for the rest of society. Engels, like Marx, was to be a poor prophet of the future, but Elizabeth Gaskell saw more clearly because she had experienced more deeply, and reasoned without preconceived theory. She saw men and women, not a proletariat and a bourgeoisie.[9]

Elizabeth Gaskell always believed that capitalism could not survive unless it was modified to such an extent that the workers became profit-sharing participants. As early as *Mary Barton* she had written: '. . . the interests of one were the interests of all; and as such, required the consideration and deliberation of all; that hence it was most desirable to have educated workers, capable of judging, not mere machines of ignorant men; and to have them bound to their employers by the ties of respect and affection, not by mere money bargains alone' (Ch. 37). The terms 'affection' and 'respect' are not the language of modern industrial relations, but if this passage is purged of its sentiment and reproduced in contemporary terms it would possibly read like this: 'The interests of industry and its workers must in the long run be identical. In the interests of its own survival industry must find ways of democratising its structure so as to increase the active participation of its workers; otherwise they are in a position to block progress.'[10] That could be defined as a succinct analysis of Gaskellian socialism. It was written by the economist, Michael Shanks, and published in 1973.

In the tradition of English socialism, Elizabeth Gaskell can be seen as a predecessor of John Ruskin, G. J. Harney, William Morris, H. M. Hyndman, Emmanuel Shinwell, David

Kirkwood and Anthony Crosland—men who varied greatly in theory and attitude, but had a common purpose in the quest for an egalitarian society. Elizabeth Gaskell's social statements are invariably gradualist and call for a change in public attitude before society can be modified to any degree. It is a pattern of compromise that may be readily discerned in Charles Darwin's letter to Marx, in which he refused the dedication of the second volume of *Das Kapital*. Darwin stated simply: '. . . freedom of thought is best promoted by the gradual illumination of men's minds, which follows from the advance of science'.[11] And for Darwin, the erstwhile Unitarian, the word science was used in its older sense of general knowledge. The same belief in education and progress can be found in 'My Lady Ludlow' and *Wives and Daughters*. It also happens to be quintessentially English in its avoidance of violence and affirmation of social optimism.

Elizabeth Gaskell possessed the gift that Anatole France discerned in Balzac: she had seen the shape of the future in contemporary events. The Cumnors are with us still, but Nicholas Higgins cannot be silenced and must be heard. The oligarchy will yield, but it will never wholly relinquish power, for in England, power has always been indirect and wielded obliquely. The aristocracy has long learned not to be offensive in public. To read Engels is to read a theoretical exposition of the working class of Manchester; to read Elizabeth Gaskell is to see a social historian of unusual prescience using fiction as her analytical method. Time has proved her accurate.

Notes

1. The woman, the writer and the Unitarian

1 Claud Welch, *Protestant Thought in the Nineteenth Century*, 2 vols, New Haven, 1972, Vol. 1, p. 184.
2 Quoted in *The Dissidence of Dissent* by Francis E. Mineka, Chapel Hill, 1944, p. 19.
3 Quoted in *Harriet Martineau* by R. K. Webb, New York, 1960, p. 65.
4 Thomas Belsham, *Memoirs of the late Reverend Theophilus Lindsey M.A.*, London, 1873, p. 279.
5 Letter to Mrs Long, April 1850, quoted in *James Anthony Froude* by Waldo Hilary Dunn, Oxford, 1961, p. 167.
6 Quoted in *Life and Correspondence of Major Cartwright* ed. F. D. Cartwright, 2 vols, London, 1826, Vol. 1, p. 300.
7 Cambridge, Mass., 1950.
8 *Ibid.*, p. 17.
9 It was possibly a part of this diary composed between March 10, 1835 to October 28, 1838 and recording the early years of her daughters Marianne and Margaret (Meta) that was privately published by Clement King Shorter in London in 1923 as *My Diary: The early years of my daughter Marianne.*
10 All references to Elizabeth Gaskell's letters are to the *Letters of Mrs Gaskell* ed. by J. A. V. Chapple and A. Pollard, Manchester, 1966.
11 *New Letters and Memorials of Jane Welsh Carlyle* ed. by Alexander Carlyle, 2 vols, London, 1903, Vol. 2, p. 29.
12 Thomas Carlyle, *Chartism*, London, 1840, p. 5.
13 Quoted in 'Natural Knowledge in Cultural Context: the Manchester Model', Arnold Thackray, *The American Historical Review*, Vol. 79, No 3, June 1974, pp. 681–709.

2. *Mary Barton*

1 W. R. Greg, 'Mary Barton', *The Edinburgh Review*, LXXXIX (1849).
2 Raymond Williams, *The Country and the City*, New York, 1973, p. 92.
3 P. Gaskell, Esq., *The Manufacturing Population of England. . . .* London, 1833, p. 27.

4   Quoted in *Household and Family in Past Time* ed. Peter
     Laslett and Richard Wall, Cambridge, 1972, p. 172.
5   Peter Gaskell, p. 26.
6   Friedrich Engels, *The Condition of the Working Class in
     England* tr. and ed. W. O. Henderson and W. H. Chaloner,
     Oxford, 1958, p. 12.
7   E. J. Hobsbawn and George Rudé, *Captain Swing*, London,
     1969, p. 216.
8   *Puritanism and Liberty* ed. and intr. A. S. P. Woodhouse,
     London, 1950, p. 71.
9   W. H. Oliver, 'Tolpuddle Martyrs and Trade Union Oaths',
     Labour History, 10, May 1966.
10   Peter Gaskell, p. 299.
11   Asa Briggs, *The Age of Improvement*, London, 1960, p. 298.
12   George Watson, *The English Ideology*, London, 1973, p.
     221.
13   *Memoirs of a Revolutionist*, London, 1899, p. 179.
14   European socialists were shocked by the combination of reli-
     gious and social optimism. Trotsky recalled: 'One Sunday
     I went with Lenin and Krupskaya to a Social Democratic
     meeting in a church, where speeches alternated with the
     singing of hymns. The principal speaker was a compositor
     who had just returned from Australia. He spoke of the
     social revolution. Thereupon everybody rose and sang:
     "Lord Almighty, let there be no more kings or rich men!"
     I could scarcely believe my eyes or ears.' Leon Trotsky, *My
     Life*, London, 1930, p. 127.

3. *Ruth*

1   Derek Hudson, *Munby. Man of Two Worlds*, London, 1972,
     pp. 40–41.
2   Charles Mackay, 'The Working Classes', *Blackwood's Maga-
     zine*, Vol. 101, 1867.
3   Quoted in *The Dissidence of Dissent* by Francis E. Mineka,
     Chapel Hill, 1944, p. 262.
4   R. B. Walker, 'The Growth of Wesleyan Methodism in Vic-
     torian England and Wales', *The Journal of Ecclesiastical
     History*, XXIV, No 3, July 1973, p. 283.
5   Cecil Woodham-Smith, *Florence Nightingale*, New York,
     1951, p. 41.
6   Sir Edward Cook, *The Life of Florence Nightingale*, 2 vols,
     London, 1914, Vol. 1, p. 500.

4. *Cranford*

1 *The Letters of Charles Dickens* ed. Walter Dexter, 3 vols. London, 1938, Vol. 2, p. 428.
2 Anthony Trollope, *An Autobiography*, London, 1950, p. 357.

5. *North and South*

1 Quoted in *Charles Dickens, His Tragedy and Triumph* by Edgar Johnson, 2 vols, London, 1953, Vol. 2, p. 704.
2 *Ibid.*, p. 823.
3 R. and E. Frow and Michael Katanka, *Strikes*, London, 1971, p. 59.
4 'Mechanics' Combinations', *The St James's Magazine*, October 8, 1825, p. 9.
5 T. S. Wise and J. A. Symington, *The Brontës: Their Lives, Friendships and Correspondence*, 4 vols, Oxford, 1932, Vol. 4, p. 153.
6 C. Wilson, 'The Entrepreneur in the Industrial Revolution in Britain', *History*, XLII, 1957, p. 103.
7 E. S. Haldane, *Mrs. Gaskell and Her Friends*, London, 1930, p. 105.
8 *Condition of the Working Class in England*, Ch. 1.
9 Quoted in *The Cotton Industry in the Industrial Revolution* by S. D. Chapman, London, 1972, p. 54.
10 S. G. Checkland, *The Rise of Industrial Society in England 1815–1885*, London, 1964, p. 395.
11 Pietr Kropotkin, *Memoirs of a Revolutionist*, London, 1899, p. 500.

6. *The Life of Charlotte Brontë*

1 *Emily Brontë*, Oxford, 1971, p. 264.
2 *Mrs. Gaskell's Observation and Invention*, Sussex, 1970, pp. 575–8.
3 *The Brontës, Life and Letters* ed. Clement Shorter, 2 vols, New York, 1908, Vol. 2, Letter 704, p. 395.
4 *The Brontë Story*, London, 1953, p. 169.
5 'Further Thoughts on Branwell Brontë's Story', *Brontë Society Transactions*, No 2, Vol. 14, 1962, p. 12.
6 *The Brontës* ed. Clement Shorter, Vol. 2, Letter 681, p. 375.
7 'A Medical Appraisal of the Brontës', *Brontë Society Transactions*, Part 82, No 2, Vol. 16, 1972.

8   *Cornhill Magazine*, Vol. 1, 1860. Reprinted in *Transactions and other Publications of the Brontë Society*, Vol. 2, Parts IX to XV, 1965.

7. *Sylvia's Lovers*

1   Margaret Lane, *The Brontë Story*, London, 1953, p. 258.
2   Daniel Defoe, *The Complete English Tradesman*, 2 vols, New York, 1970, first published 1745, Vol. 1, pp. 33–4.

8. *Wives and Daughters*

1   Kathleen Tillotson, *Novels of the Eighteen-Forties*, Oxford, 1954, p. 105, n. 4.
2   E. L. Jones, *The Development of English Agriculture 1815–1873*, London, 1968, p. 30.

9. Conclusion

1   'Charles Dickens', *The Collected Essays, Journalism and Letters of George Orwell*, 4 vols, ed. Sonia Orwell and Ian Angus, London, 1968, Vol. 1, p. 415.
2   P. J. Keating, *The Working Classes in Victorian Fiction*, New York, 1971, p. 166.
3   *Ibid.*, p. 52.
4   Annette B. Hopkins, 'Mrs. Gaskell in France 1849–1890', PMLA, LIII (June 1938), pp. 545–74.
5   M. C. M. Simpson, *Letters and Recollections of Julius and Mary Mohl*, London, 1887, p. 165. Unfortunately, Elizabeth Gaskell's Letters to Mary Mohl are thought to have been destroyed in the bombing of Berlin during the Second World War.
6   P. N. Furbank, 'Mendacity in Mrs Gaskell', *Encounter*, June 1973.
7   *Ibid.*
8   Michael Stevens, *V. Sackville-West*, London, 1973, 'My Manifesto', pp. 50–1.
9   Engels's depiction of Manchester is discussed at length in a review article of Steven Marcus's, *Engels, Manchester and the Working Class* by Coral Lansbury, *Yale Review*, Autumn 1974, Vol. LXIV, No 1, pp. 106–10.
10 Michael Shanks, 'Can Capitalism Survive?' *Encounter*,

August 1973. A trades-union leader like Bill Simpson argues that Marxist definitions are not applicable to English society which has never known a polarisation of the classes, or the total pauperisation of the masses. *Labour: The Unions and the Party*, London, 1973.

11 Quoted in 'Marx and Darwin' by Valentino Gerratano, *New Left Review*, 82, November–December, 1973.

Brief chronology of Elizabeth Gaskell's life and works

1810, September 29	Elizabeth Cleghorn Stevenson born at 93 Cheyne Walk, Chelsea, the eighth child of William Stevenson and his wife Elizabeth (*née* Holland).
1811, November	Her mother dies and Elizabeth is sent to her mother's sister, Aunt Lumb, at Knutsford.
1822–27	At Avonbank School, kept by Miss Maria Byerley and her sisters, Stratford-upon-Avon.
1828	Her brother, John Stevenson, disappears on a voyage to India.
1829	Goes to London to help nurse her dying father. Unhappy with her stepmother.
1829–31	Visits Newcastle with Anne Turner, then travels to Edinburgh and Manchester where she meets William Gaskell, assistant to John Robberds, Anne's brother-in-law, and minister of Cross Street Chapel.
1832, August 30	Returns to Knutsford and marries William Gaskell in the parish church.
1832	Honeymoon spent in North Wales, then returns to 14 Dover Street, Manchester.
1833	A daughter, stillborn.
1834, September 12	Marianne born, referred to in letters as Ma.
1837, January	'Sketches Among the Poor', No 1, *Blackwood's Magazine*. Margaret Emily, known as Meta, born. Aunt Lumb dies on May 1.

1841	Visits Heidelberg and the Rhineland.
1842, October 7	Florence Elizabeth born. Family moves to larger house at 121 Upper Rumford St.
1844, October 23	William born.
1845, October 10	William dies while on holiday in Wales.
1846, September 3	Julia Bradford born.
1847–48	'Libbie Marsh's Three Eras', 'The Sexton's Hero' and 'Christmas Storms and Sunshine' published in *Howitt's Journal*, the journal of William Howitt, fellow Unitarian.
1848	*Mary Barton* published in two volumes by Chapman and Hall. Visits Southport and Plas Penrhyn.
1850	Moves to new house at Plymouth Grove. Visits Kay-Shuttleworths at Windermere. Offers to visit Charlotte Brontë. 'The Moorland Cottage' published by Chapman and Hall. 'The Heart of John Middleton' in *Household Words*. Meets Charlotte Brontë August 19.
1851	'Cranford' in *Household Words*, 'Mr. Harrison's Confessions' in *The Ladies' Companion*. Visits London, Capesthorne, Knutsford, Broughton-in-Furness.
1852	'The Old Nurse's Story' in *Household Words*. Visits Silverdale, Lake District, London.
1853	*Ruth* published in three volumes by Chapman and Hall. *Cranford* published by Chapman and Hall. Visits London, Paris, North Wales. Invited to Haworth by Charlotte Brontë. 'The Squire's Story' in *Household Words*.

1854	Visit to France with Marianne. William Gaskell appointed senior minister of Cross Street Chapel. Serial publication of *North and South* in *Household Words*.
1855	Visit to Mary and Julius Mohl in Paris with Meta. Requested to write *Life of Charlotte Brontë*. *North and South* published in two volumes by Chapman and Hall. 'Half a Life-time Ago' in *Household Words*. *Lizzie Leigh and Other Stories* published by Chapman and Hall.
1856	Trips to Haworth and Brussels. 'The Poor Clare' in *Household Words*.
1857	*The Life of Charlotte Brontë* published by Smith, Elder. Travels to Italy with Marianne and Meta. Visits Oxford, Seacale, Chatsworth, Broad Leas.
1858	'The Doom of the Griffiths' in *Harper's Magazine*. 'My Lady Ludlow' in *Household Words*. Spends autumn in Heidelberg, Florence and Paris. 'Right at Last' published in *Household Words* as 'The Sin of a Father'. 'The Manchester Marriage' published in *Household Words* as 'A House to Let'.
1859	Visits Worleston, Ashbourne, London, Canterbury. 'The Crooked Branch' published in *All the Year Round* as 'The Ghost in the Garden Room'. *Round the Sofa and Other Tales* published by Sampson, Low. 'Lois the Witch' in *All the Year Round*. Holiday in Whitby (Monkshaven).
1860	*Right at Last and other Tales*, Sampson, Low. Visits Haworth, Oxford, London, Winchester, Heidelberg.
1861	'The Grey Woman' in *All the Year Round*. Travels to Normandy and Brittany with

Meta. 'Six Weeks at Heppenheim' in *Cornhill Magazine.*

1862   Visits London, Paris, Eton, Eastbourne and Oxford.

1863   Florence marries Charles Crompton, a lawyer. 'A Dark Night's Work' in *All the Year Round.* Visits Mary Mohl in Paris and then travels to Rome. 'Cousin Phillis' in *Cornhill Magazine. Sylvia's Lovers* published in three volumes by Smith, Elder. Visits Florence and Venice.

1864   Negotiates purchase of house for retirement. *Wives and Daughters* published serially in *Cornhill Magazine.*

1865   Buys The Lawn at Holybourne, Alton. *The Grey Woman and Other Tales*, Smith, Elder. Dies suddenly while talking with her daughters at Holybourne on November 12. Buried on November 16 at Brook Street Chapel in Knutsford.

Critical Bibliography

Elizabeth Gaskell scholars are indebted to J. A. V. Chapple and Arthur Pollard, editors of *The Letters of Mrs Gaskell* (Manchester, 1966), referred to throughout the text of this work as G.L., followed by the letter number. *Mrs. Gaskell's Observation and Invention* by John Geoffrey Sharps (London, 1970) is the major source for bibliographical material and contains a list of corrections to the letters in the Chapple and Pollard edition. Sharps's bibliography indicates the location of Gaskell manuscripts and primary sources of related interest. He has also noted the place of original publication for all Elizabeth Gaskell's articles and stories, and successfully withstood challenges to his scholarship in this area, viz., the response to Lawrence Jones's review of his book in *Victorian Studies*, xv, No 4, June, 1972, pp. 497–499.

The text used throughout this study has been the Knutsford Edition, with excellent introductions by A. W. Ward (8 vols, London, 1906). Ward is a critic of considerable strength and sensitivity, who should not be overlooked. A necessary note of caution has been sounded by Angus Easson in observing the deterioration of Elizabeth Gaskell's manuscripts from their initial publication to the most recent reprints in the Penguin English Library. For *Wives and Daughters*, Easson states that: 'The only printing of the novel that has authorial authority is that of the *Cornhill*, which was proofed by Elizabeth or William Gaskell until Elizabeth's death in November 1865 and afterwards, presumably, by William only' (*Times Literary Supplement*, June 14, 1974, p. 641). The text of *The Life of Charlotte Brontë* referred to throughout the work is Volume vii of *The Life and Works of Charlotte Brontë and Her Sisters* edited by Clement Shorter (the Haworth Edition, London, 1900). The first unexpurgated edition was published in two volumes by Smith, Elder and Co. (London, 1857), and contains the notorious passages about Branwell Brontë and Mrs Robinson.

The Victorian Bibliography of *Victorian Studies* is the most reliable source for recent articles and books on Elizabeth Gaskell. A full and useful bibliography with pertinent comments on respective works is to be found in Margaret Granz's *Elizabeth Gaskell: the Artist in Conflict* (New York, 1969). Among more recent works Edgar Wright, *Mrs. Gaskell: The Basis for Reassess-*

ment (London, 1965) offers a traditional but sympathetic view of the author's work, and John McVeagh, *Elizabeth Gaskell* (London, 1970) provides the most concise and illuminating introduction to the novels. The introductions to the Penguin English Library editions of Elizabeth Gaskell's novels vary in depth and insight, but should all be consulted by the serious Gaskell scholar. Stephen Gill's introduction to *Mary Barton* contains useful social background but does not supersede Kathleen Tillotson's study of that novel in *Novels of the Eighteen-Forties* (London, 1961).

A study of Elizabeth Gaskell leads one inevitably into Brontë country, still a tangle of conflicting evidence since the heyday of Clement Shorter and T. J. Wise. The critic moves with discretion here and it is advisable to travel with a guide. The best available at this time is Tom Winnifrith, whose *The Brontës and their Background* (London, 1973) has clearly defined the main pitfalls awaiting the trusting and unwary. In conjunction with Winnifrith, the standard works remain those of Margaret Lane and Winifred Gérin. Margaret Lane, *The Brontë Story: A Reconsideration of Mrs Gaskell's Life of Charlotte Brontë* (London, 1953) is an edited version of Elizabeth Gaskell's biography, with some emendations that I find unlikely. The cheery version of Charlotte Brontë's marriage has more affinity with the desire for 'happy endings' than with reality, for example. Winifred Gérin, in her biographies of the four Brontës, *Anne Brontë* (London, 1959); *Branwell Brontë* (London, 1961); *Charlotte Brontë: The Evolution of Genius* (Oxford, 1967); and *Emily Brontë* (Oxford, 1971), gives dimension and significance to the Brontës that Elizabeth Gaskell never met and knew only from Charlotte Brontë and her friends. Clement Shorter, *The Brontës: Life and Letters*, 2 vols, (London, 1905) should be consulted with Winnifrith's comments in mind. The *Brontë Society Transactions* provide a continuing source of reference for Brontean research.

The best background study of Unitarianism in English intellectual life in the nineteenth century is still R. K. Webb's life of *Harriet Martineau: A Radical Victorian* (London, 1960). Scholars in this field are impatiently awaiting the publication of his history of Unitarianism. Until this work is published, Dennis G. Wigmore Beddoes, *Yesterday's Radicals: A Study of the Affinity between Unitarianism and Broad Church Anglicanism* (London, 1971) should be consulted together with Francis E. Mineka, *The Dissidence of Dissent. The Monthly Repository, 1806–1838* (Chapel Hill, 1944). In the *Memoirs and Proceedings of the Manchester Literary and Philosophical Society, 1939–41,* there is a brief account of William Gaskell's ministry by Herbert McLachlan entitled 'Cross Street Chapel in the Life of Manchester'. It is clear from this account that Elizabeth Gaskell frequently held divergent views on social issues from her husband, but such situations did not necessarily give rise to marital discord in a Unitarian household. The clearest insight into Unitarian thought of this period is still afforded by *The Monthly Repository* and *The Unitarian Herald*, the latter published in Manchester and edited for a time by William Gaskell.

The economic history of the period is better served, with S. G. Checkland, *The Rise of Industrial Society in England* (London, 1964) still providing a standard source for the general reader. Asa Briggs, *The Age of Improvement* (London, 1960) is not only brilliant social history but reveals a scholar who is at much at home with poetry and fiction as he is with market statistics. The *Studies in Economic History* edited for the Economic History Society by M. W. Flinn are useful and reliable reference guides to the continuing discussion of living standards in this period and the nature of the industrial depression. This debate is summarised by E. J. Hobsbawm and R. H. Hartwell in 'The Standard of Living during the Industrial Revolution: A Discussion', *The Economic History Review*, 2nd Series, XVI, August 1963. When assessing the impact of Marxism upon English unions it would be unwise to overlook a work by Bill Simpson, *Labour: The Unions and the Party* (London, 1973), which is written from within the union movement and not from a doctrinaire, academic stance. William D. Grampp, *The Manchester School of Economics* (Stanford, 1960) offers clarification of this confused and emotionally comprehended field of economic thought. *Rural Discontent in Nineteenth-Century Britain* edited by J. P. D. Dunbabin (London, 1974) should dispel the last remnants of rural arcadianism that have descended to us from Carlyle and Disraeli. Margaret Hale was wise not to encourage Nicholas Higgins's plan to return to a life on the land.

Index